FIGURAL LANGUAGE
IN THE NOVEL

FIGURAL LANGUAGE IN THE NOVEL

The Flowers of Speech from Cervantes to Joyce

RAMÓN SALDÍVAR

PRINCETON UNIVERSITY PRESS
PRINCETON, NEW JERSEY

Published by Princeton University Press,
41 William Street, Princeton, New Jersey
In the United Kingdom: Princeton University Press,
Guildford, Surrey

Library of Congress Cataloging in Publication Data will be
found on the last printed page of this book

ISBN 0-691-06587-X

This book has been composed in Linotron Aldus

Clothbound editions of Princeton University Press books
are printed on acid-free paper, and binding materials
are chosen for strength and durability

Printed in the United States of America
by Princeton University Press
Princeton, New Jersey

For Paulette

Table of Contents

For there is a language of flowers.
For there is a sound reasoning upon
all flowers.

CHRISTOPHER SMART
Jubilate Agno

Now, to be on anew and basking again
in the panaroma of all flores of speech.

JAMES JOYCE
Finnegans Wake

Such a flower [the heliotrope of Plato or Hegel, Nietzsche or Bataille] always bears its double within itself, whether it be seed or type. . . . The heliotrope can always be *relevé*. And it can always become a dried flower in a book. There is always, absent from every garden, a dried flower in a book.

JACQUES DERRIDA
White Mythology

Preface

> Every novel, every didactic poem that is truly poetic, establishes first its peculiar individuality.
>
> FRIEDRICH SCHLEGEL
> *Werke 8:150*

My idea for this book rose from a passage in Melville, in which the naive young Ishmael, faced with the fantastic and awesome circumstances of the hunt for Moby Dick, admits that the entire situation was "so mystical and well nigh ineffable . . . that I almost despair of putting it in comprehensible form." These words made me consider whether the wonder of the story Ishmael relates in *Moby-Dick* is finally caused less by the whale than by Ishmael's dogged but successful attempts to represent an aspect of the unknowable and ineffable in narrative.

What kind of "despair" was this, and what kind of "comprehensible form" does Ishmael provide? At base, the questions seemed to involve not just the formal features of the narrative, but also the entire enterprise of storytelling, of narration itself. Ishmael could not understand the meaning of those fabulous events without first naming the "ineffable" and taming the "mystical." This could be done only by constructing a "syntax" to organize sentences and to establish the most basic links between subjects and objects, between words and things. His task was to formulate the very possibility of a grammar by which the mythical and subjective lyricism of his oceanic visions might be meaningfully communicated.

It then struck me that it is this very possibility of expression and representation through narration which forms the fundamental assumption of all narrative fiction. All "poor fictionalists," to use Trollope's phrase, must be in fact first the authors of a *system* of expression before they can be authors of particular expressions. In an interview published shortly before the appearance of *Swann's Way* in 1913, Marcel Proust expressed precisely this idea in remarkably similar terms: "I first perceived [the elements of my book] deep within me without understanding them, and have had as much difficulty putting them into intelligible form as if they were alien to the intelligence. . . ." The present study analyzes the assumptions behind such statements in order to examine the processes by which narrative establishes the grammar and syntax proper to the expression of its particular meaning. Following Nietzsche and Charles Sanders Peirce, I have termed these processes the creation of rhetorical form. My book investigates the enabling conditions of narrative fiction and the various ways in which modern narrative seeks to create an epistemological ground upon which coherent versions of the world may be produced. In detailed readings, I trace this central problem of narrative from Cervantes, to Stendhal, Herman Melville, Thomas Hardy, and James Joyce.

These readings, however, are based on assumptions of a more general nature. First, I assume that at the center of each literary text stands the central question of "how can the story be told?" Every novel in its own way attempts to answer this question by creating figures and narrative stances that will allow the truth of the story to shine forth. While each novel is distinct and attempts to locate its own procedure for the expression of meaning, the interpretation of any text will always appeal to *narrative* as the path to knowledge.

Second, since literary language seems persistently tempted to fulfill itself in one single moment, in the unique expression which would explain its ineffable mysteries, we are constantly faced with the frustration of attempting to define something that continually resists definition. The novel is always "novel," always something new, and constantly subverts our generalizing tendencies. As soon as one definition for the genre is offered, a series of texts arises to belie the definition. Again the notion of storytelling is at issue: how is one to specify the history of the relations among the various elements of this subversive genre?

Third, the problem of interpretation is never simply one among others; it is the problem of problems. Literary theory has always taken the stand that the interpretation of narrative may be accomplished simply by reading through the language of the text toward some external, non-linguistic object of interest. I would like to propose in contrast a theory of reading which concerns itself in practical terms with the texture and the rhetorical resources of language, as well as with the formal and referential aspects of the work at hand. To read is to question and to understand these resources, to see them "forcing, adjusting, abbreviating, omitting, padding, inventing, falsifying, and whatever else is of the *essence* of interpreting" (*On the Genealogy of Morals*, III, 24). It is to see the *aesthetic* structure of knowledge. I do not claim a special privilege for my readings. No point of view, including my own, can ever be entirely free from the rhetorical screening of the real which interpretation necessarily imposes upon us. But I do claim that a critical awareness of this rhetorical screen can provide insight into the validity of any statement which seeks to describe or prescribe the real.

My procedure is a basic one. I reevaluate the texts in the light of their own individual concerns with the story to be told. I allow the text to formulate its own theory of interpretation. I then place these distinctive data about the novel in a literary history, a generic story. To discuss these and related issues, I turn in the following chapters of this study to close readings of Cervantes, Stendhal, Melville, Hardy, and Joyce after a brief consideration of the nature and limitations of critical discourse. While it is comforting to assume that critical discourse is neutral and does not affect the subject it considers, we have reached a point in literary studies where it is no longer possible nor fruitful to ignore the fact that the assumptions and conventions of literary criticism affect, support, and to some extent condition the results of our reading. "To pretend that we can go direct to the text," argues Colin MacCabe, "is to take literary criticism at its word and believe that the text is a simple and definable object. But every text is already articulated with other texts which determine its possible meaning and no text can escape the discourses of literary criticism in which it is referred to, named, and identified." Nowhere is insight into the relationships between literary and critical discourse clearer than in the works of Charles Sanders Peirce and Friedrich Nietzsche.

I am grateful to colleagues and friends who read various drafts or sections of this book. Paul de Man and J. Hillis Miller read the book in early drafts and made many beneficial comments. Charles Sherry, Walter L. Reed, Warwick Wadlington, Larry Carver, and Wayne Lesser helped me overcome difficulties in the argument. I made many changes of both substance and style in response to their objections. The main part of the book was written in 1979 during a research leave of absence from the University of Texas at Austin. The National Council on Chicanos in Higher Education and the University Research Institute of the University of Texas at Austin supported my research and writing with generous grants, and I am grateful to these institutions for their assistance.

Portions of Chapters Two, Five, and Six appeared in *MLN*, *ELH*, and *The James Joyce Quarterly* respectively. I am grateful to the editors and publishers concerned for permission to reprint this material.

For the sake of convenience and economy, I cite the German, Spanish, and French texts of Nietzsche, Cervantes, and Stendhal in translation where translations exist. In those cases where my argument depends on the original phrasing, or where in my opinion the existing translations depart too radically from the letter of the original, I offer my own translations. I have used the standard primary language critical editions.

I wish to dedicate this book with love to Paulette, *estrella y norte de mis caminos*.

FIGURAL LANGUAGE
IN THE NOVEL

ONE

Rhetoric and the Figures of Form: Peirce, Nietzsche, and the Novel

> The symbol may, with Emerson's Sphynx,
> say to man:
> Of thine eye I am eyebeam.
> CHARLES SANDERS PEIRCE

Echoing the sentiments of many literary figures, Gustave Flaubert once wrote that "Criticism occupies the lowest place in the literary hierarchy; as regards form, almost always; and as regards 'moral value,' incontestably. It comes after rhyming games and acrostics, which at least require a certain inventiveness."[1] Understandably, Flaubert's statement is not one that literary critics have wished to face in the hundred years since it was written. Blunt and forthright as his words are, and without a trace of mitigating irony, Flaubert's accusation seems all too uncomfortably close to the mark. And yet, the literary vocation which Flaubert himself did so much to raise to the highest of "literary hierarchies" has itself not escaped the sting of truth. Friedrich Nietzsche, himself not one to mince words, claimed in his "Attempt at a Self-Criticism" in *The Birth of Tragedy* that while "art and *not* morality is . . . the truly *metaphysical* activity of man," it is still the case that "the existence of the world is *justified* only as an aesthetic phenomenon." He then adds, however, that all life and art depend on "deception, points

[1] Gustave Flaubert, *Correspondance*; cited and trans. by Francis Steegmuller in the introduction to *The Letters of Gustave Flaubert 1830-1857* (Cambridge, Mass.: The Belknap Press of Harvard University Press, 1980), p. xv. Here, as in other chapters of my study, I will cite the original language in the body of the text only when the argument depends on the original phrasing.

of view, and the necessity of perspectives and error."[2] Without exploring at this point the implications of Nietzche's claim that life and art depend on "the necessity of error," it is worth our while to note that Nietzsche's most literary texts, *The Birth of Tragedy* and *On the Genealogy of Morals*, examine the nature of the critical act and conclude with a position that, while not inconsistent with Flaubert's, allows to the critic a justifiable base for his error and a modest share in the novelist's world. In fact, it is one of Nietzsche's more interesting conclusions that the critical thinker, represented on a worldly level by Socrates and on a more refined plane by Apollo, stands in the same relation to the reality of existence as the aesthetically sensitive man, the Dionysian poet, stands in relation to the reality of appearances. Both are willing inventors of the relations among the images they see.

Nietzsche's parable of the split between the Apollonian and the Dionysian tempers might well serve to illustrate the implications of the assumed dichotomy between the creative and the critical act and of its relevance to the study of meaning in the novel. Flaubert once again provides the pertinent text. Writing to Louise Colet, Flaubert notes a moment in his writing during which he seems to have attained the ideal impersonality he has sought to achieve in his work: ". . . it is a delicious thing to write," he says, "to be no longer yourself but to move in an entire universe of your own creating. Today, for instance, as man and woman, both lover and mistress, I rode in a forest on an autumn afternoon under the yellow leaves, and I was also the horses, the leaves, the wind, the words my people uttered, even the red sun that made them almost close their love-drowned

[2] Friedrich Nietzsche, *The Birth of Tragedy*, trans. Walter Kaufmann (New York: Random House, Vintage Books, 1967), pp. 22-23 (hereafter cited as *BT*). I have also consulted the new *Nietzsche Werke Kritische Gesamtausgabe* (*WKG*), ed. Giorgio Colli and Mazzino Montinari, 5 vols. to date (New York: Walter de Gruyter, 1972-), *Die Geburt der Tragödie*, vol. 3:1:11-12.

eyes."[3] In this "delicious" moment, the line between self and other, between subject and object disappears, and the writer dissolves into the blissful unity of the universe. It is a mood Nietzsche describes as Dionysian, in which "everything subjective vanishes into self-forgetfulness. . . . Under the charm of the Dionysian not only is the union between man and man reaffirmed, but nature which has become alienated, hostile, or subjugated, celebrates once more her reconciliation with her lost son, man" (*BT*, p. 37). As Flaubert will later realize, and as Nietzsche now explains, this ecstatic moment brings with it, however, the unexpectedly negative result that *individual* existence, divorced from Dionysian unity with the world, now seems meaningless and absurd: "In this sense the Dionysian man resembles Hamlet: both have looked truly into the essence of things, they have *gained knowledge,* and nausea inhibits action; for their action could not change anything in the eternal nature of things" (*BT*, p. 60). In the light of this existential knowledge concerning his worldly isolation, man loses the ability to act: "Knowledge kills action," writes Nietzsche, because "action requires the veil of illusion." Apollo, "Der Scheinende," as the god of appearances and dreams, now arises to represent for Nietzsche the creative integration of truth and illusion which makes human action possible. "When the danger to will is greatest," Nietzsche argues, Dionysian insight and Apollonian veiling merge to create the grandest of illusions, *art* itself: "art approaches as a saving sorceress, expert at healing. She alone knows how to turn these nauseous thoughts about the horror or absurdity of existence into notions with which one could live" (*BT*, p. 60).

The conjoined Dionysian and Apollonian aspects of the human imagination, creating "notions with which one can live," thus represent for Nietzsche one enlightened form of the union

[3] Steegmuller, *The Letters of Gustave Flaubert*, p. 203. Letter of 23 December 1853 (no. 446) in *Oeuvres complètes de Gustave Flaubert, Correspondance 1852-1854*, vol. 3 (Paris: Louis Conard, 1927), pp. 404-405.

between creative action and critical insight. This union is of course a mythical one and thus not necessarily one which we the inhabitants of the historical world are likely to experience. And, indeed, Nietzsche thereafter introduces into this happy marriage of illusion and truth the disrupting figure of Socrates, the *theoretical man,* who also suffers the malaise of illusion but not at the Apollonian level, where illusion is an act of willful self-deception. Apollonian insight stresses the doubly fantastic quality of narrative realism. It not only recognizes that all representation is an imitation of a thing or an event and not the represented thing or event itself, but also that empirical reality is itself already a representation, a fantastic creation of the human imagination.

Socratic knowledge is a construction based on empirically given elements and the empirically observed correlations among them. In contrast to the Apollonian vision, which never forgets that its representations are but the *signs* of appearance and not the represented *things,* the Socratic view imagines that its insights reveal what actually "is": "Whenever the truth is uncovered, the artist will always cling with rapt gaze to what still remains covering even after such uncovering; but the theoretical man enjoys and finds satisfaction in the discarded covering and finds the highest object of his pleasure in the process of an ever happy uncovering that succeeds through his own efforts" (*BT,* p. 94). Thus, while Apollo and Dionysos continue to veil and unveil for the sake of truth this image of the "one nude goddess" of truth, the critical thinker is perversely enraptured by the fetish of the search rather than by its ends. This is the case even of Lessing, writes Nietzsche, "the most honest of theoretical men, [who] dared to announce that he cared more for the search after truth than for truth itself" (*BT,* p. 95). Lessing had thereby revealed the secret of critical discourse to be its profound illusion that its cognitive powers could penetrate the deepest mysteries represented in art, to illuminate and correct them. This "sublime metaphysical illusion," as Nietzsche calls it, accompanies cognitive discourse and "leads it to its limits at which it must turn into *art—which is really the aim of this mechanism*" (*BT*, pp. 95-96). It is thus Nietzsche's belief that, despite their divergent levels of insight in relation to truth, the forms of Dionysos, Apollo, and Socrates are always simultaneously present in the creative and the critical acts. They form a shifting interplay among truth, illusion, and delusion, and aid and abet one another in constructing "notions with which one could live."

It has always been one of the implicit purposes of literary criticism to eliminate ambiguity and error from the reading of a text. Whether we face problems of a surface nature, such as intricacies of plot development and character interaction, or whether the ambivalences are more deeply situated in the linguistic network of the text, the work of the critic is often viewed as fulfilling a function similar to that performed by Nietzsche's theoretical man in *The Birth of Tragedy*: his is the "unshakable faith that thought, using the thread of logic," can "separate true knowledge from appearance and error" (*BT*, p. 95). As Socratic analogue, the critic thus reduces the ambiguities of a text into harmonious tensions or reorders the value systems operating within a text in order to arrive at a satisfying statement of the meaning of the work.

Developments in the philosophy of language throughout our century have almost universally demonstrated, however, that "ambiguity" is often not simply a surface blemish of language but is instead an essential basis of language and is thus implicit in any act of communication.[4] Moreover, "ambiguity," as defined by theoretical linguistics, does not simply mean "vague" or "polysemous."[5] Rather, it alludes to a continuing operation

[4] Noam Chomsky, "Recent Contributions to the Theory of Innate Ideas," in *The Philosophy of Language*, ed., John R. Searle (New York: Oxford University Press, 1971), p. 126.

[5] Chomsky, "The Theory of Transformational Generative Grammar," in *Philosophy of Language*, p. 78.

of semantic self-generation on the part of the linguistic sign throughout the signifying process.[6] "Meaning" exists now not as an independent concept, ruling from transcendent levels the workings of mundane speech, but as a contingent element. "Ideas" as represented by our linguistic signs are no longer conceived as standing in logical relation to one another before we have signs to represent them.[7] The logical outcome of this progression has been that the possibility of "interpretation" has itself become no longer the marginal concern of philosophers but the central problem of all who would read judiciously and write intelligibly.

The significance of these and like problems of language for the student of literature should thus be clear. Concern with literature entails a necessary confrontation with problems of meaning and ambiguity in language because these problems do not merely lie inert within the medium of the text, but are often manifested in the formal patterns of the literary work of art. In fact, some contemporary theories of narrative have postulated that formal problems in narrative fiction, such as those posed by multiple or unreliable narrators, by disrupted plot sequences, by delayed or omitted expositional sections, or by the presence of conflicting modes of narration within a single work, are essentially symptomatic of deeper language problems, which in fact they figure. To say that problems of narrative form are symptomatic of linguistic issues is not to deny that these formal patterns exist because an author wishes to create a certain artistic effect—the notion of intentionality is not at issue here. What is at issue is that the possibility of the creation of a particular effect by figural manipulation is governed *in the*

[6] Chomsky, "Deep Structure, Surface Structure, and Semantic Interpretation," in *Semantics: An Interdisciplinary Reader in Philosophy, Linguistics and Psychology*, ed. D. D. Steinberg and L. A. Jakobovits (Cambridge: Cambridge University Press, 1973), p. 214.

[7] Newton Garver makes this point in his Preface to Jacques Derrida's *Speech and Phenomena and Other Essays on Husserl's Theory of Signs*, trans. David B. Allison (Evanston: Northwestern University Press, 1973), p. ix.

first place by the nature of poetic language and by the kind of meaning which it can conceivably represent.

American "New Criticism" attempted to create a critical methodology which investigated literary texts as self-contained units of meaning. W. K. Wimsatt, Cleanth Brooks, and other New Critics rejected traditional ideologies that saw the literary text as a kind of riddle dissembling a hidden meaning and a prevailing truth. Yet they continued to allow traditional values to creep back into the evaluating process by measuring the success or failure of a literary work in terms of its abilities to harmonize or disguise its moments of dissonance and ambiguity. As it was based on traditional notions of philosophical empiricism, New Criticism could not but assume a continuity between sense impressions and the essence of things, on the one hand, and an organic continuity between the meaning of any perceivable structure and its understanding by a transcendental subject, on the other hand. The New Critics were thus hampered from seeing that literature is significantly conditioned, internally as well as externally, by historical processes, and that some of their most vital generalizations and interpretations derived from a pre-existing ideological position.[8]

The case for structuralism's own failure to deal adequately with the relationships between the synchronic and the diachronic, the conceptual and the particular, planes of language is put forth most forcefully by Frank Lentricchia.[9] Briefly stated,

[8] American "New Criticism" was of course no monolith, but the similarities among the New Critics were real. See Murray Krieger's fine account in *The New Apologists for Poetry* (Minneapolis: University of Minnesota Press, 1956) of the unifying elements among the various New Critics. René Wellek's essay, "The New Criticism: Pro and Contra," *Critical Inquiry* 4 (Summer 1978): 611-624, discusses the four most frequent accusations made against the New Criticism: its alleged esoteric aestheticism, its unhistorical base, its attempt to make criticism scientific, and its origins as primarily a pedagogical tool.

[9] Lentricchia, *After the New Criticism* (Chicago: University of Chicago Press, 1980), pp. 114-120. Tzvetan Todorov, *Qu'est-ce que le structuralism?: Poétique* (Paris: Seuil, 1968); and *Grammaire du Decaméron* (The Hague: Mouton, 1969) exemplify many of structuralism's basic tenets. See also, Gérard Genette,

Lentricchia argues that the basis of current structuralist thought, Ferdinand de Saussure's *Course in General Linguistics* (1916), affirms "a wholly relational and differential view of discourse as system." Literary structuralists such as Todorov, Greimas, and Bremond understand Saussure to be saying that this systematic dimension of language is all that can be known by the human intellect. But in this acceptance of the limitation of human knowledge, structuralism might be viewed as a flight from "romantic irrationalism," a flight which can lead to the kind of platonized readings of Saussure which Todorov offers in his *Grammaire du Decaméron*. Todorov writes: ". . . universal grammar is the source of all universals and it gives definition even to man himself. Not only all languages but all signifying systems obey the same grammar. It is universal not only because it informs all the languages of the universe, but because it coincides with the structures of the universe itself."[10] In Todorov's reading, language (*langue*), as a universal paradigm of all signifying structures, is made to stand over and above any particular speech act (*parole*). But crucial passages in the *Course in General Linguistics* deny this hierarchy between *langue* and *parole* and attempt instead to integrate the

Figures III (Paris: Seuil, 1972); A. J. Greimas, *Sémantique structurale* (Paris: Larousse, 1966); and Vladimir Propp, *Morphology of the Folktale*, trans. Laurence Scott; 2nd rev. ed. Louis A. Wagner (Austin: University of Texas Press, 1968). The first section of Claude Bremond's *Logique du récit* (Paris: Seuil, 1973) is a critique of Greimas and Todorov. In these few pages I do not intend to summarize or to offer an "introduction" to structuralism, for that work has already been admirably done by several scholars, among them, in this country, Robert Scholes, *Structuralism in Literature* (New Haven: Yale University Press, 1974); Fredric Jameson, *The Prison-House of Language* (Princeton: Princeton University Press, 1974); Edward Said, *Beginnings: Intention and Method* (Baltimore: Johns Hopkins University Press, 1975); Frank Lentricchia, *After the New Criticism*; Jonathan Culler, *Structuralist Poetics* (Ithaca: Cornell University Press, 1975); *The Pursuit of Signs: Semiotics, Literature, Deconstruction* (Ithaca: Cornell Unversity Press, 1981); and *On Deconstruction: Theory and Criticism after Structuralism* (Ithaca: Cornell University Press, 1982). I do intend, however, to place my work within a specific critical context.

[10] Cited by Lentricchia, *After the New Criticism*, p. 116.

two, *langue* and *parole*, synchrony and diachrony, into a rigorous dialectic. Saussure thus writes: "Language and speaking are then interdependent; the former is both the instrument and the product of the latter." Lentricchia goes on to argue that quite in contrast to the notion offered by Todorov and other literary structuralists of a universal grammar ruling particular speech acts, Saussure seems to develop "a notion of system and history as an integrated and dialectically controlled field of linguistic phenomena."[11] Saussure's dialectical move, inadequately investigated by the structuralists, serves to situate discourse, literary or otherwise, in human space and cultural time while subverting "the formalist *telos* of timelessness."

My own analysis seeks a method of interpretation which will provide a firm ground for the development of a way of reading literary language while distinguishing among logical, semiotic, and rhetorical notions of the linguistic sign and articulating its relation to cultural time. In developing a working model, however, there are at least two notions of rhetoric which must be clarified and distinguished.

The first notion of rhetoric is that which is tied in everyday use to methods of persuasion or manipulation through particular kinds of language. This notion deals with the aptness or ineptness of particular types of discourse in particular circumstances. When "rhetoric" is defined in this way, the continuity from grammar as logic to grammar as rhetoric is simple and direct. Rhetoric becomes simply a subset of the categories of logic: operational definitions of modern science, J. L. Austin's illocutionary and perlocutionary speech acts, and Wittgenstein's language games are functions of language that can be analyzed under the heading of "rhetoric." In this guise, rhetoric is not a matter of linguistic form, but is the relation of linguistic expressions to the specific circumstances in which their use makes sense. Charles Sanders Peirce's emphasis on interpretation and

[11] Lentricchia, *After the New Criticism*, p. 117.

reading, for instance, is *rhetorical* when he suggests that meanings are to be explained in terms of the human context which names them.[12]

In the article "Logic as Semiotic. The Theory of Signs" from the manuscripts c. 1897, Peirce points out that communication in language involves a triadic structure: "A sign, or *representamen,* is something which stands to somebody for something in some respect or capacity." In addressing somebody, the sign creates in the mind of that person another sign, and that second sign which it creates "is the *interpretant* of the first sign." The sign stands for something, its *object,* "not in all respects, but in reference to a sort of idea, which I have sometimes called the *ground* of the representamen."[13] Because every representamen is thus connected with three things, the ground, the object, and the interpretant, the science of semiotics has three branches. The first Peirce terms *pure grammar.* Its task is to ascertain what must be true of the representamen used by every rational intelligence in order that it may embody a *meaning.* The second branch is *logic,* which is the formal science of determining the conditions necessary for the representation of a universal truth. The third aspect, *pure rhetoric,* most directly concerns this discussion. Its task, writes Peirce, is to ascertain the laws by which "one sign gives birth to another."[14] For Peirce, the interpretation of the sign is not a meaning, but another sign, and, hence, his preoccupation with *reading* as interpretation. The semantics of the sign lead us continually from one sign to another, and

[12] See Charles Sanders Peirce, *Philosophical Writings,* ed. Justus Buchler; appeared originally (1940) as *The Philosophy of Peirce: Selected Writings* (rpt. New York: Dover Publications, 1955), pp. 99-113; also in *Collected Papers of Charles Sanders Peirce,* ed. Charles Hartshorne and Paul Weiss (Cambridge, Mass.: Harvard University Press, 1931-1935): 2: paragraphs 227-229. On Peirce's concern with the sign and the laws governing systems of signs in their use in societies, see W. B. Gallie, *Peirce and Pragmatism* (New York: Dover Publications, 1966).

[13] Peirce, *Philosophical Writings,* pp. 99-113.

[14] Peirce, *Philosophical Writings,* p. 99.

never to a final, transcendental truth. Since people think only in signs, it is only in this exchange of signs that a new "meaning" can develop. "Meanings," however, cannot be stable, for in the continual exchange of signs in daily life, "meanings" are so altered and defaced that they become in effect like newly coined words. This process of linguistic self-sufficiency is for Peirce regulated by rhetoric. Rhetoric is thus a non-disjunctive, transformational system which has no ideological, ethical, or veridical support outside itself.

With Peirce, we move into fields from which radiate paths to problem areas of practical criticism and to a second notion of rhetoric. This other notion of rhetoric is the study of tropes and figures. In this sense, rhetoric is considered solely within an intra-linguistic context; but, as Nietzsche has shown, that context is immense. Together with Peirce's analysis, which participates in the rejection of organic totalizations of meaning associated with romantic idealism, and leads in the direction of the "deconstruction" of the transcendental signified, Nietzsche's work initiates the critique of the metaphysics of truth as the desire for such a transcendental signified.

Two texts by Nietzsche, *Das Philosophenbuch* and "Rhetorik," are especially useful to an understanding of the problem of narrative. These texts discuss the relationship between language and rhetoric in a manner which underlines the essential tie between problems caused by the ambiguity of meaning in both natural and literary discourse. The first of these texts, *Das Philosophenbuch*, is a collection of essays and notes written in 1872, 1873, and 1875. They are concerned with the figure of the Philosopher. In them Nietzsche poses for himself the project of sketching the outlines of his conception of philosophy and its relations to art, science, and civilization in general.[15] Two

[15] Friedrich Nietzsche, *Das Philosophenbuch / Le Livre du philosophe*, ed. and trans. Angèle K. Marietti (Paris: Aubier-Flammarion, 1969), p. 9. Marietti cites Ernst Holzer and August Horneffer, the editors of vol. 10 of the Kröner edition of Nietzsche's works.

sections in particular from this unfinished work will concern our discussion: section 1, "The Ultimate Philosopher," and section 3, "On Truth and Falsehood in Their Extra-Moral Sense."[16]

"The ultimate philosopher," writes Nietzsche, "demonstrates the necessity of illusion, of art, and especially, of an art dominated life" (*WKG* 3:4:16). From the beginning, the theme is one of the common necessity of illusion and art in human life. In fact, civilization began, according to Nietzsche, with an act of deception. The infinite quantity of individual characteristics was reduced to general concepts by the veil of the trope of similarity. The necessity of social communication created the situation whereby unlike things were given metaphorically one name. Thus, what later came to be considered "truth," the truth of the identity of two different objects under a common rubric, for instance, emerged originally only as a social necessity: "How truth matters to man! To possess the truth in confidence is the highest and purest life possible. Belief in truth is necessary to man. Truth appears as a social necessity: through a metastasis, truth is applied to everything, even where it is not needed" (*WKG* 3:4:61). The processes of everyday life and the need to believe in truth force people to assign a common, figurative label to what are, in fact and literally, different things. Only after countless repetitions and through the rhetorical process of "metastasis," the rapid transition from one expression to another, is the metaphoric name taken literally. The repetition of a metaphor in time, compounded by the rhetorical process of metastasis, thus establishes a "truth" where before there was none.

This same process, by which the metaphorical becomes literal, explains for Nietzsche the creation of such notions as causality,

[16] The series of aphorisms, notes, and fragments which were to have become *Das Philosophenbuch* are gathered, partially, in Nietzsche, *Gesammelte Werke* 6 (Munich: Musarion Verlag, 1922). A more complete collection is now available in the *Nietzsche Werke Kritische Gesamtausgabe* of Colli and Montinari, *Nachgelassene Fragmente*, Sommer 1872 bis Ende 1874, vol. 3 (4), hereafter cited in the text by *WKG*. All translations are my own.

identity, will, and action, and is also the structure which will later lead to the revaluation, the "deconstruction," of all values in *The Will to Power*.[17] In this text, however, Nietzsche explains how a sensed stimulus and a glance at a certain motion, occur-

[17] "Deconstruction" is the term Jacques Derrida introduces to contemporary philosophy and applies to Nietzsche's revaluation of such ideas as the *text, writing*, and *interpretation*. See, for instance, the essay "Differance," in *Speech and Phenomena*, pp. 129-160. David Allison notes in his "Translator's Introduction" that "the term 'deconstruction' (*déconstruction*), while perhaps unusual, should present no difficulties here. It signifies a project of critical thought whose task is to locate and 'take apart' those concepts which serve as the axioms or rules for a period of thought, those concepts which command the unfolding of an entire epoch of metaphysics." Allison adds that "the work of deconstruction does not consist in simply pointing out the structural limits of metaphysics. Rather, in breaking down and disassembling the ground of this tradition, its task is both to exhibit the source of paradox and contradiction within the system, within the very axioms themselves, and to set forth the possibilities for a new kind of mediation, one no longer founded on the metaphysics of presence" (pp. xxxii-xxxiii). Deconstruction does not simply subvert these systems. It exhibits the clash of forces of signification within the system and denies the claim to domination of one mode of signification over another. Michael Ryan in *Marxism and Deconstruction: A Critical Articulation* (Baltimore: Johns Hopkins University Press, 1982) thus argues: "Deconstruction consists of a series of polemics with philosophy rather than of the elaboration of a philosophical system, and its point is to show that all philosophical systematizing is a matter of strategy which pretends to be based on a complete system of self-evident or transcendental axioms" (pp. 33-34).

For in-depth accounts and critiques of the concept and of its implications for literary criticism, see Paul de Man, "The Rhetoric of Blindness," in *Blindness and Insight: Essays in the Rhetoric of Contemporary Criticism* (New York: Oxford University Press, 1971), pp. 102-141, and *Allegories of Reading; Figural Language in Rousseau, Nietzsche, Rilke and Proust* (New Haven: Yale University Press, 1979); Gayatri Chakravorty Spivak, "Translator's Preface to Jacques Derrida's *Of Grammatology*" (Baltimore: Johns Hopkins University Press, 1976), pp. lxii-lxvii; Barbara Johnson, *The Critical Difference* (Baltimore: Johns Hopkins University Press, 1981); Rudolph Gasché, "Deconstruction as Criticism," *Glyph* 6 (1979): 177-215; Jonathan Culler, "Jacques Derrida," in *Structuralism and Since: From Lévi-Strauss to Derrida*, ed. John Sturrock (New York: Oxford University Press, 1979), pp. 154-180, and *The Pursuit of Signs*, pp. 18-43; and Christopher Norris, *Deconstruction: Theory & Practice* (London: Methuen, 1982). Two useful anthologies of deconstructive criticism are Harold Bloom et al., *Deconstruction and Criticism* (New York: The Seabury Press, 1979) and Robert Young, ed., *Untying the Text: A Post-Structuralist Reader* (Boston and London: Routledge & Kegan Paul, 1981), pp. 223-316.

ring one immediately after the other, can produce the idea of causality as an action founded upon common empirical experience. When two things, a determinate sensation and a visual image, appear together, argues Nietzsche, we conclude that one is the cause of the other. The conclusion, however, "that the one is the cause of the other, is a metaphor borrowed from the notions of Will and Action" (*WKG* 3:4:71) and is, furthermore, a reasoning by analogy. Time, space, and causality are but metaphors by which people account to themselves the things around them:

> Our only way of mastering the multiplicity is by creating general categories, for example, terming "bold" a quantity of different modes of action. These actions become understandable for us when we gather them under the rubric "bold." All understanding and knowledge are, properly speaking, acts of denomination. Now, with a bold leap: The multiplicity of things is brought into accord once we consider them as the innumerable expressions of *one* quality. . . . An abstraction gathers innumerable versions of one quality together and acquires value as a cause. What is the abstraction (quality) capable of gathering the multiplicity of things? . . . Metonymy! A false syllogism. A predicate is confused with a sum of predicates (definition). (*WKG* 3:4:74)

In these somewhat cryptic early notes, Nietzsche is preparing an argument to be fully developed in later texts. His point is that words become ideas and concepts, not by serving as reminders of an original, individual thing or experience, but by seeking to fit innumerable, similar (but never altogether equal) cases under one name. Ideas thus originate through the equating of the unequal. We truly do not know, argues Nietzsche, what might be the *essential quality* of any concept ("boldness," "honesty," "truth," and the rest). But we do know about the many separate, unequal actions which, by omitting their differences, we term, for instance, "bold." From these unequal actions we then create the general concept "Boldness." In all cases, therefore, the disregarding of the individual and the real furnishes us only with metaphorical similarities and metastatic generalizations, which, in forming "sign-chains" of ever new interpretations, represent, and distort, the real.

In "On Truth and Falsehood in Their Extra-Moral Sense," Nietzsche explicitly poses the now familiar question:

> What therefore is truth? A mobile army of metaphors, metonymies, anthropomorphisms: in short, a sum of human relations which became poetically and rhetorically intensified, metamorphosed, adorned, and after long usage seem to a nation fixed, canonic and binding; truths are illusions of which one has forgotten that they *are* illusions; worn-out metaphors which have become powerless to affect the senses; coins which have their obverse effaced and now are no longer of account as coins but merely as metal.[18]

General concepts and names arise from the multiplicity of individual qualities only if the substantial differences among individual entities are forgotten. As a consequence, Nietzsche will continue to argue, the synthetic quality of human judgment, which describes things according to the contingent qualities of their appearances, and then generalizes and identifies them as essential qualities, is really only a rhetorical process, a metonymic and metaphoric process, of false substitutions. For Nietzsche, then, all rhetorical figuration, the very basis of language, is based on false syllogism. Reason and judgment begin, however, with rhetorical figures. Thus emerges what Nietzsche elsewhere will term "the pathos of truth": truth statements cannot announce a transcendental condition or state of logical

[18] Nietzsche, "On Truth and Falsehood in Their Extra-Moral Sense," in *The Complete Works of Nietzsche*, vol. 2 *Early Greek Philosophy*, ed. Oscar Levy, trans. Maximilian A. Mügge (London: T. N. Foulis, 1911), p. 180. *WKG* 3:2:374-375.

certainty; they can only claim that no linguistic illusion is consciously committed. Consequently, "illusion" is already present as the very "ground" of philosophy and language. Art comes to the possibility of standing in a privileged position on that ground only if the artist understands that language is based on the priority of tropological structures: "Art, therefore, treats *appearance* as *appearance*; it precisely does *not* intend to deceive, and is, consequently, *true*."[19] The art work as representation offers the world as mere appearance and, in so doing, comes closer to the nature of reality than can either ordinary or philosophic discourse. As the metaphors of ordinary discourse are compounded by the metaphors of poetic representation, the folds in the veil of illusion are plied one upon the other and the mechanics of truth-creation are revealed.

In valuing "natural" language and "realistic" art, we forget, claims Nietzsche, that the process we call "rhetorical" to designate the tricks of an overly self-conscious art, is always *already* present and at work in all acts of conceptualization and linguistic expression. Nietzsche's later notes from his "Course on Rhetoric," offered to two students at the University of Basel during the winter term of 1872-1873,[20] not unexpectedly re-

[19] Nietzsche, *Gesammelte Werke* (Munich: Musarion Verlag, 1922): 6:98. See also on Nietzsche's tropological structures, Hayden White, "Myth and History," *Metahistory: The Historical Imagination in Nineteenth-Century Europe* (Baltimore: Johns Hopkins University Press, 1973), pp. 333-346; and Michel Foucault, "Nietzsche, Genealogy, History," in *Language, Counter-Memory, Practice: Selected Essays and Interviews* (Ithaca: Cornell University Press, 1977), pp. 139-164.

[20] Philippe Lacoue-Labarthe and Jean-Luc Nancy, "Rhétorique et langage," *Poétique* 5 (1972): 101. Here and in the essay, "Le détour," *Poétique* 5 (1972): 53-76, Lacoue-Labarthe discusses the background to Nietzsche's theory of language and to the debate concerning Nietzsche's originality. It is clear that Nietzsche used the works of his contemporaries, especially of Richard Volkmann, *Die Rhetorik der Griechen und Römer in systematischer Uebersicht dargestellt* (Berlin: Ebeling und Plahn, 1872) and of Gustav Gerber, *Die Sprache als Kunst* (Brombert: Mittler'sche Buchhandlung, 1871-1872). The crucial points of the discussion, however, those having to do with the future use of rhetoric as the deconstructive element in *The Will to Power*, are completely original with Nietzsche and, as we have seen, were already present in the notes for the

affirm his earlier pronouncements on the rhetorical aspects of language:

> It is not difficult to demonstrate . . . that *rhetoric is an extension of the devices imbedded in language* at the clear light of reason. There is no unrhetorical, "natural" language to which one could appeal: language is itself the result of purely rhetorical devices. . . . Language-inventing man does not apprehend things or events as such, but only *stimuli*: he does not reproduce sensations, but rather images of sensations. . . . Instead of the thing itself, the sensation receives only the *mark* of the thing. That is the *first* aspect: *language is rhetoric,* for it only intends to convey a *doxa,* and not an *episteme.*[21]

The most important tools of rhetoric are tropes, improper designations. It is essential to remember that for Nietzsche all words are in themselves from the very beginning of their signification, tropes. Although he announces that he will discuss metaphor, synecdoche, metonymy, onomatopoeia, catachresis, metalepsis, allegory, and irony, Nietzsche speaks on only three tropes in the "Course on Rhetoric."

Beginning with *synecdoche,* which he defines as the introduction of a partial vision for a complete, whole vision, Nietzsche points out that synecdoche shows that language never can express something in a complete manner. It always attempts only to exhibit that whole allusively, by displaying its most salient parts. He then defines *metaphor,* the second trope in his hi-

---

unfinished *Das Philosophenbuch* (1872). For full development of this idea, see Paul de Man, "Nietzsche's Theory of Rhetoric," *Symposium* 28 (1974): 33-51; also in *Allegories of Reading,* pp. 103-118. See also the recent re-readings of Nietzsche collected by David Allison, *The New Nietzsche* (New York: Dell Publishing Co., Delta Books, 1977), as well as Bernard Pautrat, *Versions du soleil: Figures et systèmes de Nietzsche* (Paris: Seuil, 1971).

21 Nietzsche, "Rhetorik," *Gesammelte Werke* (Musarion Verlag): 5:298; hereafter cited in the text by *GW.* Paul de Man cites this passage in *Allegories of Reading,* p. 105.

erarchy, as a short comparison, a transposition (*metapherein*) of a habitual signification from one word to another. Metaphor does not create new meanings; it simply displaces significations. The third and most important figure which Nietzsche mentions is *metonymy*, the radical transposition of cause and effect. (This is *metalepsis* in classical rhetoric.) Metonymy is of special importance because Nietzsche's critiques of the origin of the notions of cause and effect, of truth and moral value, and even of the concept of a stable and self-identical subjectivity, use the structure of metonymy as the deconstructive element in the following manner: Abstract qualities provoke the illusion that they are the essences of things, that is, the causes of particular properties, while, in fact, argues Nietzsche, it is only *in virtue* of those same particular properties that figurative existence is attributed to abstractions.[22] Now he says: "In short, tropes do not simply approach words now and then; instead, they form the very nature of words. There is no such thing as a 'proper meaning' that can be communicated only in particular cases."[23]

As there is no difference for Nietzsche between words and tropes, he likewise sees no difference between "normal" and "rhetorical" (that is, "literary") discourse; for, as he never ceases to claim, normal discourse is simply rhetoric in syntactic form. For Nietzsche, rhetoric can no longer be conceived as a guide to techniques of persuasion or manipulation. It *characterizes* language proper by forming the foundation of all semantic interpretations. In short, tropes are not derivative from, but constitute, the very structure of language. With this theory, Nietzsche reorders the priorities which make mimetic representation of an extra-linguistic referent the determinant of

[22] Elsewhere, Nietzsche had written: "Die Abstraktionen sind Metonymien d. h. Vertauschungen von Ursache und Wirkung" (*WKG* 3:4:69).

[23] Nietzsche, *Gesammelte Werke* 5:300. Hayden White has demonstrated how an investigation of the principle modes of historical consciousness based on the prefigurative (tropological) linguistic protocols that inform them may be conducted. See *Metahistory*, pp. 31-38 on "The Theory of Tropes," and pp. 331-374 on Nietzsche's use of the metaphorical mode of prefiguration.

meaning in language. Now the intra-linguistic elements of figures are primary. In Nietzsche's view, the artist who recognizes the "rhetorical form" of language in general will stand in a privileged position insofar as the artist can succeed in resisting the logical seductions by which metaphorical discourse is made literal. The artist must ceaselessly strive to retain the difficult insight that language is metaphorical at base and creates literal meanings only by its ability to forge semantic chains from unending figural links.

Nietzsche's discussion provides a model for the analysis of narrative because it can be demonstrated that the general process of the mystified substitution and reversal of properties to create epistemological authority which characterizes language is also the pattern which determines the representational form and structure of narratives. This is the pattern I will refer to as "rhetorical form." It is the rhetorical structure to which Nietzsche points as the origin of all meaning in natural, philosophic, and literary discourse. As when Ishmael attempts to translate his "mystical and well nigh ineffable" experiences into "comprehensible form," narrative emerges from the deconstruction of all metaphors which seek to create semantic equivalences among the multiple and irreducible differences of the real world. The literary text traces the implications of normal discourse in a way which calls attention to this procedure of meaning-creation in the guise of a story about everyday intersubjective relationships. The formal and representational elements of the story invite and allow an understanding of these human relationships. At the same time, however, the rhetorical force of language undermines and finally obscures the literal meaning of a narrative's representations in order to reveal the tropological quality of that understanding. This is the process we will term, following Paul de Man, the *allegory* of narrative.[24] Narratives

[24] De Man explains that: "The paradigm for all texts consists of a figure (or a system of figures) and its deconstruction. But since this model cannot be closed off by a final reading, it engenders, in its turn, a supplementary figural

negate their own representational truths in order to represent the undecidability which undermines all acts of understanding. This epistemological concern becomes a humanistic concern when it is manifested "allegorically" in narrative as the passions of love, desire, fear, pity, and other emotions.

These emotions have a *metaphorical* structure, in Nietzsche's sense of the term, because they establish a figural relationship between "inner" feelings and "outer" realities. Each passion participates in a process which displaces the referential meaning of a subjective phenomenon into an objective situation. To take one example: "Love" denotes the displacement of the feeling that the self lacks completion by the conviction that, in possessing another, the self will be fulfilled. "Love" thus has a precritical referential meaning—the desire for fulfillment—but since we can know this desire only as a possibility and not as a certainty, the expression of love's desire changes metaphorically into a literal (but unwarranted) fact: the fact of love as self-fulfillment. "Love" is thus subjectively true, since it expresses a truthful desire, but objectively false, insofar as it forgets its own referential meaning. To the extent that human passion may be conceptualized and named in language, I wish to suggest that those passions will always denote epistemological and linguistic, as well as psychological, structures. This is a subject to which we will return in greater detail in the following chapters.

I would stress that the analysis of narrative as a phenomenal

---

superposition which narrates the unreadability of the prior narration. As distinguished from primary deconstructive narratives centered on figures and ultimately always on metaphor, we can call such narratives to the second (or the third) degree *allegories*. Allegorical narratives tell the story of the failure to read whereas tropological narratives . . . tell the story of the failure to denominate" (*Allegories of Reading*, p. 205). These "unreadable" allegorical stories are not to be understood in opposition to "readable" metaphorical ones. Rather, they function as the differential outcome of the ongoing dialectic between precritically "readable" narratives and metaphorically readable ones. They are "unreadable" to the extent that while they can point out the unwarranted reconciliation achieved by figures of speech, they are unable to resist the force of rhetoric and undo its effects.

event cannot proceed under the illusion that it can lead to a definitive reading, to transcendental perception, or to any kind of organizing sign. Nietzsche's Zarathustran poses notwithstanding, we cannot forget that criticism can only unveil the system of reference which places signs in relation to one another. It cannot claim to have mastered any text by fixing the dynamics of its semantic structure in relation to any one specific meaning.

But while criticism cannot presume to stabilize a text, it is not any more nor any less liable to the inventive force of language than is the literary text about which it speaks. Nietzsche's theory of rhetoric, which lies at the foundation of his entire metaphysics and which claims that both "art and life depend on the necessity of error," can thus stand as the model for our own reading of narrative. That act of critical reading is necessarily an "inventive" act, as Nietzsche argues in contrast to Flaubert, and is most nearly true to its subject when it engages that other discourse in creative dialogue, allowing it to represent what the author commands and what he does not command of the language he uses. This process is, as Jacques Derrida notes, not a quantitative distribution of truth and error, or of force and weakness, "but a signifying structure that critical reading should *produce*."[25]

The purpose of Nietzsche's theory of rhetoric is therefore not to retain the privileged status of the literary work, nor to establish the ascendancy of the critical performance, but to allow a new kind of demystified reading to occur. This new reading is a conversation among author, reader, and text to the extent that it incites the complex interaction among the authorial intentions, the programmatic rhetorical structure of a literary text, and the equally complex possibilities of response latent within a historically determinate reader. It follows from the foregoing discussion, therefore, that the already besieged notion of the

[25] Derrida, *Of Grammatology*, p. 158.

text as a container of a retrievable gem of meaning must be set aside completely. The clash of concepts articulated within the borders of this authorial, readerly, and textual system continues to break up the apparently unitary pattern of the text and the act of reading. Instead of reified gems of meaning, we find heterogeneous and paradoxical forms of forces, ontologically unfounded but historically powerful and transformable. It is the task of literary criticism to investigate the parameters and values of these discursive forces in their cultural-historical and textual settings.

❦ TWO ❦

In Quest of Authority: Cervantes, *Don Quijote*, and the Grammar of Proper Language

> To be true, one must use the accepted metaphors.
>
> FRIEDRICH NIETZSCHE
> "On Truth and Falsehood in Their Extra-Moral Sense"

> The true paradises are the paradises one has lost.
>
> PROUST
> *Le Temps retrouvé*

The Prologue to Miguel de Cervantes' *Don Quijote* is probably one of the most self-conscious and significant moments of creation in all Western literary history. Cervantes there alludes to the controlling principles which will regulate the development not only of his own magnificent text, but also of the genre of the novel itself. And, apart from the Prologue, *Don Quijote* offers us a series of literary discussions, critical commentaries, and philological notes which, despite their random dispersal, converge toward a single topic: that of defining a proper, truthful, and exemplary language for narrative fiction.

This preoccupation with language reveals, as Cervantes criticism has shown, a portrait of an artist profoundly situated within the philosophic and aesthetic ideologies of his time.[1] For

[1] See, for instance, the fine studies by Américo Castro, *El Pensamiento de Cervantes* (1925; rpt. Madrid: Noguer, 1972) and *Hacia Cervantes* (Madrid: Taurus, 1960); Joaquín Casalduero, *Sentido y forma del "Quijote"* (Madrid: Insula, 1959); Jean-François Cannavaggio, "Alonso López Pinciano y la Estética Literaria de Cervantes en el *Quijote*," *Anales Cervantinos* 7 (1958): 13-107; E. C. Riley, *Cervantes' Theory of the Novel* (Oxford: Oxford University Press, 1968); Alban Forcione, *Cervantes, Aristotle, and the Persiles* (Princeton: Princeton University Press, 1970); Ruth El Saffar, *Distance and Control in Don*

Renaissance Spain in particular, these precepts were expressed primarily by the Italian and Spanish commentaries on Aristotle's *Poetics*.[2] Although we can hardly assume that Cervantes began writing the mad Hidalgo's story with the intent of transforming Aristotelean precepts into the protocols of a new literary genre, we cannot doubt that when Cervantes assimilated and applied them in his text, he also directly incorporated into it the formal, historical, psychological, and linguistic concerns which were to emerge as the informing features of the novel in its later "developing" stages. In fact, one could even argue that the inter-subjective and temporal dimensions explored by the modern novel are also at least implicitly indicated in Cervantes' novel.

These claims are tenable, I think, even when we consider that one of the distinctive features of the novel seems to be its very resistance to constraining principles, for *Don Quijote* is exemplary in a non-exemplary way.[3] It does not prescribe a genre

---

Quixote (North Carolina Studies in the Romance Languages and Literatures, no. 147, 1972); John J. Allen, *Don Quixote, Hero or Fool* (Gainesville: University Presses of Florida, 1979); and Alexander Welsh, *Reflections on the Hero as Quixote* (Princeton: Princeton University Press, 1981).

[2] Castro, for example, argues that Cervantes' Aristotelean concepts are not simply superimposed on the text but in fact form "parte constitutiva de la misma orientación que le guiaba en la selección y construcción de su propia senda." He also remarks that in Cervantes "la teoría y la práctica son inseparable" (*El Pensamiento de Cervantes*, p. 30).

[3] The notion of the novel as the protean genre was first advanced by Victor Shklovsky in the essay "Sterne's *Tristram Shandy*," trans. and rpt. in *Russian Formalist Criticism*, eds. L. Lemon and M. Reis (Lincoln: University of Nebraska Press, 1965), pp. 27-57. More recently, Michael Holquist in *Dostoevsky and the Novel* (Princeton: Princeton University Press, 1977), and Walter L. Reed in the chapter entitled "The Problem with a Poetics of the Novel," of his *An Exemplary History of the Novel: The Quixotic versus the Picaresque* (Chicago: University of Chicago Press, 1981), pp. 1-18, have proposed convincing elaborations of a similar idea. See also, Holquist and Reed, "Six Theses on the Novel—and Some Metaphors," *New Literary History* 11 (1979-1980): 413-423. The idea that the "novelness" of novels derives from their impulse to transcribe the dialectical tensions among the meanings of human utterances is derived in part from the work of M. M. Bakhtin, *The Dialogic Imagination: Four Essays*, ed. and trans. by Caryl Emerson and Michael Holquist (Austin: University of Texas Press, 1981).

so much as it underwrites one. As it narrates the story of don Quijote's attempt to re-enact the ideals of the Golden Age of chivalric romance, it also reveals the conditions under which the immanent potential of literary language to be meaningful might be actualized.

I would like to suggest that significant new perspectives concerning Cervantes' novel use of language might be gained by reading those instances in *Don Quijote* where the issues of the "reading," "interpretation," and "criticism" of literature are dramatized. By directing attention to the Prologue and to recurring metaphors in some of the numerous discourses on literary criticism and on the nature of "proper language," we can recognize the features and possible applications of the hermeneutic model the text constructs for its own proper reading. The work of my essay will thus be primarily philological.[4] It will concern itself with the grammatical, rhetorical, and formal rules elaborated by Cervantes' novel.

❦ ❦ ❦

Cast in the form of an imaginary dialogue with a fictive reader, the Prologue to Cervantes' novel begins with an innocuous metaphor about the relationship the author bears to his text: "Idle reader, you can believe without any oath of mine that I would wish this book, as the child of my understanding, to be the most beautiful, the most sprightly, and the cleverest imaginable" (p. 25).[5] But, given the "law of Nature," which dictates similarities between fathers and sons, say Cervantes,

[4] I use the word in Leo Spitzer's sense of it: "The philological character of the discipline of literary history . . . is concerned with ideas couched in linguistic and literary form . . ." (*Linguistics and Literary History* [1948; Princeton: Princeton University Press, 1974], p. 32, n. 8).

[5] I use the revised critical edition of *Don Quijote* by Francisco Rodríguez Marín, 10 vols. (Madrid: Tip. de la "revista de archs., bibls., y museos," Ediciones Atlas, 1947), and the translation of J. M. Cohen in the Penguin Classics Edition (Harmondsworth: Penguin Books, 1974). In some cases, I have modified the translation slightly. Passages from the Prologue to *Don Quijote* will be indicated by page number, while those from the text proper will be identified simply by Part and chapter.

the progeny of his "understanding" could yield only a "lean, shrivelled, whimsical child full of varied fancies that no one else has ever imagined."[6] And while a father's love for his offspring may blind him to its faults, Cervantes at least is fully aware of his child's faults because "though I may seem don Quijote's father, I am really his step-father."[7] As part of the ongoing parody of rhetorical commonplaces, the author renounces his paternal role and orphans the text so that he might offer us an objective and dispassionate view of it. But an objective and dispassionate view is precisely what we are not allowed. Cervantes first cajoles, "dearest reader," and then flatters the reader, "you have free will . . . and you are in your own home where you are lord as the king is over his dominion" (p. 25), in a transparent attempt to gain his sympathy.[8]

This new metaphor of reader/king turns out to be blaming praise, for it is immediately followed by the pointed refrain, "under my cloak, a fig for the king" (*debajo de mi manto, al Rey mato*) (p. 25). Depending on the interpretation one chooses, the reader is either being encouraged to criticize or is himself, as king, being duped. "Thus," adds Cervantes, "you may say whatever seems necessary about the history, without fear of

[6] *Prologue*, p. 25. Fully aware of the novelty of his word, Cervantes expressed a similar thought in the Prologue of his *Novelas Ejemplares* (1613): "Yo soy el primero que ha novelado en lengua castellana; . . . estas son mías proprias, no imitadas ni hurtadas: mi ingenio las engendró y las parió mi pluma" (*Obras completas de Cervantes*, ed. Angel Valbuena Prat, 18th ed. [1940; rpt. Madrid: Aguilar, 1975], II: 10).

[7] *Prologue*, p. 25. Don Quijote, too, will later use this metaphor: "For there is no father or mother to whom their children seem ugly; and this delusion is even more prevalent in respect to the children of the brain" (*DQ* II, 18).

[8] See Américo Castro, "Los Prólogos al Quijote," *Hacia Cervantes*, pp. 231-266, and the more recent work of Mario Socrate, *Prologhi al "Don Chisciotte"* (Venice: Marsilio, 1974), for compatible readings of the rhetorical intent of Cervantes' prologue. See also, on the preoccupation in the picaresque with the emergence of writing and its relation to authority, Harry Sieber, *Language and Society in "La Vida de Lazarillo de Tormes"* (Baltimore: Johns Hopkins University Press, 1978); and the review-essay by Roberto González Echevarría, "The Life and Adventures of Cipion: Cervantes and the Picaresque," *Diacritics* 10 (Fall 1980): 15-26.

being abused for a bad opinion or rewarded for a good one" (p. 25). In renouncing his paternal duties and obligations as procreator of don Quijote, Cervantes thus leaves the reader the exciting liberty to establish his own unconstrained reading of the text.

But we are not as unconstrained as we might desire, as becomes apparent when Cervantes' dialogue continues with a consideration of the difficulty of fabricating Prologues. Concerning those difficulties, Cervantes says:

> I would have wished to present it to you naked and unadorned, without the ornament of a prologue or the countless train of customary sonnets, epigrams and eulogies it is the fashion to place at the beginning of books. For I can tell you that, much toil though it cost me to compose, I found none greater than the making of this preface you are reading. Many times I took up my pen to write it, and many times I put it down, not knowing what to say. And once when I was in this quandary, with the paper before me, my pen on my ear, my elbow on the desk and my hand on my cheek, thinking what to write, a lively and very intelligent friend of mine came in unexpectedly. (p. 26)

Although the authorial voice speaks from the Prologue directly to the reader as if from outside the fiction of the novel and as if describing a real situation beyond the pages of the written text, the authorial voice in fact already speaks from within the fiction. The Prologue author has assumed a role which allows him to write words which stand in direct contradiction to the words of the preceding "Dedication to the Duke of Bejar." That dedication claims that the author has determined to bring forth "into the light" the "ingenious Hidalgo" protected from all inclemencies by the "cloak of the Duke of Bejar's most excellent name." It further states that *Don Quijote* will appear "naked of that precious adornment of elegance and erudition in which works composed in the houses of the learned usually go clothed." The author has lent these dedicatory words considerable authority by virtue of his proper signature, "Miguel de Cervantes Saavedra." In direct opposition, however, the Prologue insists on the necessity of the ornate clothing of erudition, and seeks to dress *Don Quijote* in fitting elegance. The force of the Prologue thus works against the Dedication and undoes the privileged status that non–fictional statements logically enjoy over fictional ones. It thus proclaims a substantial victory by fiction over the expressed will of the real author, under whose name it has been written that such supplementary affectation will not be allowed in this text.

This insistence on the primacy of artifice is of course but the first of many future transformations of "real" and "fictive" events, the last and most important of which will occur only after don Quijote's renunciation of knight errantry in the apostrophe to the narrator's pen in Chapter 74 of Part II. There the pen acquires its own voice to proclaim that "for me alone was Don Quijote born, and I for him" (*para me sola nació don Quijote, y yo para él*). At this point, however, the pen remains silent and the rhetorical discrepancies caused by the translation of reality into art cede to the appearance of the author's "gracious and witty friend." Sitting with pen in hand before the blank page, musing on the direction his Prologue should take, the author now directs his attention to the friend and announces that he has almost decided not to publish his book:

> For how could you expect me not to be worried . . . at what that ancient lawgiver they call the public will say when it sees me now, after all these years . . . come out with all my years on my back, with a tale as dry as a rush, barren of invention, devoid of style, poor in wit and lacking in all learning and instruction, without the quotations in the margins or notes at the end of the book; whereas I see other works, never mind how fabulous and profane, so full

of sentences from Aristotle, Plato and the whole herd of philosophers, as to impress their readers and get their authors a reputation for wide reading, erudition and eloquence? (p. 26)

Because he will not adorn *Don Quijote* with the jewels of erudition, because of his inadequacy and scanty learning, and because he is too spiritless to seek out authors "to say what I can well say without them" (p. 27), the author has almost decided not to allow the History of don Quijote to see "the light of the world." The lack "Cervantes" ironically bemoans is simply that of inter-textual authority.

To meet this lack, to "fill the void of [your] fear and reduce the chaos of confusion to clarity" (p. 27), the gracious and witty friend offers a novel solution: fiction, in the form of an innocent deception. He suggests that the author write the mandatory sonnets, epigrams, elegies, learned quotations, and annotations himself, "baptizing" them as he chooses and "attributing" them to whomever he pleases. By suggesting such an arbitrary solution to this central issue, the friend aligns himself as we shall see with the polyonomatic spirit of the mad don Quijote.[9] Citing Horace, Divine Scripture, and Ovid in sardonic bad faith, the friend shows the author how the demands of critics and pedants for truth in fiction can be circumvented by the creation of the illusion of authority. Reference to other authors, even if transparently inappropriate, he claims, "will serve . . . to give immediate authority to the book" (p. 29).

And since the book is intended solely as an attack on the romances of chivalry, continues the disingenuous friend, it has no need for "the niceties of truth or the calculations of Astrology; nor is it concerned with geometrical measurements; nor with the arguments which can be confuted by Rhetoric; nor does it set out to preach to anyone, mingling the human

[9] Leo Spitzer, "Linguistic Perspectivism in the *Don Quijote*," *Linguistics and Literary History*, p. 41.

with the divine'' (pp. 29-30). Although it is difficult to measure intent when dealing with such an obviously rhetorical situation, it seems that the friend sets here the need for truth, scientific observation, mathematical proof, rhetorical manipulation, and theological reference outside the context of Cervantes' book. The friend's refusal of textual authority and traditional expressions of empirical truth is in effect a refusal of the authority of referential language. For him that authority can always be produced from the resources available to literary discourse and the artistic imagination. And when he dictates a more perfect *imitación* (p. 30), he does so in a qualified sense. Since the aim of the book is to overthrow ''the ill-founded machinery of these books of chivalry'' (p. 30), it should use literary means (imitation) only to the extent that they serve its anti-literary end (the destruction of a genre of fiction). Accordingly, the friend counsels that the author strive ''but for simplicity, with significant, honest and well-ordered words (*palabras significantes, honestas y bien colocadas*) . . . setting out your ideas without intricacies and obscurities (*dando a entender vuestros conceptos sin intricarlos y escurecerlos*)'' (p. 30).

But the author, who accepts these words ''without question'' and appropriates them for his Prologue, in effect *rejects* the spirit of his friend's advice, for he has accepted an empirically present authority, figured in the words of the friend, over a linguistically created one, ''Cervantes' '' own still unwritten Prologue. The voice of the friend, advising the author to reject the seduction of mimetic representation and to invent freely the requisite words from the resources of his imagination, as a result, is betrayed by being captured *verbatim* in the written text of the Prologue.

While the pattern of this betrayal may be overly ingenious, it points out clearly one of the underlying issues of the text: at what level and by whom is this betrayal initiated? By Cervantes? the represented author? the friend? or by language itself? It is a point that will shortly have even clearer manifestations. Traditionally, it has been the critic's role to pose these questions and to make their differences significant; Cervantes here usurps that role by dramatizing the question of authority. Michel Foucault's interest in Cervantes is thus understandable.[10] In Cervantes he has located an anterior version of his own attempt to demonstrate that authority is either a property of discourse and not of writing, or that authority is an analytic construct and not an empirical presence. At stake in the Prologue is the possibility that, as Edward Said puts it, ". . . within the discontinuous system of quotation, reference, duplication, parallel, and allusion which makes up writing, authority—or the specific power of a specific writing—can be thought of as something whole and as something invented—as something inclusive and made up . . . for the occasion."[11]

Furthermore, when the author ends his Prologue by saying that in the figure of Sancho Panza he presents the reader with the emblematized "signs" (*cifradas*) of squirehood, he also puts in abeyance the notion that the *Quijote* is a rejection of the books of chivalry. It is represented now as but their *substitute* sign, that is, as an encroachment upon the ground of chivalric romance. With this rhetorical turn, the language of the Prologue seems to find itself unable to fulfill its promise to destroy the language of chivalric romance, as it realizes that in repeating that discourse it has become another allegorical link in the tradition and unable to participate in a radical, new, beginning.

The statement of Sancho's status as paradigm is thus itself also in need of explication. If we consider all the possible metaphoric transformations which occur in the Prologue to describe the forthcoming text, we are still left with a troubling residue, namely the explanation of the need for so many possible metaphors for the one text: child and orphan, history and romance, negation and paradigm. The supplementary desire to make San-

[10] See, for instance, *Les mots et les choses* (Paris: Gallimard, 1966), pp. 60-64.

[11] *Beginnings*, p. 23.

cho the "sign" of the ideal Squire, for instance (a desire which can never be reduced to the status of complement to the preceding negation of that metaphor), never allows the final, unequivocal description of the text to emerge. In the Prologue, then, the ambiguity of authority in language is indicated by the failure of the text's own various statements to constrain the text within any one context.[12] It is most significant, that, from the outset, the author and his fictional voices establish this dialogue of contradictions concerning the nature of literary language in general, and concerning the manner in which to create a proper language for the expression of the history of don Quijote in particular.

❦ ❦ ❦

The theme of the quest for a proper and exemplary language announces itself within the tradition of the critique of affectation and pedantry. This idea courses throughout Cervantes' work, but attains its clearest expression in Chapter 16 of Part II in *Don Quijote*. There, Quijote meets don Diego de Miranda, a gentleman whose poet-son has belittled the dignity of the vernacular for poetic expression. Don Quijote, appropriating the role of the defender of natural language, argues:

> [A]ll the ancient poets wrote in the tongues they sucked with their mother's milk, and did not go out to seek strange ones to express the greatness of their conceptions. . . . But your son, sir, as I imagine, does not dislike vernacular poetry, but poets who are merely vernacular and know no other tongues nor sciences. . . . You should let your son travel where his star calls him; for if he is as good a scholar as he should be, and if he has successfully mounted the first step of learning, which is that of languages, with them

[12] Thus, Mario Socrate notes: "E allo stesso tempo, parallelamente, [il *Prólogo*] se è volto come storia del libro, della sua nascita, della sua peculiare natura, del suo diverso linguaggio" (*Prologhi al "Don Chisciotte,"* p. 123).

> by his own diligence will he ascend to the summit of humane letters. . . . The pen is the tongue of the soul: and as ideas are there engendered, so will his writings be. (*DQ* II, 16)

For don Quijote, the study of language is the primary science, serving to establish a base for the expression of truth. The poet's pen, as the voice of the source of truth, is thus an instrument of truth. His elegant statement also provides, however, an example of the rhetoric of exchange which characterizes Quijote's linguistic habits. Through the process rhetoricians term metastasis, don Quijote transfers authority unproblematically from the literal statements about the "mother tongue" to the figural notion of a "tongue of the soul." This is the process by which Cervantes' novel operates. A "real" concept is made metaphoric, and through rhetorical manipulation, is spoken of as real but in a new, "ideal" sense.[13] A few chapters later, the Licentiate concludes a similar discussion by noting: "You will find the pure, correct, elegant and clear language among the wise courtiers . . . ; I said *wise* because there are many who are not so, and wisdom is the grammar of proper language" (*El lenguaje puro, el proprio, el elegante y claro, está en los discretos cortesanos . . . ; dije discretos porque hay muchos que no lo son, y la discreción es la gramática del buen lenguaje*) (*DQ* II, 16).[14]

[13] The reader must of course avoid assuming that passages such as this one represent authoritative expressions of Cervantes' own intentions or theories of language. In fact, at one point or another, don Quijote, Sancho, the Canon, the Priest, the Barber, Sanson Carrasco, and don Diego all express distinct, complementary, or even contradictory opinions. This multiplicity of voices is one indication of the dialectical nature of Cervantes' proposed exemplary discourse.

[14] *Discreto* and *discreción*, the problematic words in this passage, may be rendered into English in various ways: intelligent, clever, educated, discreet, wise; it is the quality attributed to the "friend" in the Prologue. The *Diccionario crítico etimológico de la lengua castellana*, ed. Juan Corominas, 4 vols. (Madrid: Gredos, c. 1954-1957) gives the following derivation: "discreto: tomado del lat. *discrētus*, participo de *discernere*, 'distinguir, discernir'; *discreción* tomado del lat. *discretio, -onis*, 'discernimiento, selección.' " Damasio de Frías, a contemporary of Cervantes, defines it in his *Diálogo de la discreción* (1579) thus:

Ambiguity arises from the fact that "natural" language is here attributed to those who, by virtue of their exposure to "culture," are most un-natural.[15]

In the Prologue to *La Galatea* of 1585 Cervantes had already given the figure of the Poet the faculty of "enriching his proper language, and of mastering the artifice of eloquence which dwells within it" in order that other men, imitating the Poet, might understand that their language allows them "an open, fertile and spacious field through which they might course with sweetness, gravity, eloquence, and liberty."[16] The problem *La Galatea* goes on to make thematic, however, is precisely that of limiting the power of language in order to keep it from entering into an anarchy of nonsense. At issue in the Prologue to *La Galatea* as in both discussions here in *Don Quijote* is the question of what constitutes a "pure" and "proper" natural language. Is natural language a negation of literary language? And if a proper language does exist, then who might possess it?

Despite his competence as a philologist, don Quijote himself possesses a curious kind of *discreción*.[17] As a product of the

---

"no es otra cosa *discreción* que un hábito del entendimiento práctico mediante el cual obramos en las cosas *cuando* y *cómo*, *dónde* y *con quién*, y con las demás *circunstancias* que debemos. Y este hábito, como tan universal que es, participan de él los demás hábitos morales y aun especulativos todos." Cited by Margaret Bates, *"Discreción" in the Works of Cervantes* (Washington, D. C.: The Catholic University of America Press, 1945), pp. 2-3. *Discreción* is thus an intellectual habit of the rational mind which allows the practical decisions of the understanding to be made. As we shall see, *discreción*, as the possibility of discerning and selecting out what is proper to a thing or situation, will soon become for don Quijote the most elusive and problematic of qualities.

15 This is another instance where the authority of the speaker may be properly questioned. Another character remarks later that since the Licentiate graduated *last* in his class, he is hardly one to dictate a definition of proper language.

16 *La Galatea*, in *Obras completas*, I:737. My translation.

17 On Quijote's linguistic peculiarities, see the stylistic investigations of Helmut Hatzfeld, *El "Quijote" como obra de arte del lenguaje* (Madrid: *Revista de Filología Española*—Anejo lxxxiii, 1966); and Ángel Rosenblat, *La lengua del Quijote*, Biblioteca Románica Hispánica (Madrid: Gredos, 1971). Throughout his lifetime, Quijote remains a lover of language. He is careful to choose "resonant and significant" names for himself, his horse, and his lady (I, 1); he

Renaissance, Quijote respects the necessity of cultivating linguistic abilities and accepts the notion that linguistic modalities can serve as indicators of gentle breeding. In frustration over his failure to influence Sancho's peculiar usages, don Quijote thus declares at one point that his squire is "a perverter of proper language" (*un prevaricador del buen lenguaje*) (*DQ* II, 19).

Although Sancho's speech is the most frequent target of Quijote's corrections, it is not the only one. In I, 12, Quijote interrupts the Goatherd's story to correct that narrator's words: "*Eclipse* it is called, my friend, not *clipse*—the obscuration of those two great luminaries." Later, he adds: "*Sterile*, you mean, friend"; and again: "Say *Sarah*—replied Don Quixote, who could not bear the goatherd's mistakes." Completely out of patience with these impolite interruptions of his story, the Goatherd finally explodes with the exclamation: "Long may the itch (*sarna*) live . . . and if you make me correct my words at every turn, sir, we shan't be done in a year."

In II, 7, Quijote's desire for linguistic purity leads to this comedy of linguistic error:

> "Sir, I have concerted my wife to let me go with your worship."
>
> " '*Converted*,' you mean, Sancho," said Don Quixote, "not '*concerted*.' "
>
> "I've implored your worship once or twice, if I remember rightly," answered Sancho, "not to correct my words, if you don't understand what I mean by them, but just to say when you don't understand: '*Sancho*, or *Devil*, I don't understand you.' And if I don't make myself clear, then you can correct me, for I am so *focile*."
>
> "I don't understand you, Sancho," replied Don Quixote promptly. "I do not know what *so focile* means."

---

carries on extended commentaries of words (II, 48); and he justifies certain usages (II, 32); he also proposes etymologies (II, 67) and flaunts his knowledge of Latin (II, 29), Arabic (II, 47), and Italian (II, 62).

"So focile," replied Sancho, "means *I am so-so.*"
"Now I understand you even less," said Don Quixote.
"Well if you can't understand me . . . I don't know how to say it. I can't say anymore."

Quijote's insistence on the propriety of speech is contingent upon his unquestioning faith in the conventions of language. He thus demands, and sometimes receives, unequivocal precision on the formal and grammatical levels of speech. Thus when Sancho naively ignores formal and grammatical conventions, the course of Cervantes' narrative is sidetracked and becomes that of the telling of the search for an unequivocal foundation, a primary *Logos,* which might order speech and allow the narrative to proceed toward its proper conclusion. In II, 3, for example, after the Bachelor has corrected Sancho's improper *presonajes* with *personajes,* Sancho retorts by saying: "Do we have another reproacher of words (*voquiblos*)? Well, if we pursue that, we won't be done in a whole lifetime." In alluding to the possibility of entering upon an infinite regression with the minute criticism of every particle of error, both the Goatherd and Sancho naively intuit that meaning is possible only by an *uncritical* acceptance of the propriety of arbitrary linguistic signs. In this passage, for instance, Sancho's defense of *presonajes* incurs another error, *voquiblos* for *vocablos,* which if pursued could open still other digressive paths.

The constant interruptions of the numerous interpolated tales by don Quijote's mad actions offer another important aspect of this narrative process of displacement and digression.[18] Sancho's unfinished story in I, 20, for example, could well serve as an emblematic instance of the novel's entire narrative pattern. In order to forestall Quijote from yet another headlong rush into disaster, Sancho begins to tell a story which requires the listener's active participation. When Quijote interrupts the telling

[18] See the interruptions of the Goatherd's tale in I, 12; Sancho's unfinished tale in I, 20; Cardenio's interrupted story in I, 24; the interruptions of "The Tale of Foolish Curiosity" in I, 35, and the rest.

to complain about Sancho's digressive manner, and as a result fails to keep an accurate count of the goats that have been rowed across a stream in the story, Sancho abruptly ends his story. Quijote's failure to keep count, to participate in the fiction, means an end to the narrative. Sancho's story is an exemplary one. It is firmly rooted in the folktale tradition of the *cuento sin fin* (tale without end) and has definite Medieval precedents.[19] It also emphasizes the developing theme of the importance to fiction of the reader/listener's participatory role. More importantly, however, it points out that Quijote's numerous interruptions of the various interpolated tales affect those stories in much the same way as his grammatical and lexical corrections affect Sancho's individual sentences. In both cases, Quijote's well-meaning interruptions displace the issue of the narrative from thematic to linguistic concerns and delay the expression of the story's concluding terms. Similarly, on the larger structural level of the novel as a whole, the interpolated tales themselves also divert the narrative from its apparent goal, namely, the story of don Quijote's madness.

Between the beginning and the end of narration in *Don Quijote* lies, then, the dilatory area of *reticentia,* the rhetorical figure which interrupts, suspends, and turns meaning aside. This rhetorical design brings the entire narrative structure of the novel very closely in line with the structure of don Quijote's own interrupting sentences. The dynamics of storytelling impel a narrative toward conclusions; in *Don Quijote,* however, narratives continually set up delays, stoppages, and deviations in the flow of discourse in an attempt to keep the story open, in an attempt to delay the subject from predicating a definitive and restrictive end to the text's plurality. By deferring the end of

[19] See, as a possible model of Sancho's narrative, the story by the twelfth century Aragonese, Petrus Alphonsus, "Rex quidam habuit fabulatorem suum" ("A Storyteller's Ruse"), which sets up a similar structure of audience-participation as a diversionary tactic. In K. P. Harrington, ed. *Mediaeval Latin* (Chicago: University of Chicago Press, 1972), pp. 419-420.

narration, Cervantes and his various narrators dramatize the inability of the sentence to constitute a total meaning. The total, the summation of meaning, can be glimpsed at the break of speech, but cannot be represented as a synthetic whole. Any movement toward such a completion is always displaced onto yet another track in search of an authoritative end. Thus, on the level of individual sentences, of individual stories, and even of the novel as a whole, the processes of displacement and deferral seem to form the essential characteristics of *Don Quijote*'s meaning and narrative structure.

This "reticency" of the narrative is also a clue to perhaps the single most significant difference between don Quijote and Sancho Panza. Don Quijote's speech acts continually reflect his will to structure, to provide definitive endings and dependable meanings to events in the world. Sancho, in contrast, presents a will to unstructure definitions and meanings. For Sancho, definitions and meanings are exorbitant desires and not implacable realities. Quijote reacts quickly to interrupt what he considers misuses of proper speech. Yet he often does not respect "proper" significations. His concern is always with the lexicological rather than with the tropological considerations of *el buen lenguaje*. Whereas Sancho abuses grammar, Quijote abuses rhetoric. In both cases, the attempted expression of meaning is displaced and finally postponed indefinitely. Quijote's errors, however, are considerably graver than Sancho's, for his occur at the primary level of language creation, the level of *figuration*.

❦ ❦ ❦

The most celebrated instances of don Quijote's displacements of meaning occur in I, 8, with the Adventure of the Windmills, and in I, 21, with the Helmut of Mambrino episode: "At that moment, they caught sight of some thirty or forty windmills (*molinos*), which stand on that plain, and as soon as Don Quixote saw them, he said to his squire: 'Fortune is guiding our affairs. . . . Look over there, friend Sancho Panza, where more than thirty monstrous giants (*gigantes*) appear. I intend to do battle with them and take their lives. With their spoils we will begin to get rich, for this is a fair war, and it is a great service to God to wipe such a wicked brood from the face of the earth.' 'What giants?' asked Sancho Panza" (*DQ* I, 8).

Don Quijote's pivotal substitution of the word *gigantes* for *molinos* is an interruption of the proper relationship which should obtain between a word and its referent. It marks out the first major instance of what will become a constant process of displacement or detour in his statements. From this point forward, don Quijote's language seems to develop sense of its own accord, detached from the object to which his word is apparently pointed, liberated from the truth which could bring the word into harmony with its proper referent. Don Quijote institutionalizes the latent similarity between *molinos* and *gigantes* into the radical identity, that the windmills *are* giants.[20] Sancho's incredulous "What giants?" cannot dispel the Quixotic vision because, while Sancho attempts to explain away the similarities ("Those are not arms, but sails . . ." etc.), for don Quijote the process has already surpassed analysis. The sense of the word "gigante," instead of designating the thing which the word should normally designate (a sense which for this particular word is already in the realm of metaphor), goes elsewhere.

Whereas the writers of the Middle Ages could depend on an essential connection between a given word and its referent, as words were the repositories of a divinely ordained truth, Cer-

[20] This assimilation of differences into similarities is, as we should recall, for Nietzsche the figural basis of all rational discourse; it is also one of the characteristics Jacques Derrida ascribes to metaphor in "La Mythologie blanche: la métaphore dans le texte philosophique," *Marges de la philosophie* (Paris: Minuit, 1972), pp. 288 *passim*. The essay has been translated as "White Mythology" by F.C.T. Moore, *New Literary History* 6 (1974); Alan Bass' translation is included in his translation of the entire volume, *Margins of Philosophy* (Chicago: University of Chicago Press, 1982), pp. 207-271. Hereafter, I refer to Bass' translation.

vantes exploits here the idea that words are sources of ambiguity, deception, and error. Signification, by its capacity for metaphorical displacement, will thus remain for don Quijote in a constantly latent state of subversion, as the subversive element always lies ready to emerge from the space between a "thing" and its everyday "name." This possibility of the redirection of any signification will become the essential characteristic of language in *Don Quijote*: The performative aspect of the language of quest, which posits the production of meaning in the mode of a prolepsis, is always postponed and made secondary to the delaying rhetoric of displacement.

The second major instance of this process of metaphoric displacement concerns "Mambrino's Helmet":

> Before too long Don Quixote caught sight of a man on a horse wearing something on his head which shone like gold (*traía en la cabeza una cosa que relumbraba como si fuera de oro*). . . .
>
> "If I am not mistaken, someone approaches us wearing on his head the Helmet of Mambrino, about which I swore the oath you know of."
>
> "Take good care of what you say, and even greater care of what you do," said Sancho. . . . "If I might talk as I used to, I could probably give you some reasons that would make your worship see that you are mistaken."
>
> "How can I be mistaken, unbelieving traitor?" asked Don Quixote. "Tell me, can you not see the knight coming toward us . . . wearing a gold helmet on his head?" (*¿no ves aquel caballero que hacia nosotros viene . . . que trae puesto en la cabeza un yelmo de oro?*) (*DQ* I, 21)

This passage describes a progressive transformation of perceptions. The narrator first perceives the approaching object ambiguously as "something which shone like gold"; don Quijote's perception of it then implies the possibility of error, "if I am not mistaken"; but finally actualizes that error fully, "can you not see . . . a gold helmet on his head?"

Several chapters later the issue is still unsettled, for as don Quijote asks Sancho whether he has taken proper care of "Mambrino's helmet," the squire impatiently asks whether anyone hearing don Quijote say that "a barber's bowl is Mambrino's helmet, and that he has not emerged from this error in more than four days" (*DQ* I, 25) might not justly question his sanity. Quijote, equally impatient, answers: "Look Sancho . . . is it possible that in all the time that you have been with me you have not noticed that all things pertaining to knight errantry seem chimeras, stupidities or nonsense, and that they are all done backwards?. . . And thus, what seems (*parece*) to you a barber's bowl, seems (*parece*) to me Mambrino's helmet, and will seem (*parecerá*) something else to someone else." The ambiguity in the determination of the "real" nature of the shining golden object is resolved to don Quijote's satisfaction by the assimilation of differences of perception under the word "seems" (*parecer*) in its various paradigmatic forms. Don Quijote thus creates "Mambrino's helmet" as he has created Dulcinea and himself—out of the spirit of his metaphoric word.

By the end of I, 44, having reconciled himself to the impossibility of calling the basin a basin, and following the rules of Spanish word-formation,[21] Sancho coins a new word for the golden object: *baciyelmo* (bowlmet), thus attempting to assimilate all variant signs under a single signifier. This neologism indicates, moreover, all the paradigmatic exigencies of which don Quijote has always availed himself. And Sancho's capacity for linguistic creativity is the rhetorical equivalent of his own capacity to follow don Quijote's errant path. Once Sancho has accepted the initial transposition of Quijote for Quijana, the pattern for other, more radical transpositions is established. When don Quijote rebukes Sancho for his perversions of "Mam-

[21] See Spitzer, "Linguistic Perspectivism in *Don Quijote*," p. 81, n. 27, for the rules of word-formation.

brino" into "Malino," "Malandrino," and "Martino," don Quijote shifts the issue from the central point: Sancho's errors are in the second degree. They occur only after he has accepted as truth the error in the first degree of calling the bowl (*bacía*) a helmet (*yelmo*).

From the moment in the Prologue that the "friend" advises the author to make use of *imitación* and *palabras significantes, honestas, y bien colocadas,* to the Canon's indictment of the books of chivalry in I, 47 and 48 on the basis of verisimilitude,[22] to don Quijote's own statements in II, 3, about the essential truth of history,[23] and in II, 16, about the relationship between art and nature,[24] the standard of judgment used by the various characters and narrators is *mimetic*. The authority of a narrative is contingent upon the status of its mode of representation as defined by "a natural manner of speaking" (*una manera de decir como natural*) (II, i). But what exactly does the text represent as this "natural manner of speaking"? As we have seen, neither don Quijote, nor Sancho Panza, nor the multitude of characters, nor the author (represented as the language of the translation of Cide Hamete Benengeli's Arabic text as reported by the Second Author), can finally be described as possessing the paradigm upon which all other modes of discourse are patterned. The very real possibility which the text proceeds to explore is that no manner or mode of speaking may be entirely "natural." At best, one can say that the various options of language offered by the text of *El Ingenioso hidalgo Don Quijote*

[22] See, for instance: ". . . he who flees verisimilitude will not be able to moderate excesses" (I, 47); "Having imitated Ulysses, Aeneas, Achilles, Hector . . . he will display such perfection" (I, 47); and, "According to Tully, comedy should be the mirror of life, and exemplum of the image of truth" (I, 48).

[23] "The historians who lie should be burned, in the manner of those who coin false money" (II, 3); and also: "History is something sacred; because it should be truthful, and where truth is, there God is" (II, 3).

[24] Don Quijote says that "the natural poet who makes use of art will be a much better poet . . . [because] art is not better than Nature, but perfects it; so, Nature combined with art, and art with Nature, will produce a most perfect poet . . ." (II, 16).

de la Mancha are more or less conscious attempts to discover *la gramática del buen lenguaje.*

The element common to the various examples of this natural language is always a discreet *imitación* of simple and unadorned Nature, as in Quijote's harangue to the goatherds in I, 11, concerning the Golden Age. These are the social and linguistic conditions which don Quijote seeks:

> Fortunate the age and fortunate the times on which the ancients bestowed the name of golden . . . because the people of that time did not know those two words *thine* and *mine*. . . . All was peace then, all amity, all concord. . . . In those days the soul's amorous conceits were clothed simply and plainly, exactly as they were conceived, without any search for artificial elaborations to enhance them. Nor had fraud, deceit, or malice mingled with truth and sincerity. Justice pursued her own proper interest. . . . The law did not then depend on the judge's understanding for interpretation because there was yet nothing to judge, nor anyone to be judged. (*DQ* I, 11)

Anticipating don Quijote's later "Discourse on Arms and Letters" (I, 29-30) in which he states that the goal of the knight errant's path is the re-establishment of *concord* and *peace*, one may say that don Quijote's quest is the re-attainment of the state of fullness and stability which language, as the voice of the truth of Nature, possessed in the Golden Age. In don Quijote's vision of the present age as a perversion of the Golden Age, interpretation of meaning becomes a matter of making present what is now absent in language, of restoring an original, unmediated relationship between words and things. The loss of innocence and truth in don Quijote's version of the myth is thus directly tied to linguistic categories: the introduction of the pronominal (and economic) distinctions *yours* and *mine*, the lover's loss of the unmediated access to the "conceits of the soul," and the introduction of the elaboration of words which resulted in the artificial consolidation of the power to interpret the word as law in the understanding of the judge. Quijote's notions of truth, reality, and plenitude are here based on a longing for a mythic world in which there was no gap between the expression and the understanding of meaning, in which there was, in short, no need for the mediation of language.[25]

According to don Quijote, the natural poet, whose pen is the "tongue of the soul" (II, 16), can free language and approximate the return to this lost paradise of semantic fullness by the simple imitation of nature. Unproblematic discourse is said to lie latent in the book of nature, ready to be transcribed. But as don Quijote rightly understands, *imitación* cannot occur without an at least theoretical awareness of resemblances or likenesses, that is, of what will always be the condition of metaphor. As soon as this possibility of metaphor is introduced, the perversion of the Golden Age is already at hand, for the immediacy of absolute reference is dissolved with the introduction of a metaphor's supplementary reference. Don Quijote's attempt to recreate the Golden Age by imitating the words, which are themselves already imitations, of the books of chivalry is thus a self-negating enterprise. His attempt to recover unmediated language must be performed through mediating language. As a consequence, the ironic situation arises whereby the champion of linguistic purity is also its most violent enemy.

The linguistic model which is valorized throughout *Don Quijote* belongs to the traditional system of interpretation in which *metaphor* and *mimesis* are constantly linked. Aristotle's *Poetics*, which provides the most important theory of rhetoric for the

[25] See Murray Cohen's discussion in *Sensible Words* (Baltimore: Johns Hopkins University Press, 1977), pp. 1-42, on seventeenth-century theories of language and universal grammar. On the importance in seventeenth-century literature of language as a social indicator and of the theme of linguistic ability, see Américo Castro, *El Pensamiento de Cervantes*, pp. 184-185; Rosenblat, *La Lengua del Quijote*, pp. 14-16; and Amado Alonso, "Las prevaricaciones idiomáticas de Sancho," *Nueva Revista de Filología Hispánica* 2 (1948): 1-20.

Spanish Renaissance,[26] defines *metaphor* thus: "Metaphor consists in giving a name that belongs to something else; the transference being either from genus to species, or from species to genus, or from species to species, or on grounds of analogy."[27] It is noteworthy, as Jacques Derrida points out in "White Mythology," that Aristotle's definition of metaphor occurs in the *Poetics*, a work which starts out as a study of mimesis.[28] By the seventeenth century it is a commonplace notion in literary theory that mimesis, as the imitation of nature, is connected with the possibility of meaning and truth in poetic discourse.[29] Cide Hamete, the Second Author, the various readers of texts within the novel, and even don Quijote himself postulate the

[26] E. C. Riley, *Cervantes' Theory of the Novel*, pp. 2-3; and Armando Durán, "Teoría y práctica de la novela en España durante el Siglo de Oro," in Santos Sanz Villanueva and Carlos J. Barbáchano, eds., *Teoría de la novela*, Colección "Temas" 6 (Madrid: Sociedad Gen. Española de Librería, 1976). Riley notes that although the *Poetics* was not translated into Spanish until 1623 (by Antonio Ordonez), it was available indirectly through Italian sources and its statements were contained in many of the contemporary Spanish rhetorics. See also Aubrey Bell, "Cervantes and the Renaissance," *Hispanic Review* 2 (1934): 87-101; and Cesáreo Bandera, *Mímesis conflictiva: Ficción literaria y violencia en Cervantes y Calderón* (Madrid: Gredos, 1975); and especially, Jean-François Cannavaggio, "Alonso López Pinciano y la Estética Literaria de Cervantes en el *Quijote*," pp. 13-107, which argues convincingly for the importance of López Pinciano's *Philosophía Antigua Poética* (1596) as a possible source of Cervantes' poetic precepts.

[27] *De Poetica* 1457^b 6-9, in *Works of Aristotle*, vol. 11, under the editorship of W. D. Ross; *De Poetica*, trans. Ingram Bywater (London: Clarenden Press, 1924). Citations from this translation of Aristotle will be identified in the text. López Pinciano too defines metaphor in these terms in *Philosophía Antigua Poética* (*PhAP*), ed. A. Carballo Picazo, 3 vols. (Madrid: CSIC, 1953), II:132 *passim*. Hereafter cited by volume and page number.

[28] This conjunction of figures, argues Derrida, is not mere coincidence. While mimesis is an ambivalent process, it generally functions as a mnemotechnic sign that brings back in altered form something that is not immediately present ("White Mythology," pp. 237-238). The power of the mimetic imagination is such that it is able to convert even nonsensory experiences, such as passions and emotions, into objects of perception. Mimesis is thus, at least in part, man's natural ability to make the imperceptible world perceptible.

[29] See López Pinciano, who argues that imitation is the formal cause of poetry: "Poesía . . . no es otra cosa que arte que enseña a imitar con la lengua o lenguaje" (*PhAP* I: 195).

Aristotelean notion that mimesis is in some respects a possibility inherent in nature which can unveil nature. When don Quijote says, for example, that "the natural poet who makes use of art will be a much better poet than the poet who relies only on his knowledge of the art: the reason for this is that art is not better than Nature, but perfects it. In this manner, Nature combined with art, and art with Nature, will produce a most perfect poet" (DQ II, 16), he is on perfectly stable theoretical grounds. Don Quijote expounds the classical argument that the poetic word can "combine" with Nature, thus forming a bridge between perceptible external and imperceptible internal themes, because he understands that mimesis is not something extraneous to Nature, but rather belongs to it in the form of human speech.

This concept of the "natural," explains Derrida, is reduced and confined by Aristotle to human speech: ". . . naturality in general says itself, reassembles itself, knows itself, appears to itself, reflects itself, and 'mimics' itself par excellence and *in truth* in human nature. *Mimēsis* is proper to man. Only man imitates properly. . . . The power of truth, as the unveiling of nature by *mimēsis*, congenitally belongs to the physics of man, to anthropophysics. Such is the natural origin of poetry, and such is the natural origin of metaphor."[30] This is as much to say that man's ability to see resemblances is not only one of his constitutive properties, it is also the very basis of his will to see the truth. "To produce a good metaphor," writes Aristotle, "is to see a likeness" (*De Poetica* 1459[a] 7-8). And this ability to see likenesses is also what makes the representation of truth possible: ". . . midway between the unintelligible and the commonplace, it is metaphor which most produces knowledge" (*Rhetoric* III, 1410[b]). *Mimēsis*, in conjunction with metaphor, thus produces knowledge by allowing us to reduce the complexly differential quality of things and concepts into a structure of intelligible similarities.

[30] Derrida, "White Mythology," p. 237. Cf. López Pinciano's detailed discussion of "*imitación*" (*PhAP* I: 195).

But as we have seen in our reading of the Adventure of the Windmills and of Mambrino's Helmet, this ability to see resemblance within difference is precisely the source of don Quijote's delusions. Rather than providing him with clear and certain "knowledge," don Quijote's perceptions of resemblance always lead him astray. But Cervantes' aim is not to indict don Quijote's propensity for metaphors, nor to condemn metaphor as such. Instead, he wishes to show that, to the extent that don Quijote's metaphors share in the same processes of "imitation" on which the truth of everyday discourse is based, his metaphors put in question the "purity" and "propriety" of discourse in general.[31]

While the reduction of differences into similarities has been a thematic presence from the first, Chapter 25 of Part I provides the specific pattern by which don Quijote's metaphorical speech acts are organized. Alluding there to his intended imitation of Amadís de Gaula and to his desire for Dulcinea del Toboso, Quijote names Amadís as "the north-star, the morning star, the sun of all valiant knights and lovers" and Dulcinea as "the day of my night, . . . north-star of my quest, star of my fate." The dual figures of Amadís, as the paradigmatic "sun" and "north-star" of knight errantry, and of Dulcinea, as the exemplary "north-star" of courtly love, are assimilated as the single representation of don Quijote's quest. In effect, the desire to be Amadís is but another expression of his desire for Dulcinea. And the reverse of this statement is also valid. But once this chiasmus has been performed, there is no reason why it cannot be performed again and again, in an ironic spiral of indefinite

[31] Quijote forgets (in a literal sense) the metaphoric nature of his language of quest. He metaphorizes the metaphors of ordinary discourse, which are no longer seen as metaphors, and thus deconstructs by negative example the truth of traditional discourse. Don Quijote does at an exponential level what others do on a primary level: "Er vergisst also die originalen Anschauungsmetaphern als Metaphern und nimmt sie als die Dinge selbst." (He thus forgets that his original, informing metaphors are metaphors and takes them as things in themselves) (Nietzsche, *GW* 6: 84).

regression. The absorption of the sense of "north-star" and "sun" by both Amadís and Dulcinea is a further expression of the chaos at the center of don Quijote's linguistic habits. It negates the concept of an organizing center which might validate the imitation, for in each case the unique and central source of life-sustaining energy is shown to be susceptible to displacement by another figure, equally unique and vital.

By Part II, these metaphoric displacements have proceeded at such a pace that don Quijote no longer requires the substantial presence of Aldonza Lorenzo to sustain his belief in the metaphoric Dulcinea. He can thus freely admit that "God knows whether or not there is a Dulcinea in the world, or whether she is fantastic or not fantastic; . . . I contemplate her as befits a lady to be contemplated who is in herself beauty of the highest degrees of perfection" (*DQ* II, 32). Dulcinea is now as don Quijote would be without her—"a shadow without a body to cast it" (II, 32). Language, having attained truth, should be "filled, achieved, actualized, to the point of erasing itself" before the object or thought to which it refers and makes manifest. Metaphor, however, is "the moment of possible meaning as the possibility of non-truth . . . the moment of the detour in which the truth might still be lost."[32] Don Quijote's metaphors, the mimetic representations of his desires, enact this detour from truth, for instead of revealing Dulcinea's immediate presence, they continously allude to her absence: "God knows whether or not there is a Dulcinea in the world."

The double suns of don Quijote's solar system revolve around the empty center of his illusions. And since there is no properly ordering reference in such a metaphor, don Quijote, who is himself the mark of a figure of speech, can only continue on his errant path down the long digressive sentence which is his life, with no assurance that he will ever reach the source of

[32] Derrida, "White Mythology," p. 241.

clarity and light which signifies his desires.[33] The indeterminability of metaphor, the metaphorization of metaphor, seems to be written into the very script of his linguistic acts. In this situation, don Quijote is different from those other metaphorical wanderers who populate Cervantes' fictive landscape only insofar as his natural genius to see hidden resemblances, and hence to substitute one term for another, has run away with him. In the *Poetics* Aristotle had written that "the greatest thing by far is to be a master of metaphor. It is the one thing that cannot be learned from others; and it is also a sign of genius, since a good metaphor implies an intuitive perception of the similarity in dissimilars" (*De Poetica* 1459[a] 5-8). Don Quijote's "genius" for metaphor, however, has led to an aberrant semantics, a code of uncontrolled substitution, a rhetoric which continues to baffle others, as he well realizes when he notes that "my history . . . will need a commentary to be understood" (*DQ* II, 3). His discourse baffles precisely because in attempting to approach the ideal of language, it reveals the metaphoric structure of everyday discourse and its pragmatic rhetoric. The commentary on the text, consequently, will itself be susceptible to the maladies of the primary text.

❦ ❦ ❦

While our discussion has led repeatedly to the notion of metaphor, we have yet to see the exact nature of don Quijote's figures. For the sake of economy, the "Helmet of Mambrino" episode and the "Amadís-Dulcinea-north-star-sun" metaphor cluster can provide the textual examples for a closer reading of his figures of speech.

In the first example, Quijote is not saying that the barber's basin is a helmet. Such a statement would not be a metaphor

[33] Foucault thus argues that "Don Quichotte . . . était devenue un signe errant" (*Les mots et les choses*, p. 62).

but merely a manifestly wrong use of language.[34] Don Quijote's "madness" has not alienated him from nature to quite such an extent. What he is saying is that the golden, shining object on the approaching man's head is Mambrino's helmet. This is a metaphor as defined by Aristotle, the substitution by analogy of similar qualities (golden, shining, head-piece) between different things (Mambrino's helmet and the barber's basin). The meanings transferred concern the properties of each thing. Derrida points out in "White Mythology" that in order for it to be possible to replace one property by another, without bringing the thing itself into the play of substitutions, it is necessary that these properties belong to the same essence of one thing, or have been taken from different essences of one thing.[35] This is the operation, writes Derrida, which Aristotle calls *antikatēgoreisthai*: "the predicate of the essence and the predicate of the proper can be exchanged without the statement becoming false."[36]

Don Quijote's metaphors thus do not simply designate the legitimacy of the inversion of subject (S) and predicate (P), but rather point to a process of reciprocal substitutions between two predicates applied to one and the same subject. In other words, don Quijote's metaphor is not structured such that

where S – is a barber's basin
and P – is Mambrino's helmet
that, *S* is *P* and *P* is *S*,

but rather is patterned so that:

[34] The standards for deciding what are "good" versus "bad" metaphors are, unfortunately, not easily decidable. Max Black points out, for instance, that while "Man is a Wolf" is a wrong use of language, it is a perfectly acceptable metaphor (*Models and Metaphors: Studies in Language and Philosophy* [Ithaca: Cornell University Press, 1962]). "Bad" metaphors are, of course, nothing more than "good" catachreses.

[35] "White Mythology," p. 249.

[36] Ibid., p. 249, n. 55. Aristotle's definition, *Topics* I.5 102a 18-19.

if X – the object on the approaching man's head
and S – is golden, shining head-gear
and P – it is Mambrino's helmet
then, for X, if *X* is *S*, then *X* is *P*, and
if *X* is *P*, then *X* is *S*.

It follows, then, that don Quijote's madness will not force him to create helmets from every barber's basin he encounters. Instead, the structure of his linguistic habits will lead him to perceive Mambrino's helmet for any golden, shining head-gear. The process is always due simply to the exchange of similar attributes of different things. For this reason, Quijote can imagine that "what seems to you to be a barber's basin appears to me to be Mambrino's helmet, and to another as something else" (I, 25).

Our statement of the problem of metaphor in this manner is useful because it helps us differentiate three possible levels of meaning in the metaphor: (a) the *literal*—"golden, shining basin"; (b) the *proper*—"golden, shining head-piece"; and (c) the *figural*—"Mambrino's golden helmet." The literal and the figural meanings share the proper sense.[37] At the moment the barber's basin can become Mambrino's helmet without having lost any of its properties as a basin, the world of reality as represented by Cide Hamete also becomes susceptable to quixotic transformations without necessarily losing any of its qualities as "reality."

We can also discern a similar pattern in the "sun" metaphor cluster of I, 25, where the properties of the analogy may be written in this fashion:

[37] This distinction among the figural, proper, and literal senses of a metaphor is a familiar one to rhetoricians. See Paul de Man's discussion, "Proust et l'allegorie de la lecture," in *Mouvements premièrs* (Paris: José Cortí, 1972), pp. 231-250, trans. by the author as "Reading (Proust)" in his *Allegories of Reading*, pp. 57-58.

if X – the guiding ideal "sun," and "north-star"
and S – Amadís, the "sun" is one expression of the ideal
and P – Dulcinea, the "north-star" is another
then, for X, if *X* is *S*, then *X* is *P* and
if *X* is *P*, then *X* is *S*.

The necessary condition of these abstractions and exchanges is that the essence of a subject should admit of several properties, and then that between the essence of a thing and what is proper to it there should be a specific possibility of inversion so that the elements can be exchanged for each other. These simple rules govern the process of metaphorization. However, the complexity implicit in the sensation of specific properties and their proper expression can lead to "bad" metaphors. And indeed, in our last example, it is difficult to know what is proper to the central idea (Amadís, Dulcinea, sun, star) since none of these is intrinsically, directly *sensible*. They can be discerned only indirectly. As a consequence, the metaphor implying the source of all meaning for don Quijote fails to bring clear and certain knowledge. The best one can expect is *palabras honestas, significantes y bien colocadas*. The structure of don Quijote's metaphors as *antikatēgoreisthai* reveals therefore a law of ambiguity which governs the possibility of meaning creation. And it is under this solar metaphor that the history of don Quijote is brought forth into the "light of the world" (Prologue).[38]

[38] The sun metaphor occurs widely throughout the novel. Some examples: Amadís has been called "the Knight of the Sun"; Dulcinea is "the sun of . . . beauty" (II, 8), and the "light of the sun of beauty" (II, 10); Sancho describes the "Enchanted Dulcinea" as being like "the very sun at noon" (II, 10)—an ambiguous metaphor indeed; Don Quijote is often named by such terms as "the pole-star and the morning star of knight errantry" (II, 49). Carrasco accuses critics in II,3 of scolding "at specks in the bright sun of the work they review." The metaphor has already been applied to books by the Canon in I, 48, when he describes the new mode of writing he proposes as causing "the old books to be eclipsed in the presence of the new." Quijote, who has not heard this, says that "to attempt to convince anyone that there were no such persons as Amadís and the other knights . . . would be like trying to persuade one that the sun does not shine."

Our examples of the sun metaphor have one function—to show that the appeals to criteria of "clarity" and the negations of "obscurity" throughout the text of *Don Quijote de la Mancha* are already constructed by metaphors. The novel seems to answer the question of the clarity or obscurity of language by saying that, properly speaking, language cannot be either "clear" or "obscure." The concepts which play a part in the definition of the ideal language always have an origin and a force which are themselves nameable only by indirection or periphrasis. Don Quijote's "madness," consequently, is but the paradigm of the very process of metaphorization (that is, idealization and appropriation) which constitutes everyday discourse.[39] He consistently finds that the truth of the ideal can be expressed only through the detour of tropes. This does not mean, however, that his speech acts are meaningless. While he does not create new signs, nor enrich the existing codes, as Sancho does in the "baciyelmo" episode, don Quijote does expose the functions of language. From the material of everyday discourse he produces new rules and new meanings. And because the metaphorical is not exhausted by an account of its sense but gives rise to new metaphors, themselves in need of interpretation, don Quijote's use of metaphor gives rise to a *text*. One major aspect of don Quijote's story is then essentially the art of establishing a syntax for the transformations and deviations of his metaphoric language, in which the differences among the things of the world are forgotten and assimilated into an organic unity of sense.

❦ ❦ ❦

This process of displacement of meaning is always made present to the reader both by the narrator's comments and by the in-

[39] As we noted in Chapter One, this is Nietzsche's argument about creating "notions with which one could live." Derrida summarizes: "The recourse to a metaphor in order to give the 'idea' of metaphor: this is what prohibits a definition, but nevertheless metaphorically assigns a check-point, a fixed place: the metaphor/dwelling. . . . [M]etaphor can always be deciphered simultaneously as a particular figure and as a paradigm of the very process of metaphorization: *idealization* and *reappropriation*" ("White Mythology," p. 253).

sistence throughout the text on the "literary" or "illiterate." Quijote, as we have seen, is an insatiable reader and has even felt urges to write (I, 2 and 3). The Priest and the Barber both read and criticize literature with a vengeance (I, 6). In all of don Quijote's various adventures, the shepherds and goatherds he happens to meet are always either students, poets, or singers. Dulcinea, in Sancho's false account of his embassy to her, has not read don Quijote's letter because, according to Sancho, "she said that she could neither read nor write." Sancho himself of course is illiterate, as are several of the characters to whom the Priest reads the manuscript of "The Tale of Foolish Curiosity" (I, 32). The Canon reveals his vast reading of chivalric fiction (I, 47), his intentions to write a chivalric story (I, 48), and urges don Quijote to read history (I, 49).

The "Second Author" describes himself as being such an avid reader that he is driven by a "natural disposition" to read even scraps of paper in the streets (I, 9). In fact, this insistent disposition to reading can actually be said to have given us the novel itself. There would be no story to tell in the first place had not don Quijano been driven mad by his readings of chivalric novels. And the greater part of the text of *Don Quijote* (everything after I, 8) would have remained unknown had it not been for the reading habits of the Second Author, who searches for and finds the lost portions of the manuscript: "In the first part of this history, we left the valiant Basque and the famous Don Quixote with naked swords aloft. . . . At this critical point, our delightful history ended and remained as if dismembered, our author failing to inform us where to find the missing part. . . . This caused me great annoyance" (*DQ* I, 9).

In high suspense over what will happen next, the Second Author cannot bring himself to believe that the missing text is not to be found. Thus, in compensation for the "work and diligence" (I, 9) he invests in locating the missing sections of the manuscript, the Second Author now claims part of the glory of don Quijote's adventures, and part of the fame of Cide Hamete's narrative.

Arguing for the authenticity of the newly discovered manuscript of the *Historia de Don Quijote de la Mancha, escrita por Cide Hamete Benengeli, historiador arábigo* (I, 9), the narrator claims that the only objection that might be raised against its veracity is that its author is an Arab, from a nation of liars. Hence, should the story prove to be deficient in truth, he argues, "for my part, I hold that it was the fault of that dog of an author, rather than any fault of the subject matter" (*DQ* I, 9).

From I, 10, on, this narrator, the "Second Author" as he has identified himself, cedes the bulk of the narration to the "First Author" (I, 9), Cide Hamete Benengeli's inscribed voice, as translated from the Arabic by an anonymous Moorish translator. This digressive episode concerning the discovery of the Arabic manuscript in the Toledan marketplace turns the telling of don Quijote's adventure into a story about the narration of *Don Quijote*, and is the circumstance which first calls attention to the synchronic problematics of reading in the novel.

Without exception, the various narrators of don Quijote's story function first as critical readers of a previous version of the story. We can isolate at least four levels of reading. First, Cide Hamete addresses one hypothetical reader, made explicit by the Moorish translator. This translator then addresses the Second Author, who hired him to translate the Arabic text. The Second Author now addresses a contrived reader, who cannot always be identified with the present real reader of Cervantes' book.[40] Finally, the author of the Prologue, "Cervantes," addresses "you," presumably the real reader made explicit by the initial words of the text: "Desocupado lector." As we have seen,

[40] See Ruth El Saffar, "The Function of the Fictional Narrator in *Don Quijote*," *MLN* 83 (1968): 164-177; and *Distance and Control in Don Quixote*. See also, George Haley, "The Narrator in *Don Quijote*," *MLN* 80 (1965): 145-165; and John J. Allen, "The Narrators, the Reader, and Don Quijote," *MLN* 91 (1976): 201-212.

however, even this reader is an implied rhetorical contrivance and cannot be identified automatically with any historically determinate reader.[41] At each of these reader levels, interruptions, in the forms of critical judgments, abound. Each reader attempts to establish for him or herself the text's unequivocal truth. (These interruptions are in addition to formal or grammatical interruptions *within* the narrated story.)

The use of the first-person narrator, *yo*, in *Don Quijote* leads from the beginning to the creation of a corresponding second-person, *tú*. Émile Benveniste has shown how the presence of a *tú* is a linguistic necessity implied in every act of first-person speech.[42] The authorial voice, as *yo*, never enters the text unaccompanied. In *Don Quijote*, the presence of the authorial *yo* becomes the linguistic basis of another character, a contrived reader, who is never simply passive nor stable in identity. This "reader," in the various guises of the Second Author, the Moorish translator, the implied reader of the Prologue, or the real reader of Cervantes' text, is the source of doubtings, corrections, and qualifications.

The Moorish translator, for example, declares Chapter 5 of Part II apocryphal because Sancho is said to speak there in an overly refined manner. He later also wonders why Cide Hamete, a Moor, should "swear as a Christian" (II, 27). The Second Author testifies to Cide Hamete's authority in I, 26, I, 52, II, 40, and II, 50, despite the fact that he himself has introduced Cide Hamete as a "liar." Cide Hamete, too, emerges from the Second Author's diegetic narrative to comment on his own story

[41] Wolfgang Iser has termed this rhetorically active figure, the "implied reader": "He embodies all those predispositions necessary for a literary work to exercise its effects—predispositions laid down, not by an empirical outside reality, but by the text itself. Consequently, the implied reader as a concept has his roots firmly planted in the structure of the text; he is a construct and in no way to be identified with any real reader" (*The Act of Reading*, p. 34). See also Iser's *The Implied Reader: Patterns of Communication in Prose Fiction from Bunyan to Beckett* (Baltimore: Johns Hopkins University Press, 1974).

[42] Émile Benveniste, *Problèmes de linguistique générale* (Paris: Gallimard, 1966), pp. 252-253.

in II, 8, II, 24, II, 29 and II, 47. Whatever the causes of these interruptions may be, their results are always the same and resemble don Quijote's linguistic corrections and critical commentaries: they incessantly divert the issue away from the central narrative.

One can thus justly say that, in this novel, the moment which marks the passage from "life" to writing about life corresponds to the features of the act of reading. Both acts require the critical separation from the undifferentiated mass of detail those distinctively "true and significant" elements which can constitute a text. In II, 44, the mediating voice of the Second Author points out Cide Hamete's recognition of just this process. There, Cide Hamete is reported to have asked for praise "in the proper original of this story," not simply for what he has written, "but also for what he has not written." The readings described within the novel, and the preceding instance which defines Cide Hamete's method of reductive writing, display this attempted process of critical interpretation. If the writing, like the reading and interpretation, of a text involves a paring away of the supplementary elements which seduce away from the ascetic goal of understanding, one must read the sense of *imitación* (mimesis) in this text in a sense other than as the duplication of reality. *Mimesis* here always cedes to *poesis*, that is, fabrication or invention. At every point that the narrative claims authority by reference to the truth of history (a diegetic instance), it thus also names the opposite and contradictory moment of poetic creation, as the text continues to deconstruct their difference.

❦ ❦ ❦

This unavoidable decay of differences, which by Part II clearly structures the language of the text, is especially evident in Cide Hamete's invocation of the "sun" at the beginning of II, 45:

> O perpetual discoverer of the Antipodes! Torch of the world! Eye of heaven! Sweet stirrer of wine coolers! Here Thym-

> brius, there Phoebus, now archer, now physician! Father of Poetry, inventor of Music, you who always rise and—though you seem to—never set! On you I call, sun, by whose aid man engenders man. On you I call to favor me and to light the darkness of my mind . . . for without you I feel myself timid, faint-hearted and confused. (*DQ* II, 45)

In this apostrophe, the historian par excellence becomes a *poet* and aligns himself with that other sun-gazer, don Quijote. The image of the sun, whether as guide to historical truth, as sign of the ideal of imitation, or as emblem of desire, orients the text toward the seduction of literary language as metaphor. It is at textual moments such as this, which dramatize the assimilation of differences, that traditional interpretations have posed the possibility of transforming the contradictions of the act of reading *Don Quijote* into a narrative which will contain them in enveloping them. Thus, one may find statements such as the following by Ángel del Río: "Cervantes gives poetic form to the vision of a problematic reality. He seeks a foundation from which to distinguish reality and illusion, and to establish unambiguous truth."[43] Del Río conceives of this novel as a perfect mimetic imitation of a problematic world. In a similar manner, Manuel Durán writes: "Ambiguity is nothing more than a secondary by-product of Cervantes' novel. It is a partial result within the artistic totality that is produced by the new rules that Cervantes invents, and it is interesting only insofar as it helps to clarify those complicated and elastic rules which are to transcend the older rules of fiction."[44] And Américo Castro has written: "Cervantes' impressionism is something profoundly rooted within his ideal system. . . . Men of great genius know that truth cannot be born out from the critique of experience. Cervantes will present his figures enveloped and resolved within

[43] Ángel del Río, "El Equívoco del Quijote," *Hispanic Review* 27 (1959), rpt. in *El Equívoco del Quijote* (San Juan, P. R.: Cordillera, 1972), p. 25.

[44] Manuel Durán, *La Ambigüedad en el Quijote* (Xalapa, Veracruz: Univ. Veracruzana, Biblioteca de la Fac. de Filosofía y Letras, 1960), pp. 268-269.

the impression which they create in each observer who approaches the work, in the various points of view they create."[45]

Such readings of *Don Quijote* imply the promise of a narrative which, having reconciled its inner contradictions, might serve as a model for reading this and other texts. As a narrative about resolved contradictory interpretations of what constitutes truth and falsehood (history and fiction) within the act of reading, the model would itself escape the destructive elements of that complication. The resolution of the play of truth and falsehood by perspectivism and impressionism would itself be truth, and would thus be the cornerstone for Del Río's "foundation to distinguish reality and illusion, and to establish the recognition of truth." One would have to follow out the entire string of instances of assimilations of differences into resemblances, of mergings of truth and error, fiction and reality, in *Don Quijote* in order to decide whether the novel in fact corresponds to such a model.

We have already seen how don Quijote, himself the metaphoric figure par excellence and blessed with the genius for discerning likenesses, has aligned himself with the fictional *exemplum*, Amadís de Gaula, and how he has created an ideal expression of plenitude in the equally fictional figure of Dulcinea del Toboso. The figural logic of the narrative thus requires that we see Amadís and Dulcinea, assimilated into one by the substitution of their common features with those of the "sun," as symbols of don Quijote's quest. Their figural senses (Dulcinea is the "sun of beauty"; Amadís is the "sun of knight errantry") allow this reduction to the implicit proper sense (the attributes of "light," "life-giving power and source," "center"), which in turn allows don Quijote to make them the emblems of his desire for the plenitude of the Golden Age. But if we inquire into how Dulcinea becomes such an organizing symbol, we will see the unsuitability of regarding this symbol as a point of reference

[45] Américo Castro, *El Pensamiento de Cervantes*, pp. 183-184.

from which we might harmonize distinct perspectives and give coherence to the narrative as a whole. Here again Cervantes is very subtle, for when the existence of Dulcinea is questioned in II, 32, and don Quijote admits the possibility of her metaphoric status, the narrative poses the distinct possibility that this symbolic entity is not a sign of a transcendental truth, but is simply a metaphor of a metaphor. As such, it can provide us with no more stable point for establishing an authoritative interpretation than can any other metaphor.

I say that "Dulcinea" is a metaphor of a metaphor because her name is, first of all, itself already the figural sign of Quijote's love for Aldonza Lorenzo. Secondly, Dulcinea, with Amadís, also represents the ideal "sun," which is the source sustaining Quijote's imaginative life. Recalling our earlier distinction among the *figural, proper,* and *literal* senses of metaphor, we can therefore say that, as a metaphor, the name of "Dulcinea" displaces its own proper sense: the *figural* Dulcinea is simultaneously the *proper* center of Quijote's desires. The *proper* and *figural* tenors thus collapse into the one *literal* vehicle.[46] This composite "Dulcinea" does indeed represent a certain sense. But the figural Dulcinea (Aldonza Lorenzo as transformed by Quijote's romantic imagination) announces that proper sense (the ideal solar center) by means of a literal sense (Aldonza Lorenzo as others actually see her) to which the proper and figural senses bear no resemblance at all.[47]

Furthermore, Aldonza as the figure for the "enchanted Dulcinea" of Part II, chapter 10, in Sancho's deceptive account of

[46] Schematically, we have, then, these possible levels of meaning: (a) the *literal*—Aldonza Lorenzo, and later, the peasant girl of II, 10; (b) the *proper*—the ideal solar center of "beauty" and "light"; the "pole-star" and "north star"; and (c) the *figural*—Dulcinea del Toboso. The *proper* is no longer the shared quality, as the *figural* and *proper* levels collapse, provoking the *literal* level to dominate the meaning of the metaphor. See Quintillian, *Institutio Oratoria*, trans. H. E. Butler (Cambridge, Mass.: Harvard University Press, 1966), VIII, vi, 4-10.

[47] I follow here the pattern of reading Paul de Man describes in "Reading (Proust)," *Allegories of Reading*, pp. 67-68.

his visit to El Toboso, represents yet another sense, which is also proper to her (that is, the *loss* of beauty, the *eclipsing* of the sun, the *chaos* of the center). But this tertiary sense no longer coincides at all with the original emblematic sign of the transcendent sun of truth.

The situation pointed out by the "Dulcinea-north-star" metaphor is not simply that symbols and metaphors contain separate and distinct layers of meaning. This is certainly true, but not entirely to the point here. Rather, the several meanings of this metaphor cluster are constitutively contradictory. No possible reconciliation among them can occur: at the moment one meaning predominates, the others are negated. Nor can this opposition of conflicting readings be ignored. Representing Dulcinea allegorically as the Ideal necessarily leads to the oxymoron which can name Aldonza as the Ideal. This latter possibility diverges from the initial meaning of the figure to the point of negating it as a valid representation. The negation stems from the necessary tropological factor that the one literal and representational figure (Aldonza) engenders at least two meanings, one figural and metaphorical (Dulcinea), the other proper and allegorical (the Ideal north-star), and that the relationship among the levels of meaning is one of radical incongruity.

The history of don Quijote can always be reduced to a confrontation of incongruent meanings: history/fiction, mad/sane, foolish/wise, proper/improper, literal/figural, etc. At the same time, however, it is virtually impossible to define at any one instance in the novel any of these polarities in the precise terms of truth or error. Each element of the polarity shares in truth and error and thereby eliminates its relationship to its opposite as a polarity.[48] Whenever the text is described in terms of the truthful expression of any one of these polarities, it is always

[48] Thus we have, for example, the string of passages which both affirm and deny the truth of don Quijote's visions. See II, 24-25, in particular. Cf. the discussion by Alexander A. Parker, "El concepto de la verdad en el Quijote," *Revista de Filología Española* 33 (1948): 287-305.

possible to point to the presence of the opposite term inextricably tied to it, deconstructing its supposed truth value. But since the figural logic of the text makes it impossible to accept even this deconstructed sense as a demystified truth, the text proceeds to engender still other supplementary figural patterns which undo the logic of the prior patterns. Quijote's view that things can seem something to one person and something else to another is thus reflected anew in the very structure of his metaphors, whose words can "mean" one thing and simultaneously imply their opposite. I am saying, of course, that the narrative of *Don Quijote* always says something about itself and about how it should be read. But at each point that it seems to establish the ground for its own *authoritative* reading, the means for the undoing of that stable foundation are also established. As a consequence, no proper reading (perspectival or otherwise) can emerge from the text to guide us to the transcendental sun of truth. When we feel that we have arrived at such a perspectival synthesis, the words expressing the synthesis will continue to imply some other, perhaps subversive, dialectic. The narrative of *Don Quijote* thus *allegorizes* its own deconstruction: at every point that the text speaks about history, poetry, arms and letters, chivalry, imitation, or desire, something else is metaphorically signified. That other signified concept is always the flowing chain of language and its metaphoric words, which will continue to eliminate the value system upon which their authority is founded.

Such an interpretation accounts for the coherence of the text, which, despite its narratival *reticentia*, will recover, at the limits of its negations, the adequation between its enunciated meanings and the historical structure upon which the possibility of all exhaustive thematic readings depends. But since don Quijote's metaphors do not simply represent the exchange of two distinct realities (the ideal vs. the real, say), but represent the structure of metaphor itself, the difficulty pointed out in this analysis is a grave one. We shall never be able to deduce from a glance at the literal Aldonza that she signifies the ideal of courtly beauty and truth because her attributes point in a different direction. Don Quijote "knows" her as this ideal simply because his books tell him a knight's lady should be the emblem of beauty. He has access to the proper sense by a literal act of reading. That literal reading is possible because the notion of "ideal beauty" is assigned to a referential entity who does not pertain to the world of inter-textual relations. But such is not the case for the allegorical representation of "Dulcinea" as the point of "solar" stability. Everything belonging to that allegorical representation leads us away from an understanding of the literal figure and blocks access to a correct comprehension. The allegorical narrative which denotes this situation is thus a narrative about the impossibility of complete understandings. This impossibility is not limited to don Quijote alone but, as we see in Part II especially, extends to all attempts at definitive and authoritative expressions of truth.

This discordance between the literal and the proper senses confounds don Quijote, but constitutes the site of Cervantes' own growth into full artistic maturity. In fact, the essential distance between Cervantes and his various fictional narrative voices, allegorical signs of the author's absence, is never clearer than when they claim to be able to describe faithfully, although metaphorically, don Quijote's desires and dreams. Cervantes the writer is well aware that the "truth" of any act of comprehension must always be assigned precisely to and conditioned by the parameters of metaphor.

The final elegy in which Cide Hamete's pen acquires voice to praise don Quijote resurrects the semiotic system which defines don Quijote as a graphism and a linguistic sign: *Para mí sola nació don Quijote, y yo para él: él supo obrar, y yo escribir; solos los dos somos para en uno* (*DQ* II, 74). His whole existence has been nothing but language, and in this final scene he is assimilated into the pen which writes that language into the text. While don Quijote's interpretive actions consistently show "knowledge" (as a product of metaphor) to be based on the misleading assumption of the identity of dissimilars, the utterance of this negative insight now creates a new metaphor (that don Quijote is the pen of his own writing) which engenders another proper meaning (that don Quijote is the system of fiction). The narrative thus moves us openly from a language of imitation and desire, as René Girard describes it, to a language of fiction and metaphor.[49] This final metastasis which is to supersede the value of the first metaphor is, as we have seen, even more obviously vulnerable to deconstruction than was the first and cannot, therefore, lead to a decisive end.

For the author of the Prologue, the physical presentation of a text gives it a stability which valorizes its expressions and lends dignity to its author. He seems to feel that his own "sterile" text can appropriate these qualities from other texts by incorporating them through its Prologue, marginalia, footnotes, annotations, and index. He assumes that the presence of such written authorial signs activates a metaphysics which locates truth in what is immediately present without mediation, and that words can be authorized to mean what they say. For him, the written word thus becomes transparent as it leads the reader back to the real, substantial presence which guarantees its meaning, namely the author himself.

His friend, however, ironizes this concept by inviting the implied author ("Cervantes") to create the fiction of an authoritative presence behind the word. He offers an option which seems to conform to the values of a metaphysics of presence by providing the lexical signs of presence, but which really parodies it, by cutting the word loose, and liberating it from the source

[49] René Girard, *Deceit, Desire, and the Novel*, trans. Yvonne Freccero (Baltimore: Johns Hopkins University Press, 1965; Paris: Grasset, 1961), pp. 1-4. This stricture against authoritative readings applies of course to my own reading as well, which can claim no greater authority nor any fewer errors than can other readings of Cervantes' text. Reading *Don Quijote* can be, to paraphrase Edward Said, "no more than probability and no less than error" (*Beginnings*, p. 75).

of meaning. The friend thus advises what the author has, in fact, already considered. In seeking to sever the tie, which is metaphoric, between the procreating father/author and the issued orphan-child/text, "Cervantes" had already rejected the fiction of absolute authority. From the beginning, therefore, the Prologue author and his friend dramatize the idea that the meaning of the text is not to be considered as an abstract essence made manifest by an author who stands immediately and practically behind a text, ready to assist the reader to recover that meaning. Rather, meaning in this text exists conditioned only by the dynamic system of metaphoric relations among the words of the text.

Language, as Leo Spitzer has demonstrated, forms the foundation of don Quijote's reason.[50] Its logical order, grammatical patterns, and orderly laws of construction seem to offer a base upon which other certainties can be established. Its rhetorical and figural aspects, moreover, provide it creative energy. Don Quijote's attempts to use those formal and grammatical qualities to produce an absolute and wholly independent knowledge, however, are always undermined by the rhetorical and figurative powers of language. As a consequence, don Quijote is constantly thrown into situations where all certainty is lost and where only absolute not-knowing or endless controversy remain.

Communication such as that envisioned by don Quijote, and

[50] Spitzer, "Linguistic Perspectivism in the *Don Quijote*," *op. cit.*, pp. 42-68. But far from providing, as Spitzer would have it, liberation "from the limitations of language" (p. 60), the linguistic by-play in *Don Quijote* enacts Cervantes' recognition of the chaotic possibilities inherent to the discontinuity between the linguistic sign and its conceptual referent. My own discussion, emphasizing the breakdown of the Aristotelean pattern of *antikatēgoreisthai*, the "unreadable" allegory of the "Dulcinea-Amadís-Sun" metaphor group, and the metaphorical nature of textual authority throughout the text, thus diverges from Spitzer's and Foucault's. The difference is the fundamental one between their grammatical and my own rhetorical emphasis. It is a vital difference, I think, both because grammatical analyses tend to pass over the deconstructive force of tropes in general, and because the assumed continuity between grammatical law and rhetorical order is not borne out by close analysis.

such as that postulated by the Prologue author's friend, would be Edenic in its immediacy—that is, it would not require figures and grammatical form to represent concepts. It would attempt to capture the essence of things, their purest qualities, and their sovereign identities by assuming the existence of immobile forms that precede the material world of contingency and succession. *Don Quijote* shows, however, that human speech as a whole and in its various modes of discourse is not immediate. It is rather constitutively figurative and hence burdened with ambiguity, confusion, and undecidability; it can be "truthful" therefore only about the fashioning of primordial truths. "Meanings" are parametrically linked with their narrative performances. There is no question of a decidable isolation of a "told" from the manner of the "telling." Ultimately, therefore, narrative has no non-displaceable object. Yet Cervantes also recognizes that the capabilities of language are not insignificant, for we do speak and we do write with undoubted effect. Through its very resources, through "significant, honest, and well-ordered words," Cervantes finds the possibility of creating the fiction of a satisfactorily contingent authority for alluding to the limitations discourse itself imposes upon us.

Thus, while grammatical oversight, phonological transposition, or syntactic variation constantly creep in to give rise to confusion, these errors in themselves are not the serious problem. In *Don Quijote de la Mancha* the central problem is finally that faced by the author, who, while perceiving the contradictions which beset the rhetorical quest for linguistic authority, nevertheless attempts to use that conflicting inner dialogue to enunciate a narrative about the nature of those contradictions. That Cervantes succeeds brilliantly in displaying the determinants of textuality and identity in the dialectics of *la gramática del buen lenguaje* is certainly not the least of his novel's redoubtable ironies.

❦ ❦ ❦

Don Quijote is the seminal text of the novel in more ways than even a studied glance at the history of its impact on the development of that genre might reveal. It is a point of historical fact that don Quijote's natural imitators first appeared even before Cervantes had finished composing his exemplary work. And, as Cervantes himself tells us, Part II of *Don Quijote* exists in no small part as a reaction to one such illegitimate imitation, Avellaneda's apocryphal *Don Quijote*. When in Part II Cervantes' errant knight convinces don Jerónimo, a character drawn from Avellaneda's false *Quijote*, that if there are indeed two don Quijotes in the world, he, Cervantes' creation, is the only true one, we "idle readers" are made witnesses to the conscious dramatization of the "genealogical force"[51] by which Cervantes' novel will exercise its bequeathing and disinheriting rights over all subsequent comic epics in prose. The birth of don Quijote seems to initiate a dynastic line of descent, which in its several legitimate and illegitimate branches proceeds to rule the course of modern narrative. As narrative gives birth to narrative, the authority of the "original" is strengthened and its power of influence is passed down to its succeeding generations. With *Don Quijote*, the novel acquires its overriding concerns with genealogical authority and narrative forms as it seeks a language appropriate to its transmitting ends.

Almost immediately after the appearance of *Don Quijote*, excellent translations appeared to spread the mad hidalgo's fame throughout the western world. By the middle of the eighteenth century, Cervantes' novel had been enshrined as one of the enduring, canonical texts of the western literary tradition. By then, its literary descendants were already examining fully the possibilities posed for literary language by the mad knight.

[51] This is the phrase Patricia Drechsel Tobin uses to equate "the temporal form of the classical novel—the conceptualized frame within which its acts and images find their placement—with the dynastic line that unites the diverse generations of the genealogical family" (*Time and the Novel* [Princeton: Princeton University Press, 1978], p. 6).

Marivaux's early novel, *Pharsamon: le Don Quichotte moderne* (1737), is only a poor cousin of his later, more elegant quixotic text, *La vie de Marianne* (1731-1741). In England, following a line of descent described well (even if too divorced from its European roots) by Ian Watt,[52] Richardson's *Clarissa* (1747-1748) repeats Cervantine concerns as filtered through Shelton and Marivaux,[53] and with *Pamela* (1740) in turn establishes an apparently straightforward line to Fielding. Robert Alter has shown how *The History of Joseph Andrews, Written in Imitation of the Manner of Cervantes* (1742), together with Sterne's *Tristram Shandy* and Diderot's *Jacques le fataliste et son maître* (1796), provide us with a convenient sequence of texts by which we can extend Cervantes' own metaphor from the Prologue to Part I of *Don Quijote* of the father/author and child text.[54] Walter L. Reed has recently qualified this view by showing how *Don Quijote* served as an "exemplary model for [the] dialectical redefinition of the new."[55]

But satisfaction with the self-sufficiency of a genealogical view of literary history should be at least shaken when we recall that Cervantes himself immediately dissociated himself from this paternal line by refusing to acknowledge his own authority. He is, he claims, the "stepfather," if anything at all, to this "orphan child." From this denial of authority and genealogical ties, *Don Quijote* goes on to question our most basic assumptions concerning the natural links between authors and their books, between things and their represented images, in short, between origins and their ends. Cervantes permits the introduction of a kind of historical analysis of discourse that studies,

[52] Ian Watt, *The Rise of the Novel* (Berkeley and Los Angeles: University of California Press, 1967).

[53] William Beaty Warner, *Reading Clarissa: The Struggles of Interpretation* (New Haven: Yale University Press, 1979).

[54] Robert Alter, *Partial Magic: The Novel as a Self-Conscious Genre* (Berkeley and Los Angeles: University of California Press, c. 1975). Graham Greene's novel *Monsignor Quixote* (1982) is a noble addition to the genealogy.

[55] Walter L. Reed, *An Exemplary History of the Novel*, p. 136.

as Foucault has phrased it, not only "the expressive value and formal transformations of discourse, but its mode of existence: the modifications and variations, within any culture, of modes of circulation, valorization, attribution, and appropriation."[56]

As the supremely self-created man, don Quijote has from his "beginning" separated himself from one kind of history and genealogy in order to establish another, fabulous kind. Since his forebear, Amadís de Gaula, has never existed in history but only in the unique dimension of language, don Quijote finds that he must construct himself in accordance with his own peculiar vision of what language is capable. In doing so, he allows us to consider the conditions under which a subject may appear and persist in discourse, the position it can occupy, and what rules it must follow to create the authority of meaning, as well as participate in its circulation. If *Don Quijote* has served as the model for subsequent novels, it has done so primarily by providing the most comprehensive examination of narrative as the formal equivalent of the rhetorical quest for discursive authority.

[56] Foucault, "What is an Author?" *Language, Counter-Memory, Practice*, p. 137.

❦ THREE ❦

The Rhetoric of Desire: Stendhal's *Le Rouge et le Noir*

> Love is but an illusion; it makes for itself, so to speak, an other Universe; it surrounds itself with things that are not; or to which it alone has given being; and since it offers all its sentiments in images, its language is always figural.
>
> J. J. Rousseau
> *Julie: ou La Nouvelle Héloise (II:15)*

After Cervantes, and between the comic bourgeois tales of the eighteenth century and the increasingly tragic romances of the nineteenth century, stand the novels of Henri Beyle, the quixotically self-created Baron de Stendhal. It is always surprising to find that, in bridging the eighteenth and nineteenth centuries, Stendhal stands closer in spirit and temperament to the century of enlightened revolution than to that of industrial development. Steeped as we are in the prejudices of modernism, we find it difficult to allow that a voice bred of the eighteenth century can have spoken so clearly and judiciously about the social and individual upheavals that the rise of capitalist systems would engender. On the face of it, we are justified in our initial suspicion of the perspicacity of this romantic dandy, would-be revolutionary, and minor bureaucrat. A glimpse into his journals of his formative years, from 1802 to 1806, or into the notes from this period for his grand *Filosofia nova*,[1] reveals him a

[1] Editions of Stendhal's secondary works cited in this chapter are as follows: *Pensées: Filosofia Nova*, ed. Henri Martineau, Édition du Divan, 2 vols. (Paris, 1927); *Journal; Correspondance; Souvenirs d'Egotisme;* and *La Vie de Henry Brulard*, all in *Oeuvres Intimes de Stendhal*, ed. Henri Martineau, Bibliothèque de la Pléiade (Paris, 1955); *Vie de Napoléon* and *De l'Amour* in *Oeuvres Complètes de Stendhal*, Cercle du Bibliophile (Paris, 1967). Begun simply as diaries and reading notes, Stendhal's journals, together with the *Filosofia nova*, gradually became an embellished, ready-to-hand repository of ideas: "Lorsque pour

naive youth swept up by the turmoil of Napoleonic world war, and a victim of his own erotic passions, in quest for a rhetorical medium adequate to his seemingly unbounded creative energies.[2] Even a decade later, when he begins to compose the masterpieces of his maturity, Stendhal is still the contradictory blend of eighteenth-century Enlightenment and nineteenth-century Romanticism, still celebrating with sober irony the mystic hopes of love's delusions.[3]

Molded by his education at the École Centrale in Grenoble during the transitional years of the French Revolution, and guided by the influence of his maternal grandfather, Dr. Henri Gagnon, himself a true product of the Enlightenment,[4] Stendhal

---

un concours à l'Institute, un discours, une préface, j'aurai besoin de pensées, les chercher dans mes cahiers. Ils sont mes magasins" (cited by Henri Martineau in the "Préface" to his edition of the *Filosofia nova*, vol. 1, p. ii). And as Beyle recounts in *La Vie de Henry Brulard*, he intended to codify some these notes and organize them into a philosophical schema: "J'ávais une théorie intérieure que je voulais rédiger sous le titre: *Filosofia nova*, titre moitié italien moitié latin" (p. 349).

[2] See Matthew Josephson, *Stendhal: Or the Pursuit of Happiness* (Garden City: Doubleday, 1946), pp. 1-14. This view is focused and enlarged by Joanna Richardson, *Stendhal* (London: Victor Gollancz, 1974), pp. 1-36; and by Gita May, *Stendhal and the Age of Napoleon* (New York: Columbia University Press, 1977), pp. 1-65. All of these biographical studies have now been superseded by Robert Alter's excellent new study, *A Lion for Love: A Critical Biography of Stendhal* (New York: Basic Books, 1979).

[3] "*I am* encore *in 1835 the man of 1794*," writes Stendhal (*Vie de Henry Brulard*, p. 144). See also Gita May, who notes that "[B]asically Rousseauistic in his esthetic and emotional responses to nature and matters of the heart . . . [Stendhal's] basic impulses and perspectives can best be understood as a natural outcome and continuation of the currents and forces unleashed by the *philosophes* and their revolutionary disciples" (*Stendhal and the Age of Napoleon*, pp. 5, 7). On Stendhal's position between the eighteenth and nineteenth centuries, see Harry Levin, "Stendhal," *The Gates of Horn* (New York: Oxford University Press, 1963), pp. 84-149.

[4] "Mon grand-père était et avait été depuis vingt-cinq ans, à l'époque où je l'ai connu, le promoteur de toutes les enterprises utiles (et que . . . on pourrait appeler libérales). On lui doit la Bibliothéque" (*Vie de Henry Brulard*, p. 40). Dr. Gagnon's influence on the young Beyle is discussed by Victor del Litto, *La Vie Intellectuelle de Stendhal* (Paris: P.U.F., 1962), pp. 11-29. A good recent account is Margaret Tillet's, *Stendhal: The Background to the Novels* (London: Oxford University Press, 1971).

read and absorbed the works of the Encyclopaedists, of Helvétius, of Destutt de Tracy, Montesquieu, Condillac, and John Locke.[5] "Since we see the world and men only as our sensations record them in our minds," wrote Stendhal in his notebooks, " . . . we must know this mind, . . . must know the mind and the passions."[6] But in accepting Locke's theories concerning human understanding, Stendhal also transformed them, for he had also absorbed the romances of Cervantes, of Madame de Stäel, and of Rousseau, and had lived through Napoleon's Italian campaigns, which in retrospect came to represent for him the idyllic standards of the heroic life. In Stendhal, therefore, when Locke's sensualist theories came into contact with the romantic philosophy of the post-Napoleonic era, both "ideologies"[7] became something else: a peculiar blend of organic empiricism and passionate sensibility that he was grandiloquently to term, *beylisme*.[8] It is from this clash of eighteenth-century reason and nineteenth-century passion that "Stendhal," Henri Beyle's

[5] See *La Vie de Henry Brulard*, pp. 19, 28, 188-189, and 253; and the entry "Catalogue de Tous Mes Livres" in the 1804 *Journal* (*Claix. 3 ventôse III*) in *Oeuvres Intimes*, pp. 442-443. See also, V. del Litto, *La Vie Intellectuelle*, pp. 35-51; and Robert Alter, *A Lion for Love*, pp. 29-35.

[6] Cited by Josephson, p. 82. Stendhal also writes: "*La liaison des idées ne vient que de la liaison des sensations*" (*Filosofia nova* II:65). The 1804 *Journal* entry of *1er nivôse an XIII* notes that "Le principe de Locke que toutes nos idées viennent par nos sens, et l'anatomie des passions telle que celle qui se voit dans Helvétius prouvent que nous ne voyons dans l'homme aucune effet de l'âme, qu'il n'y a que des effets de sens, que par conséquent il n'y a point d'âme" (*Oeuvres Intimes*, p. 538).

[7] "La découverte de [*Don Quichotte*] . . . est peut-être la plus grande époque de ma vie," claims Stendhal (*Vie de Henry Brulard*, p. 80). See also pp. 152-153 on Rousseau's *La Nouvelle Héloise*. Concerning his sense of the word "ideology," Stendhal wrote in *De l'Amour* I, 3 : "J'ai appelé cet essai un livre d'idéologie. . . . Je demande pardon aux philosphes d'avoir pris le mot idéologie: mon intention est une description détaillée des idées et des toutes les parties qui pouvent les composer, le présent livre est un description détaillée et minutieuse de tous les sentiments qui composent la passion nommée *l'amour*."

[8] *Beylisme* is, as Harry Levin states, "Keep[ing] one's head while losing one's heart," p. 105. León Blum's *Stendhal et le beylisme*, 3rd ed. (Paris: Albin Michele, 1974), pp. 119-164, is still the primary account of the term.

fictive masterpiece, arises to tower over the development of the modern novel.

The human experience most relevant to this clash of reason and sentiment, as Stendhal sees it, is Love: Love is the highest expression of man's energy, and the perfect form of human action, transcending all others.[9] With its nuances and complications, love is the sentiment which motivates the novels and various fictional and non-fictional works, but none more so than *Le Rouge et le Noir*. In fact, the movements to and from love are so central to Stendhal's novel that its subtitle, "Chronique de 1830," might well be altered to read "Chronique d'Amour en 1830." For the author-theorist of *De l'Amour* (1822), the psychic and physical manifestations of energy incited by love were no less possibly the cause of what both Julien Sorel and Mathilde de la Mole will refer to as "grandes actions" than to any political or economic motivations. It is this correlation offered by Stendhal in *Le Rouge et le Noir* between ways of loving and ways of acting in 1830 that I examine, for in that love story Stendhal creates the virtual rhetoric of desire for all subsequent novels of the nineteenth century.

❦ ❦ ❦

Stendhal's great, unrequited passion for Métilde Dembowski, a beautiful young Polish countess deeply involved in the nationalist revolutionary organization of the Italian *Carbonari*, became, as Stendhal openly admitted, the source of his theories of love: "That passion was my first course in logic."[10] In the unnatural association Stendhal insists upon between "passion" and "logic," the curiosity of those theories and of their relevance to *Le Rouge et le Noir* (1830) is patently clear. *De l'Amour* is important in relation to the novels because, in distinguishing

[9] *Filosofia nova* II:122: " . . . la passion la plus forte est l'amour." This notion becomes of course the main topic of *De l'Amour* and is a common theme in the *Correspondance* from 1804 on.

[10] Cited by Etienne Rey, "Préface" to *De l'Amour*, pp. i-xcix.

between four kinds of love (passionate love, mannered love, physical love, vanity-love) and seven stages of falling in love,[11] it is Stendhal's first attempt to offer the objective account of man's subjective passions which the novels, from *Armance* (1827) to *La Chartreuse de Parme* (1838), would later imaginatively enact. Perhaps the most important feature of Stendhal's tract in relation to the later novels is its analysis of the power of the imagination in love—its ability to transform both the figure of the beloved and of the lover. This is the process Stendhal termed *cristallisation* in the striking metaphor of the "Salzbourg Bough":

> Leave a lover with his thoughts for twenty-four hours, and this is what will happen:
>
> At the salt mines of Salzbourg, they throw a leafless wintry bough into one of the abandoned workings. Two or three months later they haul it out covered with a shining deposit of crystals. The smallest twig, no bigger than a tom-tit's claw, is studded with a galaxy of scintillating diamonds. The original branch is no longer recognizable.
>
> What I have called crystallization is a mental process which draws from everything that happens new proofs of the perfection of the loved one. (*De l'Amour* I, 2)

The effect of *amour-passion*, the highest form of love according to Stendhal's hierarchy, is to so alter the reality of the loved one that the new version created by love becomes for the lover the only true reality. Stendhal explains what "crystallization" means and why love is the most powerful of passions:

> In all the other [passions], desires have to adapt themselves to cold reality, but in love realities obligingly rearrange themselves to conform with desire. . . . From the moment

[11] *De l'Amour*, translated as *Love* by Gilbert and Suzanne Sale (Harmondsworth: Penguin Books, 1975), Bk. I, ch. 1; hereafter cited by *De l'Amour*, book and chapter number. The seven stages of falling in love are: admiration, desire, hope, the birth of love, first crystallization, doubt, and final crystallization (*De l'Amour* I, 4).

> he falls in love even the wisest man no longer sees anything *as it really is*. . . . Hopes and fears at once become *romantic* and WAYWARD. . . . [W]hatever he imagines becomes reality. . . . [Y]ou observe some hardly distinguishable object as white, and interpret this thing as favourable to your love. A moment later you realize that the object is black, and you now regard this as a good omen for your love.[12]

The implications of this universal transformation of the beloved by the tender action of the lover's imagination are unsettling, to say the least. Stendhal clearly signals the possibility that the pure and unadulterated consummation of authentic, passionate love can never be achieved, for in love in its various guises we necessarily eliminate the reality of the other and transform the real into an idealized and nonexistent abstraction: "I mean by crystallization a certain fever of the imagination which renders even the most ordinary objects into something unrecognizable, and in fact into an extraordinary being." The processes of "love's physiology" (*De l'Amour, Preface*) cause the lover to be enthralled by his own *wayward* transformation of the beloved's reality and to be touched by it only after he has lent it his own romantic intonation. For Stendhal, it is thus man's fundamental misfortune that at the moment he begins to move beyond himself toward another, the independent being of the other ceases to exist for him *as it really is* and becomes instead "nothing but the sum of the fulfillment of all the desires you have been able to formulate successively about her" (*De l'Amour* I, 11). And yet it is the fundamental irony of man's condition that, since Love "Still prompts the celestial sight,/ For which we wish to live, or dare to fight" (*De l'Amour* I, 3), love is also an indispensable passion, one to be tenderly cultivated, nurtured, and enjoyed.[13]

[12] *De l'Amour* I, 12. Italics are Stendhal's; capitalized words indicate Stendhal's English in the French original.

[13] Robert M. Adams has argued that "The truth one discovers by cristallizing is a truth about the errors to which one's mind is subject; but it is a way of

The celebrated scenes of chapters 9-13 of Book I of *Le Rouge et le Noir,* which detail the successive movements of the hero, Julien Sorel, during his initiation into the mysteries of love from the garden at Verrières to the heights on the nearby mountains, are at once exemplary in their portrayal of the various stages of love's delusions, and indicative of Stendhal's rhetorical strategy in portraying those delusions. In carrying out his naively detailed "plan of campaign" for the seduction of the equally naive Mme. de Rênal, Julien moves from the garden in chapter 9, to the heights in chapter 10, back to the garden in chapter 11, up to the heights in chapter 12, and back down to the garden for his final conquest over Mme. de Rênal in chapter 13. Apart from this dizzying pattern of ascent and descent, the details of the action at both the peaks and valleys of his journey are themselves remarkable. Seated with Mme. de Rênal and her confidante, Mme. Derville, in complete darkness under the graceful linden trees of the Rênal estate, Julien vows to himself at the beginning of that series of chapters that: "At the stroke of ten either I will do what I have been promising myself to do all day or I'll go upstairs and blow out my brains."[14] Having avoided the necessity of executing his melodramatically suicidal vow by successfully seizing and holding Mme. de Rênal's hap-

---

seeing clearly in the end—as Stendhal described it, of discovering the real by way of the imaginary and entering the world by way of heaven" (*Stendhal: Notes on a Novelist* [1959; rpt. Minerva Press, 1968], p. 38). But the risk involved in this reentry to the world is reemphasized later in the text: "Love is an exquisite flower, but it needs courage to pluck it on the brink of a dreadful precipice" (*De l'Amour* I, 41). Stendhal's metaphor conveys his sense of love as both an enchanting and a potentially destructive passion, and may well allude to his constant source for his erotic rhetoric, Rousseau's *La Nouvelle Héloise*: "L'amour n'est qu'illusion."

[14] Stendhal, *Le Rouge et le Noir* (*RN*), in *Stendhal, Romans et Nouvelles* vol. 1, ed. Henri Martineau, Bibliothèque de la Pléiade (Paris, 1952), (*RN* I, 9). Quotations will be identified hereafter by book and chapter number. Translations are from the Norton Critical Edition of *Red and Black,* translated and edited by Robert M. Adams (New York: W. W. Norton & Co., 1969).

less hand, Julien congratulates himself for having fulfilled, not what the narrator shows us is an act of adolescent vanity, but what he sees as his *"duty, and a heroic duty"* (*RN* I, 9).

The next chapter finds Julien on the heights, savoring his success in carrying out the strategy outlined for him by Las Cases's *Memoires de Sainte Hélene*, the Bible, and Rousseau's *La Nouvelle Héloise*, and examining his past and future life:

> Julien paused to catch his breath for a moment in the shadow of the great rocks, then resumed his climb. Soon . . . he found himself poised on an immense rocky crag. . . . This physical stance made him smile, it indicated so clearly the position he wanted to attain in morality. The pure mountain air filled his soul with serenity and even joy. . . . Julien . . . looked up into the sky, heated by an August sun. Locusts were chirring in the field below the rock; when they paused, all was silence around him. At his feet lay twenty leagues of countryside. A solitary eagle, risen from the rocks over his head, appeared from time to time, cutting immense silent circles in the sky. Julien's eye followed mechanically the bird of prey. Its calm, powerful movements struck him; he envied this power, he envied this isolation.
>
> Such had been the destiny of Napoleon; would it some day be his? (*RN* I, 10)

Here, as in the previous chapter, where the scene and style of seduction are determined by Julien's imitation of literary models of heroic passion, the mixed literary, historical, and even mythical conventions of the scene suggest that the course of love has been predetermined by the hero's and the narrator's confidence in specific models of action. The erotic implications of the enchanted pleasure garden identify Julien as a candidate for Romantic passion and Weltschmertz no less than his posture on the emblematic, sun-lit heights signals his desire to be seen as a Napoleonic hero and "bird of prey." Even Julien's ironic smile suggests his own recognition of the extent to which his life story is fated to follow a preordained course.

Together with the succeeding few chapters, which multiply the emblematic qualities of these initial scenes, the force of the romantic pattern of Julien's life is something upon which the narrator insists. This much is clear. What is not clear is the reason for the insistent use of emblems, models, and outright allegories. Novel readers are not wrong in expecting a character's actions and the end of his story to be less obviously manipulated by the author. In fact, it is our willingness to accept the author's illusion of an unconstrained, undetermined development of the hero's personality that often motivates novel-reading. Great novels, we assume, are great precisely to the extent that they allow generations of readers the opportunity to contribute their own interpretation of a character's actions and of the events of his life.[15] When these actions are insisted upon and interpreted by the author, they become literary stylization and not believable versions of human experience. Assuming, therefore, that Stendhal intended to provide more than a simplistic allegory concerning the perils of pride, ambition, and adultery in love, one must wonder why *Le Rouge et le Noir* begins and punctuates the crucial moments of its narrative with such patently emblematic moments. In answering this question, we face the very real possibility that Stendhal's aim in *Le Rouge et le Noir* is not the portrayal of character but the elucidation of something beyond character. In effect, the source of Stendhal's success in portraying character stems from his disregard of it in favor of the way in which desire, as a projection beyond the limits of the culturally and temporally defined self, affects the representation of character in literature.

At the end of chapter 12 of Book I, having finally succeeded in molding Mme. de Rênal's desires to complement his own,

[15] The most useful of works on the "emblematic images" and "allegorical topoi" of Stendhal's novels is still Stephen Gilman's "The Tower as Emblem," *Analecta Romanica*, vol. 22 (Frankfurt: Klosterman, 1967), pp. 9-63.

Julien climbs to the heights once again. But this time, the narrative's insistence on the metaphorical quality of Julien's actions transforms the original value of the scene. In the difference between the present ascent to the allegorical heights and the previous ones, a kind of rhetorical meaning arises:

> At last he rose to the crest of the great ridges he had to cross in order to reach . . . the lovely valley where lived his friend Fouqué. . . . Lurking like a bird of prey among the naked rocks which cap the great mountain, he could watch the distant ascent of any man who tried to come near him. . . . Here, said he—his eyes shining with pleasure—here people will never be able to get at me. He had the notion of indulging himself by writing down those ideas which, everywhere else, were so dangerous for him. A square block of stone served as a desk. His pen flew; he forgot his surroundings entirely. . . .
>
> Why not spend the night here? he asked himself; I have a bit of bread, and *I am free*! His soul exalted at this grand phrase, his hypocrisy prevented his feeling free even with Fouqué. . . . In the midst of an immense darkness his soul wandered, lost in the contemplation of what awaited him some day in Paris. It would be, first of all, a woman, far more beautiful and of a more exalted genius than any he had ever been able to see in the provinces. He adored her; he was beloved in return. (*RN* I, 12)

As isolated instances, the various moments within the garden and on the heights have a decided, interpretable value. But, taken as a whole, the entire series of passages between chapters 9 and 12 form a circuitous thread into the very heart of Stendhal's text. It is as if the narrator, fully conscious of his responsibility to the reader who must contend with an extensive and almost unmanageable flow of words describing the inner conflicts of a contradictory, hypocritical hero, has decided to lay a clear mnemonic track to help the reader into and out of the text.[16] The track is, as we can clearly see, an indirect one; it does not proceed in straight lines, but "scribes an infinity of zigzags" (*RN* I, 12) intricately as does that of Julien as he makes his way up to the grotto of peaceful contemplation. Thus, while the isolated scenes are significant in their own right (the eroticism of the garden, the imperious egoism of the heights, the dream of Parisian romance), it is in their considered juxtaposition that reliable meaning is apparently to be found. Rather than serving mainly as clues to character, the scenes represented in the initial chapters of Book I are, in effect, rhetorical configurations of the text's essential "syntax." In pursuing the shape and rhythm of Julien's dreams, these initial scenes clue us into the dialectical method by which the novel's represented pattern of desire is to be read.

In the present scene, the similarities to earlier scenes are apparent, but the differences as well are stark and significant. Julien is now closely associated with the "bird of prey," since we have already seen him exercise his growing faculties of "hypocrisy" in his unjust accusation of Elisa, Mme. de Rênal's lady, with "the language of a sly and prudent hypocrisy" (*RN* I, 8). At this point in the novel, Julien still relegates his love for Mme. de Rênal to the category of "a duty to be accomplished" (*RN* I, 8) and he seeks a place where he may be himself without fear of detection. As the "immense darkness" surrounds him, the hypocrisy of the garden fades, his soul wanders, and Julien begins to write.

In the security of the concealing darkness, ensconced within the matrical grotto, he conceives a fable—of himself and a woman, beloved and loving, in Paris. Like don Quijote reading in his library, Julien, here dreaming and writing, determines the errant course of his future life. Clearly, this act of writing is for Julien a compensatory act; it is explicitly intended to supplement

[16] Gilman refers to these authorial clues as "natural" emblems; they are the means by which "Great novels . . . let us inside [and] . . . invite us to come in and get to work" ("Tower as Emblem," pp. 15-16).

the ugly reality of his menial existence as a servant in a bourgeois world with a dream of an alternate world where he might be the master of his surroundings and his fate. For the reader, however, the emphatic pattern of repetitions at this early stage in the novel implies that here too we have a moment of emblematic significance. In effect, the impact of Julien's stylus upon the "square block of stone which served as a desk" already seems to trace the erotic design of his romantic dreams upon that future woman. As the narrator's ensuing words make clear, Julien has here created, by virtue of his imaginative will, the very conditions of mind necessary for the tragedy of his relationship with Mathilde de la Mole.

As in the garden scenes, which repeat the erotic topoi of the *Roman de la Rose* and *La Nouvelle Héloise*, the present action, the narrator informs us, is in no way *real*. It is instead a repetition of and an intermediary step in a series of *texts* of action: allegories of the erotic bower, of moral superiority, and of medieval chivalry. In fact, Julien's course of action is of such a conventional track that "maxims" already exist to cover it:

> Even if possessed of Julien's imagination, a young man raised amid the sad actuality (*tristes vérités*) of Paris society would have been awakened at this point in his daydream (*roman*) by a touch of chilly irony; heroic actions, and the hope of performing them, would have been supplanted by the familiar maxim: Leave your mistress alone and you'll be betrayed, alas, two or three times a day. This young peasant saw no gap between himself and the most heroic achievements except the want of opportunity. (*RN* I, 12)

The demystifying voice of the narrator arises to point out the *tristes vérités* concerning the insurmountable gap unseen by Julien between his romantic expectations and his true possibilities. The "chilly irony" of Julien's story is that, even as the author of his fate, Julien cannot control the unconscious structure of values and desires that the society against which he reacts has instilled in him. His daydream/novel (*roman* in the original), coming at the symbolic end of his childhood and marking his entry into the intersubjective structure of exchange which is love, becomes the deluding medium corrosive of "authentic" identity. The narrator's satiric comments, that "In Paris, Julien's position with regard to Mme. de Rênal would quickly have been simplified; but in Paris, love is the child of novels (*romans*). . . . The novels would have outlined for them the roles to be played" (*RN* I, 7), are thus surely ironic. Already, Julien acts as his "models" ordain that he must act. Even at the moment "that he had nothing more to desire" from Mme. de Rênal, these actions are ruled by "the ideal of behavior he had set himself" (*RN* I, 15).

Following the course of action "he had prescribed for himself" (*RN* I, 16), Julien's relationship with Mme. de Rênal can never be simply an innocent one. Quickly, both come to see it for what it is—an impossible play of contradictory forces enacted by two disparate and undisciplined wills. For Julien in particular, the act of love immediately becomes a substitute for action in a wider scope, which he feels is no longer available to the men of his age: "Ah . . . Napoleon was really the man sent by God to the youth of France! Who can take his place?" (*RN* I, 17). Apparently, Julien will, for such at least is his inexpressible desire. What the narrator continually refers to as Julien's hypocrisy, that is, his inability to reveal his desires for fear that the revelation will create the conditions which would preclude their attainment, subordinates the possibility of an authentic and reciprocal relationship of *amour-passion*. It leads instead to a deformed version of love, characterized by Mme. de Rênal's view of Julien as "her master," by her sense that she is "damned without hope" (*RN* I, 19), and by her recognition that "Their happiness now wore sometimes the expression of a crime" (*RN* I, 19). And yet, it is also the case that as desire awakens within Mme. de Rênal "the terrible idea of adultery" (*RN* I, 11) it also causes her to become aware of herself as a subjective entity apart from her roles as wife and mother. As is also true for Julien, Mme. de Rênal experiences the fact that it is not purely cognitive and passive contemplation that is at the base of self-consciousness, but *desire*.

After an exchange of anonymous letters, intended by M. Valenod to cause the overthrow of Julien from the heart of the Rênal household, and resisted by Mme. de Rênal's exquisite manipulation of her husband's response, Mme. de Rênal is as adept in the play of desire and its necessary "language of sly and prudent hypocrisy" as Julien has ever been. His own performance in support of Mme. de Rênal before the droll M. de Maugiron is so perfectly Jesuitical in using "Speech . . . to conceal his thoughts" (I, 22, epigraph), and Julien has "attained such perfect skill in this sort of eloquence, which has replaced the decisive action of the empire," that he ends by boring himself "with the sound of his own words" (*RN* I, 22). As the first erotic intrigue between Julien and Mme. de Rênal draws to a close, the themes of love and action, which motivate Julien's original desires, have come together under the spreading canopy of a necessary and universal hypocrisy, as Julien vows in the chapter entitled "Ways of Acting in 1830," "never to say anything except what seemed false to him" (*RN* I, 22).

❦ ❦ ❦

The intermediary chapters between Books I and II concerning Julien's stay in the seminary at Besançon reflect a mirror version of the world of Verrières. Whereas in the Rênal household Julien's intellectual and linguistic facilities bring about his success, those same qualities must be hypocritically suppressed for the sake of his very survival among the scheming Jesuits. Here, ignorance and linguistic crudity are the signs of character, while Julien's "look of a thinker" (*RN* I, 26) marks him as a potential threat to this community of upwardly mobile peasants.

Once again, Julien tries to adapt; it does not take him long to realize that "speech" and "gesture" might "conceal" intellectual independence as readily as they may dissemble erotic desire and social ambition. And while Julien at first "had little success in his efforts at a hypocrisy of gestures" (*RN* I, 27), he soon learns the proper rhetoric consonant with his new existence. The seminary code of insiduous dissembling teaches him that *"difference begets hatred"* and that "all good reasoning is irksome" (*RN* I, 27). After having been cleverly tricked during his doctrinal examination into revealing the extent of his erudition in the secular, and forbidden, classical authors, Julien realizes also that hypocrisy for the sake of religious asceticism requires as much will power as hypocrisy for desire and ambition: "Man's will is powerful, I read it everywhere; but is it strong enough to surmount [the] disgust [of having to pass a lifetime among such company!]" (*RN* I, 27). In acquiring the facility of the "seminary language" (*RN* I, 29), Julien has taken the first steps in bending his haughty tastes to his imperious desires. More importantly, as an exercise in self-creation by self-denial—"his task was to create for himself a whole new character" (*RN* I, 26)—the episodes in the seminary at Besançon prepare Julien well for life in the Hôtel de la Mole.

❦ ❦ ❦

Given the force of the repeated models of hypocritical action Julien has followed in his dangerous liaison with Mme. de Rênal and during his brief stay among the seminarians, it comes as no surprise that those same models also prescribe the course of action in Julien's affair with Mathilde de la Mole, the woman "far more beautiful and of a more exalted genius" foretold in Julien's mountaintop fable. Since Stendhal's emphasis seems increasingly to fall on the nature of the love relationship, rather than on the personalities of the relationship, the various figures involved may be intermittently substituted, while their actions remain more or less constant. If the pattern of desire and repulsion which Julien and Mathilde enact in Book II is more complex than that of Julien and Mme. de Rênal in Book I, it is primarily because in Mathilde Julien encounters someone as profoundly romantic and hypocritical as himself. In contrast to Mme. de Rênal's self-negating consciousness, which is quite willing to surrender body and soul to Julien, Mathilde's various attempts to negate her desires by fulfilling them through decisive action identify hers as one capable of affirming itself through self-indulgence. With her own ready-made scenario of romantic love, constructed around the Medieval romance of revolt, seduction, betrayal, and death, the story of her ancestor's love for Marguerite de Navarre, Mathilde stands before Julien as an intractable reflection of his own character. She too is ready to transform herself by becoming like the figures she envisions in the legend of Boniface de la Mole.

Again in this section of the novel, the themes of love and strength of will revolve around hypocrisy as a function of linguistic and rhetorical skills. As he enters Parisian society, Julien finds that he must learn anew in this "new Babylon" (*RN* II, 2) "the special dialect of Paris" (*RN* II, 2). In all of these renewed thematic and figural motions, as in the very title of *Le Rouge et le Noir*, the notion of gambling with an implacably prescribed fate cannot be denied.[17] And when Mathilde, early in their acquaintance, likens Julien to Jean-Jacques Rousseau, thinks of him as having "the aspect of a prince in disguise" (*RN* II, 9), and muses while studying his features that nothing but "the death sentence gives a man real distinction" (*RN* II, 8), it becomes clear that the course which lies before Julien in Paris has been significantly indicated. "Detours and details, later to be filled in freely by the author, are as yet unmarked," notes Stephen Gilman, "but the itinerary—and what is even more important, the feeling that *there is an itinerary*—is manifest."[18]

One indication of the nature of Stendhal's complex rhetorical "itinerary" is that Julien, who has been the instigator of se-

[17] See Gilman, p. 26, citing E.B.O. Borgerhoff, "The Anagram in *Le Rouge et le noir*," *MLN* 68 (1953), p. 386, on the fatality of Julien's career.

[18] Gilman, "Tower as Emblem," p. 28.

ductive acts, finds himself at the other end of the intrigue with Mathilde. From the evening she overhears Julien speaking with the condemned revolutionary, Count Altamira, on the possibility of "grand actions" (*RN* II, 9), Mathilde seeks to draw out Julien's secret heroic desires. She finally succeeds in breaking through his cautious reserve by forcing him to demand of her: ". . . shouldn't a man who wants to drive ignorance and crime from the earth pass through it like a whirlwind and do evil blindly?" (*RN* II, 9). With that wild question, Julien shows himself to Mathilde, who now wears *l'air de son esclave* (the air of being his slave) (*RN* II, 9), as perhaps the only living candidate for the role of "Boniface," opposite her own "Queen Marguerite" (as the next chapter is ominously entitled).

Their mutual recognition as fellow romantic conspirators to create a present fictive world does not of course diminish in the least their cautious approach and withdrawal from love: "the more chilly and respectful I show myself toward her, the more she seeks me out" (*RN* II, 10), observes Julien. Mathilde is equally aware that "Between Julien and me . . . everything is heroic" but also that "everything is a child of chance" (*RN* II, 12). Thus the rhetorical structure by which Julien's initial heroic/erotic impulses were dramatized is repeated. This time, however, the former pattern is complicated by the additional twist of Mathilde's wish to follow the pattern of Boniface de la Mole's love for Marguerite de Navarre. And since in this new love affair, as in the original, the desired can only be possessed by the dissembling of desire, the established pattern of approach and withdrawal actualized by Julien's earlier ascent to the heights and descent to the garden at Verrières is retraced. This time, however, the stakes to be waged between the red and the black are, literally, a matter of life and death.

That initially Mathilde herself, as an independent personality, is not the real object of Julien's desires, any more than he is the object of hers, is clear:

> This love was founded on nothing but Mathilde's rare beauty, or rather on her queenly manners and admirable style of dress. In this regard, Julien was still an upstart. . . . Certainly it was not Mathilde's character that had inspired Julien's dreaming for several days past. He had enough sense to realize that he knew nothing at all about her character. Whatever he had seen of it might just be a pretense. (*RN* II, 13)

Typically, Julien's quixotic desires appear to him to be motivated from within, but his actions reveal them to be constituted under the sign of mediation.[19] His desire has for its object the desire of the other, in the sense that there is no object of desire that is not formed without the intervention of others. Julien's assumption of the emblematic insignia of "the others" (*les autres*)—alternately, his black tutor's suit, his military coat, and now, his blue suit and Legion of Honor ribbon—are only the superficial traces of a deeper structure of desire opened up by the effect of other emblematic and literary signifiers which represent for Julien the possibility of heroic action.

[19] René Girard's now classic study of "imitative" or "triangular" desire in *Deceit, Desire, and the Novel* begins with a differentiation between "external mediation"—"when the distance [between a desired and a desirer] is sufficient to eliminate any contact between the spheres of *possibilities* of which the mediator and the subject [of desire] occupy the respective centers," as in *Don Quijote*—and "internal mediation"—"when this distance is sufficiently reduced to allow these two spheres to penetrate each other," as in *Le Rouge et le Noir* (*Deceit, Desire, and the Novel*, p. 9). For Girard, while "Imitative desire is always a desire to be Another" (p. 83), in *Le Rouge et le Noir*, the "sameness by which [the desiring subjects] are obsessed appears to them as an absolute *otherness*" (p. 106). Girard argues that it is *amour-vanité* which thus rules the world of Julien's desires. In causing the transformation of the other's being, *amour-vanité* threatens the other's individual autonomy. *Amour-passioné*, in contrast, allows the lover to see the real Beloved and to desire her true reality. Yet in *De l'Amour* Stendhal attributes the possibility of crystallization, and thus of transformation, to all levels of love, but *especially* to *amour-passioné*: "Du moment qu'il aime, l'homme le plus sage ne voit plus aucune objet *tel qu'il est*"; "[Desire nous] jette dans un plus profane . . . rêverie que sa présence elle-même"; l'être supêrieur . . . se fait illusion."

With his affinity for the word of *les autres,* Julien transforms Mathilde into more of a villainess than she really is. As their amorous battle takes shape through mutual epistolary declarations of love ("It looks as if this is going to be an epistolary novel," Julien imagines in *RN* II, 15), Julien suspects Mathilde's involvement in a plot to entrap him in his forbidden desires. In a self-defensive move, he writes of his suspicions to his friend, Fouqué, but in the process becomes again, as on the heights, the ironic author of his real fate, and, "caught up in the story he had just finished writing" (*ému de son propre conte comme un auteur dramatique*) (*RN* II, 15), he envisions Mathilde over his corpse. From the moment Julien, in the midst of his illicit tryst with Mathilde, recites tender passages from *La Nouvelle Héloise* (*RN* II, 16), to his suspicions that his actions follow the darker text of the original Heloise ("Beware the fate of Abelard, master secretary" [*RN* II, 16]), to the actual moment of love's deliverance when "Passionate love was still more a model for them than a reality" (*RN* II, 16), Julien is acutely aware that their actions are not independent but are caught in a network of allusions to fictional models. Their desires display a peculiarly progressive disappearance of the real object in favor of a prescribed, imaginary version of the self.

While Julien "was pursuing the phantom of a mistress who should . . . give not a thought to her own existence" (*RN* II, 17), Mathilde resents giving even her false self. When she does give it, she is outraged to realize that in accepting Julien she has not attained "those divine raptures that novels talk about" (*RN* II, 16) but has given herself "a master!" She now allows her romanesque imagination its almost masochistic run: "He holds immense power over me, since he reigns by terror and can punish me atrociously" (*RN* II, 17). At the precise moment Julien is about to lose Mathilde a second time, however, his natural genius in following the texts of his fate provokes him to reach for the sword of Boniface and, seeming to threaten her with it, succeeds in becoming "lord and master" (*RN* II, 17) over Mathilde.

To keep Mathilde, Julien must mask his desire to keep her, for she is perfectly willing to accept him as her lover, so long as she suspects that he does not desire her. Once again, his expressions of love change everything: "Mathilde, confident of his love, despised him completely" (*RN* II, 18). But this too is only a moment, and not an endpoint, in their love affair. Thanks to her love for music, Mathilde seduces herself and surrenders to Julien yet a third time. The step, however, from surrender—"You are my master, I am your slave" (*RN* II, 19)—to immediate resistance—"I no longer love you, sir" (*RN* II, 20)—is, psychologically and narratologically, a determined one.

In contrast to the relationship with Mme. de Rênal, the peculiarity of this affair is that love ceases to be a dialectical movement progressing through reversals and tending, finally and completely, toward a sublime coalescence of the loving couple. Here, the gap between loving and not loving, as that between desire and satisfaction, cannot be closed, nor can it be left entirely open. A semblance of closure is achieved only after Julien, feigning indifference for Mathilde in providing the illusion she has always desired, actually becomes indifferent with the resurgence of his murderous passion for Mme. de Rênal. The movement of love implicit in Julien's first affair, but made explicit with Mathilde, is one which represents a break with the deluded notion that such a totalizing passion can be achieved between two lovers, toward the notion that love forces the subordination of the beloved to the lover's imagination, and finally toward a giving way to an affirmation of both complementarity and antagonism between lover and beloved. This final movement, however, excludes the possibility of an entirely unclouded moment of mutual recognition on the part of the lovers. Love persists, not because of the natural affinity of the loving pair, but rather because their *relationship* initiates a satisfying structural process of mutual *self*-reflection. This self-reflecting love continues to offer the mystic hope of integration.

Later in the nineteenth century, Nietzsche would note: "The magic and most powerful effect of women is, in philosophical language, action at a distance, *actio in distans*; but this requires first of all, above all—*distance*."[20] Nietzsche's words describe aptly the situation Mathilde de la Mole protects, as she realizes that her seductiveness operates at a distance. Julien of course understands this too: her wiles operate upon him because she stays aloof. Without the effects of separation, she could neither seduce nor stir desire. And yet, at a distance, she is not herself but the self which desire creates: a simulacrum, a crystallized metaphor of the insubstantial essence, transcendental, inaccessible, and seductive, which might validate Julien's existence. "She became," as Stendhal writes concerning Métilde Dembowski, "like a tender phantom."[21]

But there is no essence to such a fantastic metaphor because the determinate entity which forms its literal base—Mathilde herself—is entirely separate from herself. Before Julien's desires transport her to another realm, her own self-induced desires to relive the story of Marguerite de Navarre have displaced her from whatever characteristics are basic and proper to herself. Within this series of self-displacements, Mathilde, like Mme. de Rênal, and like Julien himself, surrenders all identity, propriety, and essentiality. Love is the name Stendhal attributes to this distantiation from the essence of truth: "Passion most dissembles, yet betrays" (I:10: epigraph), and comes to share with hypocrisy, we might add, the power of its ways. This deviation from propriety, from the truth of substance, whether

[20] Friedrich Nietzsche, *The Gay Science*, trans. Walter Kaufmann (New York: Random House, Vintage Books, 1974), Section 60. Stendhal, Nietzsche says elsewhere, is "This curious epicurean, this human question mark." See also, William R. Goetz, "Nietzsche and *Le Rouge et le noir*," *Comparative Literature Studies* 18 (1981): 443-458.

[21] Stendhal, *Souvenirs d'Égotisme*, in *Oeuvres Intimes*, p. 1404.

as "hypocrisy" or as "love," is not, as René Girard has argued, the fault of *desire*, but *is* the operation of desire.[22]

Having attained an authentic mastery by feigning the role of master while actually experiencing his entire existence as a slave, Julien is finally able to transform himself into a true "romantic soul" (*âme romanesque*) (*RN* II, 38). At this moment, when Julien's "romanesque" desires are on the verge of being realized, Mme. de Rênal reappears as the necessary third element of the triangular relationship. For Mathilde, Julien's attempt to murder Mme. de Rênal transforms him fully into "Boniface de la Mole . . . reborn, . . . but in an even more heroic mold" (*RN* II, 38). The pattern of desire in Stendhal's novel is thus a dialectic of cognition, miscognition, and recognition, which, as in Hegel's discussion of the relationship between "Master and Slave,"[23] is based on what one critic has termed "the notion that through consciousness of the other, one attains consciousness of the self on the condition of being recognized by the other."[24] But in Julien's case, this recognition is further to realize that one's self *is* the other, or that the other is oneself. As if in response to his own denial of "others"—"Leave me my ideal life. . . . What do *other people* (*les autres*) matter?" (*RN* II, 40)—Julien thereafter sees clearly the fact of his own duplicity—"It's really true, man does have two spirits within him" (*RN* II, 40). He continues to decry in the absent approbation of *les autres*, as imaginary partners in the creation of the self, the validity of his suicidal self-creation: "For the others,

[22] René Girard, "*The Red and the Black*," *Deceit, Desire, and the Novel*, pp. 113-138.

[23] G.W.F. Hegel, *The Phenomenology of Mind*, trans. J. B. Baillie, rev. ed. (1931; New York: Harper Torchbooks, 1967), pp. 234, 236-237, and 239-240. See also the pertinent discussion of the concepts by Alexandre Kojève, "In Place of an Introduction," *Introduction to the Reading of Hegel*, trans. J. Nichols (New York: Basic Books, 1969) pp. 3-30.

[24] Anthony Wilden, *The Language of the Self* (Baltimore: Johns Hopkins University Press, 1968), p. 285.

I am at most nothing but a PERHAPS" (*Pour les autres, je ne suis tout au plus qu'un* PEUT ÊTRE) (*RN* II, 42).

Like don Quijote before him, Julien has made himself into an archetypal champion of forgotten ideals as he attempts to translate the romantic sentiments which animate his life into vital actions. But, as it turns out, his attempted self-creation becomes an act of self-destruction. Nowhere is this more certain than in his rhetorically charged statement to the jury hearing his case for the assault on Mme. de Rênal:

> Gentlemen of the jury:
>
> My horror of contempt, which I thought I could stand until the hour of my death, compels me to break silence. Gentlemen, I have not the honor to belong to your social class, you see in me a peasant in open revolt against his humble station.
>
> I ask no favors of you, Julien went on, his voice hardening. I have no illusions, death awaits me: I have deserved it. I have attempted to cut short the life of a woman most worthy of respect, most worthy of devotion. Mme. de Rênal had been like a mother to me. My crime was atrocious, and it was *premeditated*. I have therefore deserved the death sentence, gentlemen of the jury. But even if I were less guilty than I am, I see before me men who, without ever considering whether my youth merits some pity, are determined to punish in me and discourage forever a certain class of young men—those who, born to a lower social order, and buried by poverty, are lucky enough to get a good education and bold enough to mingle with what the arrogant rich call good society.
>
> There is my crime, gentlemen, and it will be punished all the more severely because, in reality, I am not judged by my peers. I do not see in the seats of the jury a single rich peasant, only outraged bourgeois. (*RN* II, 41)

The text of this final public message is crucial for Julien. He sees it as his last opportunity to speak what before this moment he has forbidden himself to say; it is, in short, his final bid to play out his *cause romanesque* (*RN* II, 41). Its intent must be grasped, therefore, with no possibility of misinterpretation, insofar as its function is as much to cover his shame as to reveal his guilt. But the fact remains that the ambiguity and the hypocrisy of language allow many ways of access to the secret of Julien's suicidal words.

Viewed from an optimistic perspective, Julien's speech might be seen as his determined attempt to recapture all his ambitions and desires in the form of an audacious address to *les autres*. By provoking his judges, he re-vindicates his superiority, his ability to dominate through the force of language, and his strength to endure the solitude of decisive action. But, from another perspective, we cannot forget that this speech, which seems to unmask the true Julien Sorel, also reveals his continued adherence to the role of the fatalistic romantic hero and his disguised desire for death. Invoking the name of the woman who has been "like a mother to me," Julien reveals that in striking out at this other self, it is himself whom he strikes. And beyond the atrocity of his "premeditated crime," for which he stands, like Mathilde before him, a prisoner of love, bound and ready to receive his "atrocious pain," Julien is willing to subsume the individual nature of his sin into the general social crime of "a certain class of young men—those who . . . are bold enough to mingle with what the arrogant rich call good society." In this rhetorical move, Julien's self-confidence and self-esteem, perhaps even his release from hypocrisy, emerge as the façades of his desire for negation.[25] Authentic language, like authentic

[25] The Oedipal structure of these relations has of course not escaped many *stendhaliens*. Robert Alter, for instance, correctly notes that "In *Le Rouge et le Noir*, Julien, moving between two women, finally chooses the mother figure and, perhaps partly through the unconscious logic of the incest taboo, by so doing chooses death as well" (*A Lion for Love*, p. 253).

love, free from dissembling, it seems, cannot exist but as a moment without a future.[26] If, as in the concluding scenes which depict the renewal of love between Julien and Mme. de Rênal in the prison, a rebirth toward the Other is possible, it is so only because desire continues to contravene against the bounds established by death.

Love, therefore, forms the surface matrix of human relations as Stendhal represents them in *Le Rouge et le Noir*. Beyond it, hidden beneath it, lies, as continuously demonstrated by Julien, the profundity of desire for "the true." "Love in Stendhal," notes Jean-Pierre Richard, "is the idolatry of the true."[27] The narrator's implicit stance against egoism, vanity, and hypocrisy, and for the spontaneity of natural passion, especially in love, orients the course of his narrative toward such an "idolatry." But since "in love everything is a *symbol*" (*tout est "signe" en amour*) (*De l'Amour* I, 38) whether masquerading as the desire to be the Napoleonic man of action, or the Napoleon of love, Julien's deeper desire for *le vrai* abstracts itself, and thereby suspends itself, from all possibilities of fulfillment. Thus, at the very height of his passion, at the moment just before he attains wealth, position, a child of his own, and the woman whom he has taken as the sign of his desires, Julien destroys fulfillment in his unmotivated attempt to murder Mme. de Rênal. It is unmotivated because his desires might still have been met before his felonious act; after it, those possibilities no longer exist. Julien, in effect, thus duplicates Mathilde's distancing maneuvers, and literally separates himself from fulfillment. Similarly,

[26] Georges Poulet, discussing the nature of time in *Le Rouge et le Noir*, makes this argument in "Stendhal," *Mesure de l'Instant* (Paris: Plon, 1968), pp. 250-251.

[27] "Conaissance et tendresse chez Stendhal," *Littérature et sensation* (Paris: Seuil, 1954), cited by Robert M. Adams in his Norton Critical Edition of *Red and Black*, pp. 485-503. Stendhal himself, as Georges Poulet argues, experiences this idolatry of truth as a moment of "*la ferme volonté*" (*Mesure de l'Instant*, p. 243). In the *Filosofia nova*, Stendhal had already directed his "resolute will" toward "*le vrai*": "je consacre ma vie au vrai" (II: 137).

his speech to the jury cuts short the renewal of his passion for Mme. de Rênal. That this separation from fulfillment is soon to be physically enacted upon Julien simply reinforces the emblematic force of Stendhal's rhetoric of desire and allegorizes what has been throughout the text a tropological motif. "Desire" now marks not consummation, but its inverse.

We must be cautious with this formula, of course. The inversion poses difficulties. But it also clarifies matters. As early as in his initial relations with Mme. de Rênal, Julien transfers material desires into sexual desires. With Mathilde, the transfer has been refined into the metaphysical level. Such is the circuit of desire—from a discourse surrounding a woman, to one which transforms the woman into a perceptible model of a truth which seems lacking in the everyday world. As this model of truth, Mme. de Rênal and Mathilde in turn bewilder, attract, and enchant Julien. In them the idea of fulfillment becomes seductive, but also transcendent and inaccessible. Thus arise Julien's own dissimulating responses—he dissimulates to hide the effects of both Mme. de Rênal's love and Mathilde's love and scorn. In so doing, he internalizes what he mistakenly sees as the femininity of their love, and directs it, finally and with a vengeance, upon Mme. de Rênal.

❦ ❦ ❦

It is, of course, this very possibility of dissembling the truth, of saying one thing while meaning another, which classical rhetoric terms not hypocrisy but *irony*. As is the case in his use of emblematic and allegorical language, Stendhal fully expects the reader to be aware of the rhetorical maneuvering implicit in many ironical statements of Julien and of narrator. As ironist, Stendhal depends on our acquisition of an allegorical habit of mind as we juxtapose our perceptions of the difference between Julien's expressed and intended meanings. Irony, more so than allegory, emphasizes this difference between sign and meaning and has for its function the thematization of the difference.[28] Irony is related to allegory "since irony is clearly a particular, 180 degree-reversed, instance of allegory's double meaning."[29] But while irony inverses the *inversio* of allegory, it also allows for the possibility of continued inversions. The ironic mode differs from the allegorical temper, therefore, in that the recognition of the disjunction between surface and proper meaning occurs, as Paul de Man argues, "not only *by means of* language as a privileged category, but it transfers the self [which detects this divergence] out of the empirical world into a world constituted out of, and in, language— . . . Language thus conceived divides the subject into an empirical self, immersed in the world, and a self that becomes like a sign in its attempt at differentiation and self-definition."[30] Irony affects language and personality since it comes into being at the expense of a hypothetically empirical self, who fails to recognize the ironic divergence, and another self, who exists as the language which asserts the knowledge of this failed recognition. Tropes in general say one thing and mean another. Irony, as it sets off in an infinite regress of surface and real levels of meaning, radicalizes the relationship between the substituted levels of meaning by negating the possibility of an unambiguous reading of the new, ironic relationship.

The sequential movement from sign to meaning forms the possibility of allegory and narrative in general. Irony, however,

[28] The fullest recent account of the relationship between symbolical, allegorical, and ironic modes of discourse is Paul de Man's "The Rhetoric of Temporality," in *Interpretation: Theory and Practice*, ed. Charles Singleton (Baltimore: Johns Hopkins University Press, 1969), pp. 173-209.

[29] Richard A. Lanham, *A Handlist of Rhetorical Terms* (Berkeley and Los Angeles: University of California Press, 1969), p. 61. The allegorical sign adduces an arbitrary relationship between distinct entities; it does not indicate a natural tie between a signifier and its signified, as does the symbol. "Meaning" in allegory results from the construction of analogies between the entities, rather than from the discovery of an existing natural relationship. Irony, in turn, reveals this ongoing process of analogical reflection between the related entities. See Jonathan Culler, "Literary History, Allegory, and Semiology," *New Literary History* 7 (1976): 259-270.

[30] "The Rhetoric of Temporality," p. 196.

as the interruption of that movement, can come closer than can other tropes to the actual experience of human existence, which experiences itself and the world as isolated moments factitiously linked by the human imagination. It is irony, for example, which allows Stendhal to regard the "mathematical order" in which he lists the great passions of his life as a ploy by which he may "consider them as philosophically as possible and thus remove them from within the aura which makes me *turn my eyes aside*, which dazzles me and suppresses my ability to see clearly."[31] Allegory reconstructs past events but irony interrupts to remind that the reconstruction is not the event itself. This emphasis on discontinuity—what Friedrich Schlegel terms *eine permanente Parakbase*[32]—renders irony the favored trope of the novel. It is the device Stendhal uses to figure the "duplicity" of Julien's character, the "changeability" which Fouqué remarks in Mathilde, and the "hypocrisy" of nineteenth-century life in general.

Nowhere is the force of irony as the disruption and inversion of anticipated connections more evident than in Stendhal's long parenthetical interruption of the narrative flow in II, 19. After representing a "night of madness" at the Opera Buffa during which Mathilde is transformed into the woman Mme. de Rênal has been all along, Stendhal pauses to defend the propriety of his allegory of desire:

[31] *Henry Brulard, Oeuvres Intimes*, p. 16. Stendhal then adds: "I seek to destroy the charm, the DAZZLING, of events by considering them mathematically." Grahame C. Jones, *L'Ironie dans les romans de Stendhal* (Lausanne: Éditions du Grand Chêne, 1966), is still the only full-length study of Stendhal's irony. Jones dutifully uses the available scholarship on the subject but his approach seems to me lacking the rigorous and coherent conception Stendhal's irony demands.

[32] Friedrich Schlegel, *Kritische Ausgabe Werke*, 18:85 (668), cited by Paul de Man, "The Rhetoric of Temporality," p. 200. De Man subsequently develops the notion of irony as "the permanent *parabasis* of allegory." Irony so considered is the tropological element which deconstructs the tendency of all narrative discourse to create apparently authorized temporal and logical relationships where before there were none (*Allegories of Reading*, pp. 300-301).

> The outcome of this night of madness was that she supposed she had triumphed over her love. (This page will damage the unfortunate author in more than one way. Ice-cold souls will accuse him of indecency. It does no harm to the young ladies who glitter in the drawing rooms of Paris to suppose that one of them is capable of such mad impulses as degrade the character of Mathilde. Her character is entirely imaginary, and indeed imagined at a great distance from those social customs that, among all the ages of history, will assure such a distinguished rank for the civilization of the nineteenth century.) (*RN* II, 19)

The radical suspension of the continuities assumed by the allegorical temper of the human imagination is the basis of the special mode of Stendhalian irony, and it is to a consideration of the function of this irony in relation to "desire" in Stendhal's novel that I now briefly turn.

The passage begins with an uncomplicated case of dramatic irony. We know from Mathilde's past actions and from the rhetorically weighted phrase, "this night of madness," that Mathilde has not, as she supposes, triumphed over love. As when in the Opera Buffa, Harlequin turns to the audience to remind them of the factitious nature of the domestic idyl being played out before them, [33] "Stendhal" here emerges from the anonymity of the text to disrupt the fictional illusion. The parenthetical mark is the sign of this radical turn. He wishes to point out the basic difference, which an unwary reader might overlook, between the historical world of the "young ladies who glitter in the salons of Paris" and the fictional world which Mathilde, as a "totally imaginary" character, inhabits. This separation of the real and the fictional is intentional. It serves

[33] Michele Scherillo, *L'Opera buffa napoletana durante il settecento*, 2nd ed. (Milan, 1916); see also *Henry Brulard, Oeuvres Intimes*: "Je ne puis être touché jusqu'à l'attendrissement *qu'après un passage comique*. De là mon amour presque exclusif pour l'*opera buffa*. . . . De là mon complet éloignement pour la tragédie, mon éloignement jusq'à l'*ironie* pour la tragédie en vers" (p. 351).

not to heighten the reality of the fictional (its facticity has already been granted), but to bolster our confidence in the *truth* of that separation. Thus, "no harm" can come to those "young ladies" who should recognize themselves in Mathilde, for Mathilde has no real existence. If we are made somewhat uneasy by the hyperbolic strain of the last sentence of the paragraph, which allows to the "social customs" of the "nineteenth century" such a distinguished rank among "all the ages of history," the fact that we can discern the (apparent) target of the (possible) irony is reassuring. Stendhal is, after all, simply defending his authority as a "decent" author and would not discomfit readers more than he already has. At this point, the difference between actual and fictional worlds, as that between real and apparent dupes of irony, seems clear enough. And yet, it is possible that he protests the difference too much: "It is by no means prudence that is lacking in the young ladies who have been the ornaments of this winter's balls."

Two sentences later, irony has descended into sarcasm, as Stendhal leaves no doubt that the innocent "young ladies," dreaming of "a brilliant fortune," might indeed be touched by "such mad impulses as degrade the character of Mathilde." But irony remains in force, even if it has changed direction, for one cannot help noticing that the writing intended as an apology of method has become an outright indictment of the reader's presumed bourgeois lifestyle. As if carried away by the force of his own rhetoric, the persona of the fictional narrator, in accusing the reader, begins to work against the persona of the fictional author, who wishes to regain the reader's sympathy. Once again, the identity of the dupe of irony remains in doubt, as Stendhal's aside continues to question the propriety of his text:

> (Nor is love generally the path by which young men endowed with some talent like Julien hope to gain their fortune; they attach themselves immovably to a certain

"crowd," and when the crowd arrives, all the good things of society pour down among them. Woe to the man of education who belongs to no "crowd"; even his uncertain little successes will be held against him, and the higher virtue will condemn him even as it robs him.) (*RN* II, 19)

This man without a "crowd" is of course not Julien, but might well be a certain civil servant about to lose his few remaining good ties to "society," and painfully aware that even his "little successes" are being held against him. Having unleashed the disjunctive powers of irony, Stendhal finds that conjunction of surface and real meaning, of fictional and actual worlds, and even of pseudonymal and nominal identities has become disconcertingly more difficult than one might assume. In reference to this blurring of assumed and real identities, Gérard Genette has written: "In 'Stendhal,' that *nom de guerre*, the 'person' of Henri Beyle and his 'work' are rejoined, mingled, and abolished reciprocally and ceaselessly; if for Stendhalians the work of Stendhal constantly designates Henri Beyle, Henri Beyle in turn does not truly exist but through the work of Stendhal. . . . Beyle is legitimately for us nothing but one of Stendhal's characters."[34] In mid-paragraph, this composite "Stendhal" returns to the ostensible purpose of his rhetorical aside:

[34] Gérard Genette, "Stendhal," *Figures* II (Paris: Seuil, 1969), p. 156. Genette also observes that Beyle's disposition toward pseudonymy, in both his fictional and non-fictional life, renders the notion of an "authorial presence" ambiguous and problematic: "La mani pseudonymique prend ici valeur de symbole: dans ses romans comme dans ses correspondance, dans ses éssais comme dans ses mémoires, Beyle est toujours présent, mais presque toujours masqué ou travesti. . . . Stendhal couvre Henry Brulard, qui couvre Henri Beyle—lequel à son tour confond tout à fait avec aucun des trois autres, et nous échappe à jamais" ("Stendhal," p. 157). See also Robert M. Adams, *Stendhal: Notes on a Novelist*, p. 5, listing some of the near 200 pseudonyms Beyle used at one time or another; and also, the fine essay of Jean Starobinski, "Stendhal pseudonyme," *L'Oeil vivant* (Paris: Gallimard, 1961), pp. 193-257. Grahame C. Jones, too, sees "chez Stendhal une sorte d'ironie double, une sorte d'ironie pour et contre le romancier" (*L'Ironie dans les romans de Stendhal*, p. 12), as do Albert Cook, "Stendhal's Irony," *Essays in Criticism* (1958): 355-369; and H. W. Hardeman, "*La Chartreuse de Parme*: Ironical Ambiguity," *The Kenyon Review* (1955): 449-471.

> (Look here, sir, a novel is a mirror moving along a highway. One minute you see it reflect the azure skies, next minute the mud and puddles of the road. And the man who carries the mirror in his pack will be accused by you of immorality! His mirror shows the mud and you accuse the mirror! Rather you should accuse the road in which the puddle lies, or, even better, the inspector of roads who lets the water collect and the puddles form.
>
> Now that it's fully understood that a character like Mathilde's is impossible in our age, no less prudent than virtuous, I am less afraid of distressing the reader by describing further the follies of this attractive girl). (*RN* II, 19)

We should proceed down this metaphorical road with caution. The reader's path is strewn with rhetorical potholes. With some justification, we have assumed that, as René Girard and Stephen Gilman have shown,[35] *Le Rouge et le Noir* is at least in part, formally and thematically, an allegory of desire. The narrative of this allegory describes the successive attempts by the various characters, Julien Sorel, Mme. de Rênal, and Mathilde de la Mole, in particular, to transform the possession of the desired into a bolster for identity and personal autonomy. For these characters, identity is formed in the very play of their erotic wills. The narrative proceeds to show, however, that the desired transformation of the "other" into a sign of one's own superiority is an error based on a misconception of what constitutes "fulfillment" in human relations. This error cannot be undone by a simple redirection of the course of desire from an inauthentic, narcissistic orientation toward a healthy, other-directed expression of love. As it turns out, *love itself*, as a constitutively tropological process in which the beloved is seized, transformed, and crystallized into a being of the lover's own creation, is the source of difficulties. This allegory of desire is thus simultaneously the allegory of the misunderstanding of desire. As a linear discourse liable to the protocols of narrative procedure,

[35] Girard, pp. 113-138; Gilman, pp. 16-28.

the allegory can be understood as a deconstruction of the false view that the lover's representation can coincide with the beloved's reality. The symbolical integration of isolated personalities in a sublime moment of transcendental love is the peculiarly "romantic" myth debunked by Stendhal's "realistic" discourse. All this detailing of the negative truth concerning love's duplicity is the work of allegory.

But Stendhal is much too sensitive an observer of the nuances, variations, and complexities of "love's physiology" to accept even this demystified view, which reintroduces a sense of control and mastery of love's ways, to stand as the final, crystallized word. While allegory posits a narrative duration to confine the intricate variation of amorous experience and to show that love deludes, irony resists control and puts again into question the validity of any apparently definitive answer to show that love does not *simply* delude. It simultaneously offers and removes the enchanting hope of transcendental fulfillment. Stendhal, who would have it both ways, finds, therefore, that irony, by respecting the systematic arbitrariness of love's processes, is the only trope capable of regulating the allegory of love's cognition and miscognitions.

These effects of irony are evident throughout *Le Rouge et le Noir*, but are most readily visible in the present passage. Stendhal is at once claiming mimetic perfection—that his "novel is a mirror"—and imperfection—that the reflections in his mirror, Mathilde's reflection in particular, have *no* mimetic value, since they exist in a realm inaccessible to things of this world. This is not a simple misstatement. The epigraph of I, 13, that *Un roman: c'est un miroir qu'on promène le long d'un chemin* (A novel: it's a mirror being carried along a highway), reinforces the present narrative claim to representational authority. The contradiction, which makes Mathilde simultaneously mimetically true but representationally false, is disguised beneath a rhetorical ploy which shifts the responsibility for the "indecency" of the representation from the level of the signifying text to that of the signified world: "Rather you should accuse the road in which the mud puddle lies, or even better, the inspector of roads who lets the water collect and the puddles form." Stendhal, holding the mirror which reveals society's faults, refuses the blame and assigns it to society itself, or to society's overseers. But this does not explain how his mirror can reflect what is not there, nor why, even though the initial sections of the passage expressly create the possibility of a conjunction between fiction and real life, this reflection of the non-existent cannot touch the reader. Where are we to stand, then, to judge the aptness and credibility of the author's characters if they do not impinge upon our world? And which of his rhetorical stances are we to believe? Stendhal states unequivocally that the situation can be "fully understood."

By insisting on the rhetorical form of its narrative, Stendhal's novel forces us to recognize at least four possible perspectives on the fate of the characters it creates: (a) the narrator's unclouded vision of his characters' fates; (b) the characters' own mystified vision of their conditions; (c) that of the plot, with its signs, emblems, and allegories of the characters' distinctive itineraries; and (d) that of the fictional reader, who is represented as being scandalized at the indecency of the characters' actions only to discover that those actions are based on assumptions he himself holds. *Irony* arises to show that none of these perspectives alone can organize the meaning of the text. What they do provide are guidelines originating from different points, which continue to converge and diverge, according to the play of irony, within a roughly circumscribed area. This area, delimited within the bounds of irony, may be thought of as the "meaning" of the text. The pattern of convergence and divergence of implied narrative perspectives can be felt as the rhythm of the narrative flow. This alternating movement from one rhetorically active system to another is circular and perpetual. Its infinite circularity allows any one perspective to stand momentarily in the privileged place of "meaning," but also permits that perspective to be transcribed, and thus removed from its privileged location, by other rhetorical perspectives. With regard to the text as a whole, therefore, there is no primary discourse; from the outset the text is metonymically multilingual. Moreover, this rhythm of alternating perspectives forces the reader into the same dilemma of interpretation that the characters themselves enact as they move into and out of love, from one moment of their lives to the next.

Thus the reader's sense of "meaning" in the text emerges from a shifting of vantage points from one narrative perspective to another. This systematic shifting actualized by the reading of the text is sometimes represented topographically, as in the ascending/descending scenes of Book I. It gradually evolves into a mobile pattern of truths which allows the reader to grasp the nature of the duplicitous world Stendhal portrays. Irony, however, disallows the opportunity of achieving an authorized synthesis of the differences among the various perspectives. Its movement sustains, as much as can any linguistic element, the capricious ways of love's actions. However systematic the effects of those actions may seem, irony, as the continuous inversion of love's inventing procedures, allows the mystery of their ground to remain. That Julien himself, despite his profound delusion, is often capable of sharing in the narrator's irony—"He was sick to death of all his good qualities, of all the things he had once loved with enthusiasm; and in this state of *inverse imagination* he undertook to criticize life imaginatively. It was the error of a superior man" (*RN* II, 19)—is perhaps the most important sign that his is indeed an exceptional character. His ability to retain an ironic distance from himself, an "état d'*imagination renversée*," cannot protect him from the pain created by his distance from Mathilde and Mme. de Rênal, but it does affirm the grandeur of his mistakes.

Stendhal, who was himself the transformation of a man who had so much to do with so many women, could understand these mistakes and Julien's quixotic position within the economy of desire he forms with Mathilde, Mme. de Rênal, and the crystallized abstractions their presences create.[36] As neither Julien nor Mathilde is ever a particularly fixed character type, if there is something constant about that network, it is its tendency toward variability. Even Mme. de Rênal, though surely not a model for the role of Marguerite, adds with Mathilde to the veritable typology of roles the narrative presents—mother, sister, spouse, and mistress—by and into whom Julien himself is lovingly transformed. For this reason, there is no simple reading, nor any single truth available to Stendhal's allegory of desire. The question of desire, as Jacques Derrida writes concerning a similar issue, suspends "the decidable opposition between the true and the untrue."[37] Stendhal's vision of love reflects this suspended opposition. In *Le Rouge et le Noir*, Stendhal dramatizes the implications of love's qualities, emphasizing, as in the ironic passage concerning the contradictory nature of mimetic narratives, that representations, even such self-representations as desire forces upon us, imply no one truth as such, no one representation which might substantiate the appropriation of the desired as an attempt to verify our own identity. In fact, the corrosive power of imitation, which makes the copy appear as a parody of the model, is strong enough to raise the possibility that beyond the mythology of love's integrating discourse, fragmentation is always *already* the condition of human desire.

❦ ❦ ❦

Stendhal's rhetoric of desire constitutes Julien in a perpetual dialectic of action and reaction to love. Through his desire, Julien creates Mme. de Rênal and Mathilde de la Mole as alternate

[36] Beyle lists and compares in *La Vie de Henry Brulard*, pp. 13-16, the women with whom to that date he had been amorously involved. The list is less a "*souvenir d'égotisme*" than an homage to love.

[37] Jacques Derrida, "La question du style," in *Nietzsche aujourd'hui?* Pierre Boudot et al., Publications du Centre Culturel de Cerisy-La-Salle (Paris: Union Générale d'Éditions [10/18], 1973), p. 270.

and incomplete versions of the idealized Beloved. But he, in turn, is also constituted as an object of desire in their eyes. As a result, the historically significant act which he dreams he will perform in the manner of a latter-day Napoleon is always suspended. His inability to be either himself or one of *"les autres"* continually precludes action. "As a matter of fact," Julien finally admits, "it seems that my fate is to die in a dream" (*RN* II, 40).

Insofar as Julien is always embroiled in a dialectic of narcissism and identification, his life is the acting out of this infantile dream of complete integration.[38] Reflecting on the impasse of Stendhal's own desires, Gilbert Durand remarks that "Métilde [Dembowski] reveals to Stendhal that there is no love other than the return to the mother, but paradoxically the image of Métilde dead and 'forever' lost assumes aspects which bring it singularly close to that of the dead mother. Through Métilde, the emancipation of love becomes possible, but through Métilde's death the realization of love recedes, fleeing toward an ideal and inaccessible horizon."[39] Julien's fate is thus precisely the inverse of that of Stendhal and of Rousseau's Saint-Preux: in rejecting Mathilde's play of love and hate, Julien returns to the incestual dangers of Mme. de Rênal's maternal love and the promise of spiritual integration. But since this dream of reintegration with the beloved is both realistically and symbolically impossible, narratologically, the only recourse left to the *romancier* who would bring his tale to a close is the allegorical disavowal of the impasse in the form of Julien's decapitation. That Mathilde continues to act out the story of Boniface and Marguerite by tenderly recovering and caring for Julien's sev-

[38] For full psychoanalytic readings of Julien's "Oedipal" situation, see Shoshana Felman, *La "Folie" dans l'oeuvre Romanesque de Stendhal* (Paris: José Cortí, 1971), pp. 191-216; and Leo Bersani, "The Paranoid Hero in Stendhal," *A Future for Astyanax: Character and Desire in Literature* (Boston: Little, Brown, and Co., 1969), pp. 106-127.

[39] *Le Décor mythique de la Chartreuse de Parme* (Paris, 1961), p. 149; cited by Robert Alter, *A Lion for Love*, p 254.

ered head, removing it to the mountaintop grotto where Julien first dreamed the plot of his fatal liaison, is Stendhal's final masterstroke in his portrait of desire. Julien's demanding attempts to transform, and thus disavow, present reality in favor of an aesthetically coherent fiction are displaced by his symbolic assimilation into the fiction his life has always been. Desire, which can be nothing but the nostalgic impulse toward what is not present, can be "fulfilled" only by the elimination of the lacked object, or by the interdiction of the self's extension beyond itself. In either case, it is Stendhal's shockingly modern view that the fundamental satisfaction of desire is itself a dream.

❦ FOUR ❦

The Apotheosis of Subjectivity: Performative and Constative in Melville's *Moby-Dick*

Up from the spray of thy ocean perishing—straight up, leaps thy apotheosis!

MELVILLE
Moby-Dick

Allegories are, in the realm of thoughts, what ruins are in the realm of things.

WALTER BENJAMIN
Origin of German Tragic Drama

Although Ishmael explicitly warns readers in the chapter entitled "The Affidavit" not to make a "hideous and intolerable allegory" of his preceding statements on the implacable fate which seems to drive Captain Ahab toward disaster, the fact is that generations of readers have attempted to read *Moby-Dick* as allegory. There is nothing particularly wrong in this, for despite Ishmael's stated distrust of allegory, readers find that allegory is the rhetorical form the text itself often assumes. Ishmael too constructs allegories and, as early as in the initial scenes in "The Spouter-Inn" and "The Chapel," engages in their interpretation. His very first words, "Call me Ishmael," invite, beyond their imperative tone, a turn toward other literary texts, other representations of outcast figures. Consequently, Ishmael's narrative can be, and has been, read as an extended metaphor of a quest for personal knowledge. Ishmael voyages into the world to renew his faith in its "essential meaningfulness" and to find a dependable ground for a stable sense of who he might be.

It is also a recognized fact, however, that Ishmael's narrative of self-encounter is almost immediately displaced by the powerful force of Captain Ahab's monomaniac desire to hunt out and destroy Moby Dick. Almost as if in response to Ishmael's implicit wish to find a ground for identity, Ahab arises to serve as a possible role model of unquestioned self-confidence. The narrative of *Moby-Dick* thus seems to offer two distinct versions of personal stability—Ishmael's, which is to be founded upon knowledge of the self and the world, and Ahab's, which is based on the force of human will. If a "new" Ishmael emerges from the text as narrator to tell the results of his voyage of discovery, it would seem that this new Ishmael is a synthesis of the dialectical play between the opposed personalities of Ahab and the young Ishmael. The result of this synthesis is significant indeed—the magnificent text of *Moby-Dick*. Sure of who and what he is, Ishmael can create a narrative recounting the events which lead to his certainty.

But certainty is surely not the end of Ishmael's narrative. Instead, the problematical issues of identity and action (in Ishmael's case, as narration) remain linked and unresolved throughout the novel. The dialectic between Ahab's and Ishmael's notions of what forms self-knowledge emphasizes, but does not resolve, the questions raised by their respective attitudes. The dialectic does, however, establish significant relationships in the text among action and identity, on the one hand, and the origin and performance of narrative itself, on the other. The production of narrative seems for Melville to be closely linked to the creation of a stable personality. But while imaginative invention is involved in all four concepts, the procedures by which Ahab invents the fiction of intentional actions, and by which Ishmael conceives a narrative of self-creation, are quite different. The differences between the two processes of invention seem to me crucial and indicative of a whole range of narratological issues raised by Melville's novel.

As the principal expressions of consciousness, Ahab and Ishmael form the organizing poles of the text. Ishmael attempts to draw meaning from his relationship to the world and to the persons around him. For him, human existence must be described as a "mutual, joint-stock" coordinating system, in which "nothing exists in itself." And since he conceptualizes the world in social terms, the intersections of human concerns determine for Ishmael the nature of the world. Thus, while the structure of personality may well be immanent, for Ishmael its visible features at least are socially defined. But within this contextual framework, the self can become over-determined, and Ishmael finds that he must periodically turn away from the social world and go to sea for himself, in order to recollect his own unconscious core: "I am in the habit of going to sea whenever I begin to grow hazy about the eyes, and begin to be over conscious of my lungs . . . ," he claims.[1]

Ahab too ponders the nature of personality, but seeks to draw a conclusive meaning as to its make-up through a confrontation with the world. For Ahab, personality is defined not in terms of context, but of action; not by the enveloping framework of culture, but by the movement of personal history; not in the sociability of the self, but in its isolation of an autonomous ground. "Cursed be that mortal inter-indebtedness," is Ahab's motto (392). His way of experiencing the world is thus contrary to that of Ishmael. While for Ishmael the stability of the self depends on its knowledge of contextual relations, for Ahab the self is defined simply by its ability to act. Ishmael would reestablish identity through a circular process of recollection and storytelling; Ahab would establish it through a linear process of pursuit and command.

Describing the final assimilation by man of what was previously, exclusively, the domain of God, namely the ability to create and destroy value, Friedrich Nietzsche proclaims in *The Gay Science* that we have been able to "drink up the sea,"

[1] Herman Melville, *Moby-Dick*, ed. Harrison Hayford and Hershel Parker, Norton Critical Edition (New York: W. W. Norton & Co., 1967), pp. 61, 55, and 14. Subsequent quotations will refer to this edition of Melville's 1851 English and American texts.

"wipe away the horizon," and "loosen the earth from the sun."[2] Neither historically nor conceptually is he far removed from Ahab's words in *Moby-Dick*: "I'd strike the sun if it insulted me" (144), or "What I've dared, I've willed; and what I've willed, I'll do!" (147). Once transcendent Divinity is removed from the center of the significant world, man increasingly circumscribes the horizons of meaning and interpretation.[3] Obviously, Ahab is not Nietzsche; but he does think that by striking through the "pasteboard mask" he may show that nothing is behind the mask, that the evil of this world is autonomous. For Nietzsche, as well as for Ahab and Ishmael, however, the basic question remains that of *meaning*, and each turns to man's existence in the world as the only remaining arena of the search for authentic selfhood. Only in this quest can Ishmael and Ahab find a meaning to supplement or replace the former guarantors of moral and personal stability. Ishmael, on one hand, begins with transcendental faith and ends with existential doubt; Ahab, on the other hand, begins with transcendental doubt and ends with existential faith. There is of course a world of difference constituted by that chiastic exchange of faith and doubt. But within the difference we can begin to describe and circumscribe the creation of meaning in *Moby-Dick*.

[2] *The Gay Science*, Sec. 125, pp. 180-181. J. Hillis Miller has argued in his *The Disappearance of God* (Cambridge, Mass.: Harvard University Press, 1963) that God is effectively removed from the sphere of transcendental value in the nineteenth century when man comes to look upon Him as an object among a myriad of others in the world, and therefore as susceptible to man's defining actions.

[3] The issue of Melville's movement away from traditional Judaeo-Christian metaphysics has been amply discussed by Laurance Thompson, *Melville's Quarrel with God* (Princeton: Princeton University Press, 1952); H. Bruce Franklin, *The Wake of the Gods: Melville's Mythology* (Palo Alto: Stanford University Press, 1963); R. E. Watters, "Melville's Metaphysics of Evil," *University of Toronto Quarterly* 9 (January 1940): 170-182; Thornton Booth, "*Moby-Dick*: Standing Up to God," *Nineteenth-Century Fiction* 17 (June 1962): 33-43; Martin Leonard Pops, *The Melville Archetype* (Kent, Ohio; Kent State University Press, 1970); and by Richard Slotkin in *Regeneration Through Violence* (Middletown, Conn.: Weslyan University Press, 1973), pp. 539-550.

If Ishmael as narrator desires to speak the authentic word which might define the world and cannot, and if Ahab seeks to perform his will in order to define it and cannot, are we then to assume that Melville's end is negation? Might it be possible to posit a third position between spoken identity and enacted identity from which we could speak by performing, and perform by speaking? In such a narratival sphere, the separate concepts of identity (as recovered via recollection or created by an act of the will) might be felicitously joined within the bounds of language. Whether such a synthesis is in fact possible, and what formal strategies its expression might require, may be determined by turning to Melville's text and attempting to understand the nature of its system of meaning. In what follows I examine this drama of spoken identity and enacted identity in *Moby-Dick* to consider its rhetorical and formal implications for the development of modern narrative discourse.

❦ ❦ ❦

Ishmael stands at the curious juncture of faith and faithlessness where value is not entirely lost from the human community. He speaks of his entry into the world beyond civilization as a therapeutic exercise, which will allow him to return to society well again:

> Call me Ishmael. Some years ago—never mind how long precisely— . . . I thought I would sail about a little and see the watery part of the world. It is a way I have of driving off the spleen, and regulating the circulation. Whenever I find myself grown grim about the mouth; whenever it is a damp, drizzly November in my soul; whenever I find myself involuntarily pausing before coffin warehouses, and bringing up the rear of every funeral I meet; and especially whenever my hypos get such an upper hand of me, that it requires a strong moral principle to prevent me from deliberately stepping into the street, and

> methodically knocking people's hats off—then, I account it is high time to get to sea as soon as I can. This is my substitute for pistol and ball. . . . There is nothing surprising in this. If they but knew it, almost all men in their degree, some time or other, cherish very nearly the same feelings toward the ocean with me. (12)

The initial chapter of *Moby-Dick* defines the original intent of the quest to renew the validity of the meaning of one's life, and then extends that statement to make it universally applicable to "most" men. Ishmael opens his narrative in a jocular tone fully expressive of his faith in the procedure. In that repeating "whenever" time, which he refuses to objectify for the moment, his sea-voyage-cure has proved effective. And to substantiate the validity of his faith, he presently points to the "crowds of water gazers" (12) who share his belief:

> Posted like silent sentinels all around the town, stand thousands upon thousands of mortal men fixed in ocean reveries. . . . But look! here come more crowds, pacing straight for the water, and seemingly bound for a dive. . . . There is magic in it. Let the most absent-minded of men be plunged in his deepest reveries—stand that man on his legs, set his feet a-going, and he will infallibly lead you to water. . . . Yes, as everyone knows, meditation and water are wedded for ever. (12-13)

Present within that sardonic image of humanity "fixed in ocean reveries," however, is a much more serious concept: the natural association between "meditation and water," coupled with the tone of necessity of the earlier passage, implies that this confrontation with the sea is somehow analogous to one's confrontation with one's own basic beliefs. The physically or psychologically therapeutic nature of the sea voyage thus becomes metaphysically significant. To voyage is to face the world in order to renew one's faith in its essential meaningfulness:

"Why did the old Persians hold the sea holy? Why did the Greeks give it a separate deity and make him the own brother of Jove? Surely all this is not without meaning" (14). And yet, in pursuing this meaning, Ishmael is fully aware of the fatal consequences attendant on too unguarded an examination:

> And still deeper the meaning of that story of Narcissus, who because he could not grasp the tormenting, mild image he saw in the fountain, plunged into it and was drowned. But that same image, we ourselves see in all rivers and oceans. It is the image of the ungraspable phantom of life; and this is the key to it all. (14)

The image "we" seek is not only the transcendent concomitant of physical reality, but, indeed, the embodiment of selfhood. Yet, in order to recognize the form within the pool of water as oneself, one must first know what the nature of self is. But to know the nature of the self, one must have a "reflected" idea of what the self might be. What is more, in the act of searching out a pool, a surface against which the self might be defined, one can, paradoxically, lose the self and "drown." Ishmael's tautological project, an ambiguous substitute for pistol and ball, is thus at once curative and potentially destructive. Not the least of our assumptions as to what might constitute a "self" is the notion that some genetic continuity will arise within the polarity created between the reflecting "thing" and its resultant "image." The self engenders an appearance that can be said to be identical with itself and of which it is the origin and the ground. In the same way that the self engenders appearance, so might it be said that meaning engenders a sign of itself. For Ishmael, however, this natural assumption about the integrity of self and appearance, as of sign and meaning, will become increasingly problematic.

As we continue to follow out the emerging binary logic of "Loomings," the first chapter of *Moby-Dick*, we can point to the successive description of two stages of the self and consciousness. One belongs to the past and is mystified; the other pertains to the "now" of the fiction, the stage that has recovered from the mystification of a past now revealed as being in error, present in the form of Ishmael's words.[4] "Loomings" is, like the "Epilogue," privileged in its poly-temporal grasp of the events of the quest and thus is especially significant in helping the reader to identify Ishmael's narrative stance:

> Though I cannot tell why it was exactly that those stage managers, the Fates, put me down for this shabby part of a whaling voyage, when others were set down for magnificent parts in high tragedies, and short and easy parts in genteel comedies, and jolly parts in farces—though I cannot tell why this was exactly; yet, now that I recall all the circumstances, I think I can see a little into the springs and motives which being cunningly presented to me under various disguises, induced me to set about performing the part I did, besides cajoling me into the delusion that it was a choice resulting from my own unbiased free will and discriminating judgment. (16)

The "shabby part" played by Ishmael in the "performance" was a result of his blind non-awareness: it was based on the "delusion" that his actions in the events to be narrated were a result of "unbiased free will." The event that separates that past delusion from this undeluded "now" is the radical discontinuity of a deathly tragedy that remains, for the moment at least, impersonal. Ishmael's refusal to identify the protagonist of that "high tragedy" from which he has been excluded, and the clear recognition of his own insignificance within that world of experience, cause his words to remain curiously ambiguous, with the full weight of the ambiguity concentrated in the metaphor of the drama. Within the mystified world of the past, even before the whaling voyage about which Ishmael is soon

[4] See Carl Strauch, "Ishmael: Time and Personality in *Moby-Dick*," *Studies in the Novel* 1 (1969): 468-483, for a related discussion.

to tell the listener, when the temporal reality of death was repressed or forgotten (here we must recall that the voyage is a supplanted death wish, a "substitute for pistol and ball"), the metaphor of the "Fates" and the "stage" could be used innocently, perhaps even playfully. The curious shock to Ishmael is that his innocuous metaphor has become literally true in his own eyes. He now recognizes his relative freedom within the retrospective stance (the eternal "now") of the fictive present from which be begins to narrate the story in "Loomings." He is now indeed an "actor" in the full sense of the word, a voyager in search of meaning and a performer in his own narrative.

Since the events of the novel have already happened before he begins to narrate, it is tempting to argue that the mature Ishmael's stance, existing in the "now" of resolved conflicts, is that of a subject whose insights are no longer in doubt and who is no longer vulnerable to the irony of the world. If this were the case, one could, if one wished, call his a stance of wisdom. The "now" of the narrative could then be said to designate a moment in which there was no longer any disjunction of the subject into past and present selves. Disruptions of the plenitude and stability of attained knowledge would no longer exist. The narrative could then be said to have been written from the point of view of a unified self who had recognized a past condition as one of error and stood now in a present that, however painful, at least saw things as they were and are. Having experienced a divided and finite world, the narrator could now aspire toward unity and infinity as he defined a point of view beyond himself from which to tell the story of his progression from the deluded past to the disenchanted now. Such a stance might allow for the resolution of the tension between those distinct moments.

Or so we would have it. But after all this is not the case. Reconciliation of infinite questioning with finite action can take place only on the level of *narration*, and only by the final elimination of that formerly deluded self. Instead, Ishmael is fully aware that even now, writing in the present, he can only "see a little into the springs and motives" of the drama he has just experienced. He has gained no guarantee that, whenever the concerns of daily life might again weigh upon him, the momentary glimpse of truth might be again forgotten, to be relearned anew. The dialectic between the past and the present, between delusion and wisdom, which characterizes Ishmael's narrative stance, and which designates the field upon which the events of the story take place, is therefore really an endless process ("a way I have"), which leads to no final synthesis. In this passage, Ishmael names the cyclical process "habit," the unwillingness of the mind to accept any moment in the process as a definitive or prescriptive paradigm of reality. In temporal terms, then, the narrative stance which Ishmael assumes thus designates the self and its acts of consciousness as self-generating inventions devoid of stable foundation. The present self can be radically altered by future circumstances. Seen from this perspective, the present, mature Ishmael becomes one more version of the continuously created self and not a fixed identity signaling the closure of becoming. Rather, this self-constructed artifact and its stance of wisdom is still liable to the delusions of the past, always poised to slip back into the category of error. As we read the narrative of the hunt for Moby Dick, we must keep constantly before us the fact that Ishmael's narrative voice emerges from a set of multiple and self-qualifying temporal and epistemological perspectives in a *negative* dialectic.[5]

This dialectical stance is made possible by two things: first, the "high tragedy" alluded to is not the tragedy (with its attendant death) of the speaker, but apparently that of someone

[5] On the concept of the negative dialectic, that is, a dialectic without a necessary synthesis, see Theodor Adorno, *Negative Dialectics*, trans. by E. B. Ashton (New York: The Seabury Press, 1973), pp. 134-207. The original German edition is *Negative Dialektik* (Frankfort am Main: Suhrkamp Verlag, 1966). Fredric Jameson has noted that "a negative dialectic has no choice but to affirm the notion and value of an ultimate synthesis, while negating its possibility and reality in every concrete case that comes before it" (*Marxism and Form* [Princeton: Princeton University Press, 1971], p. 56).

else. Second, the narrative is in the first person, but this first person is a narrator who can move into the minds of other characters and know what they know. Ishmael exists as narrator and as deuteragonist of his story, and his narrative depends upon the false complicity of these two roles. The concluding paragraphs of the first chapter are of great significance not only because they provide a rationale for Ishmael's motives in going to sea, but because they specifically delineate a factitious temporality which is exclusively that of *fiction* and in which the conditions of error and wisdom have become cyclical and successive. From this moment forward, Ishmael's narrative of his own attempt to discover himself, and of Ahab's to create a self, is told from a perspective of mitigating dramatic irony.

One of the most convincing discussions of Ishmael's narrative strategy is that provided by Edgar Dryden in *Melville's Thematics of Form,* which tells us that the strategy is "grounded in a supreme fiction." Ishmael constructs his life in the form of adventure stories even though he is aware that experience is in part composed of events and contingent associations without substantial significance. Organic coherence and smooth transitions do not necessarily characterize events in the real world. "This disturbing truth, which makes an orderly life possible, usually remains hidden behind the many forms which man imposes on his world, since he convinces himself that they are inherent in the nature of experience itself."[6] For this reason, as the "Extracts" imply, truth cannot be a product of an encyclopedic accumulation of worldly facts but might be best located beyond the visible world. While knowledge is open to question, truth is not. But the "truth" of the physical world which we create through the possession of knowledge might be itself an imaginative reality invented by the individual consciousness. As Dryden goes on to suggest, ". . . the experience of Ahab, the young Ishmael, and the rest of the 'Pequod's' crew

[6] Dryden, *Melville's Thematics of Form* (Baltimore: Johns Hopkins University Press, 1968), p. 83.

are not presented as a series of past events but, as . . . part of a tragic drama *composed* by the mature narrator."[7] Contained within the consciousness of the later Ishmael are a number of versions of the self which form an organic continuum through time and end in the figure of the present Ishmael. This analysis seems to me correct—a proper account of the dramatic and rhetorical structure of the novel and of its informing "book" metaphors. I would supplement Dryden's account, however, by pursuing this process of imaginative invention. Specifically, I would like to examine the procedures by which the identity of the self is invented, first by Ishmael and then by Ahab. The similarities and differences between the two seem to me crucial and indicative of a whole range of imaginative questions raised by Melville's novel.

By organizing the *cognitive* movement from delusion to wisdom into the *temporal* movement from past to present, that is, into the mythos of adventure narrative, Ishmael invites the reader to recognize the fabulous (because invented) nature of identity. Paul Brodtkorb, Jr., has noted, for instance, that the narrator permits us to *call* him Ishmael.[8] It may well be that the name Ishmael is a free creation and expresses a transitory subjective state. In any case, the obviously literary context of the *Pequod*'s voyage seems to create the possibility of a verbal continuity and of a shared identity between the separate versions of the narrating voice. For Ishmael, present identity is a product of the integrating power of narrative discourse. But since from the first Ishmael warns us that this cognitive movement is cyclical, the temporal structure of Ishmael's narrative cannot be teleologic. It is not motivated toward a conclusive end. Ironically enough, his self-perceptions do divide with the flow of time into a deluded past, a problematic and fleeting present, and a repeating future that remains liable to another version of the past. But as he proceeds to narrate his story, Ishmael recognizes that,

[7] Dryden, p. 84; italics added.

[8] *Ishmael's White World* (New Haven: Yale University Press, 1965), p. 123.

while he can now view the "circumstances" which produced that "high tragedy," he cannot control them.

Unlike Narcissus grasping for "the ungraspable phantom of life" (14) in a reflection of life, Ishmael looks at both life and reflection of life for the "key to it all." And while he can narrate the processes of delusion on increasingly conscious levels, he cannot apply his knowledge to the empirical world, thereby ordering it and controlling it through knowledge. Ishmael's narrative proceeds, therefore, fully aware from the first of its own limitations and of its own inability to designate absolutely the meaning of the events about which it speaks. Meaning, in fact, tends to disappear in that vertiginous cycle between past, present, future, and renewed past as the linguistic signs of the narrative proliferate in the attempt to grasp it.

As the voyage begins, Ishmael has returned to the mystified past. Although precipitated by an urgent need to forestall a literal and figurative death, Ishmael's voyage is not yet beset by the overriding doubts of Ahab's voyage. At this point in his story Ishmael still believes that a truth exists to be found—the difficulty is simply in the quest.

From the privileged "now" of "Loomings," Ishmael can interpret the irony of his former masthead reverie and its false security. Like Ahab, he realizes the paradoxical circumstances of a world which allows a search for absolute authenticity to be supplanted, and indeed destroyed, by the methods of that search. On the masthead, an *alter ego*, another "water gazer" stands "lost in the infinite series of the sea" (136) until,

> . . . lulled into such an opium-like listlessness of vacant, unconscious reverie is this absent-minded youth by the blending cadence of the waves with thoughts, that at last he loses his identity; takes the mystic ocean at his feet for the visible image of that deep, blue, bottomless soul, pervading mankind and nature; and every strange, half-seen, gliding, beautiful thing that eludes him; every dimly-dis-

> covered, uprising fin of some indiscernible form, seems to him the embodiment of those elusive thoughts that people the soul by continually flitting through it. In this enchanted mood, thy spirit ebbs away to whence it came; becomes diffused through time and space. . . . (140)

This unconscious blending of "waves with thoughts," as the "spirit ebbs away to whence it came," is not the moment of unity with the world, but is precisely the moment of false unity from which the quest began in Chapter 1. The "absent-minded youth" here is the reflection of that earlier "absent-minded" (13) man who drifted off toward the depths of "meditation and water" (13), as he attempted to understand himself by moving beyond and outside himself. Transcendental unity of being seems to beckon now, producing a kind of pure auto-affection in which the difference between self and not-self is effaced. And "los[ing] his identity," he seems to constitute another, from within the self, one more truly co-extensive with the ideality of the world. Yet, the unworldy character of this ideal unity is quickly unmasked as a trap for dreamers:

> But while this sleep, this dream is on ye, move your foot or hand an inch; slip your hold at all; and your identity comes back in horror. Over Descartian vortices you hover. And perhaps, at mid-day, in the fairest weather, with one half-throttled shriek you drop through that transparent air into the summer sea, no more to rise for ever. Heed it well, ye Pantheists! (140)

From the initial "water gazers" to the image of Narcissus and now here with this explicit play on "identity" and "meditation," Ishmael's attempt to generate meaning from his relationship to others and the world has centered on his subjective faith in the essential oneness of the world. But now, Descartes' God, who would not willingly deceive man, is ironically recalled. Within these "Descartian vortices" representation mingles with what it represents, to the point where their promiscuous complicity allows the self to be seduced narcissistically. Penetrating the surface of the world in an attempt to unite with the source of being, to grasp the "phantom of life," he experiences, however, not unity but loss of self. It is at moments like this that Ishmael's status as narrator standing outside this fictive past in another fictive present is exploited by Melville to the fullest in rigorous irony. This is an issue to which we will later return.

While Ishmael's temporal stance can thus be adequately described as retrospective in its fluctuations between time as "then" and "now," Ahab's is decidedly proleptic. His entire enterprise of intended vengeance is oriented toward the future moment when he will encounter the White Whale. And the ever-watchful Ishmael is quick to perceive this: "I was struck," he says, "with the singular posture [Ahab] maintained. . . . Captain Ahab stood erect, looking straight out beyond the ship's ever-pitching prow. There was an infinity of firmest fortitude, a determinate, unsurrenderable willfulness, in the fixed and fearless, forward dedication of that glance" (110-111). In that all-significant voyage, even physical attributes become figurative and readable. In fact, the symmetries of the text extend to basic linguistic levels. While Ishmael's statements of knowledge are belated and occur only retrospectively, after the fact, Ahab's words are future-oriented: the implementation of his vow of vengeance is always *about* to happen.

❦ ❦ ❦

Vows and promises, as is well known since the publication of John L. Austin's *Philosophical Papers* (1961), are complex cases of performative utterances, a variety of speech act.[9] Austin's

[9] See the essays, "The Meaning of a Word" (1940), "Other Minds" (1946), and "Performative Utterances" (1956) in the collected *Philosophical Papers*, 2nd ed., J. O. Urmson and G. J. Warnock (1961; New York: Oxford University Press, 1970), pp. 55-75, 98-103, and 233-252, respectively. See especially Austin's celebrated essay, "Performative-Constative" (March 1958), in John R. Searle, *The Philosophy of Language* pp. 13-21, where the original distinction

formulations, which distinguish performative utterances as *doings* from constative utterances as *sayings*, can help us specify some of the thematic and linguistic patterns which characterize Ishmael's and Ahab's speech acts.[10] I wish to show that Ishmael's

---

is further refined. For later revisions of the terms "performative-constative speech acts," cf. Austin's *How to Do Things with Words* (Cambridge, Mass.: Harvard University Press, 1975); and John Searle's discussion in *Speech Acts* (London: Cambridge University Press, 1969), ch. 3.

[10] Austin specifies in several places, notably in "Performative Utterances," *Philosophical Papers*, p. 235, and in the essay "Performative-Constative," that "constative" utterances might be thought of as *sayings*, assertions, descriptions, or statements, which can be either true or false. "Performative" utterances in contrast do not depend on truth value for their validity, but rather transform or effect situations when "felicitously" executed: bets, promises, warnings, vows, for instance, alter substantially the relation between a speaker and a listener simply by virtue of their having been expressed. While the constative simply *reports* situations, the performative allows the speaker to *indulge* in those situations. Performatives are thus *doings*. Here is Austin's example: "Suppose, for example, that in the course of a marriage ceremony I say, as people will, 'I do.' . . . Or again, suppose that I have a bottle of champagne in my hand and say 'I name this ship the *Queen Elizabeth*.' . . . In all these cases it would be absurd to regard the thing that I say as a report of the performance of the action which is undoubtedly done. . . . We would say rather that, in saying what I do, I actually perform that action" ("Performative Utterances," p. 235).

Austin's emphasis on the *use* of language and on the *force* of human discourse attempts to close in on the question of intention in meaningful statements. In the later text, *How to Do Things with Words*, pp. 100-108, Austin's original pair, "performative-constative," becomes the new "illocutionary-perlocutionary" polarity. His project remains one of isolating the basic conventions by which ordinary statements acquire meaning. Searle's own studies retain Austin's original insights into the importance of both the intentional and conventional aspects of language use. See *Speech Acts*, pp. 42-50. The value of these semantic theories for literary criticism is discussed by Stanley Fish in the essay "How to Do Things with Austin and Searle: Speech Act Theory and Literary Criticism," *MLN* 91 (1976): 983-1025; and also by Mary Louise Pratt, *Toward a Speech Act Theory of Literary Discourse* (Bloomington: Indiana University Press, c. 1977), pp. 152-200. In a literary text, the intentional and conventional aspects of human discourse are often purposefully flaunted, as in the case of *irony* and other rhetorical techniques, in order to affect the reader's interpretation of a particular expression or series of expressions. The reader of a literary text must therefore assume that any violations of the conventional and intentional rules of discourse that he may encounter might also be part of what he is to interpret.

words reporting his encounter with the world and Ahab's words conceiving that encounter function constatively and performatively and thus offer us important indications about the semantic structure of Melville's novel.[11]

I am not here concerned with the distinction between speech acts and nonverbal acts. I am concerned with the link between the act and the performing subject, with the principle of intentionality, and with the distinction between performative statements and speech functions that are not performative, such as statements of knowledge. Nonverbal acts will become an auxiliary issue only to the extent that an act cannot be entirely separated from the subjective intention and interpretation that necessarily accompany it. By posing the novel's issues in terms of speech act theory, we can see more sharply the nature and implications of the difference between intention and interpretation in the novel's discourse, and of the difference between Ishmael's and Ahab's verbal acts. The performative/constative distinction I offer is a convenient modern notation for the difference between Ishmael and Ahab that Melville is dramatizing more prolifically and flamboyantly in *Moby-Dick*.

In Ishmael's quest, knowledge is conceived as a transitive function. He assumes the prior existence of an entity to be known and the subject's ability of knowing the entity by way

[11] Several writers before me have pursued the close correlation between Ishmael and Ahab. Of these, I cite only those whose works have a bearing on my reformulation of the issue: William E. Sedgewick, *Herman Melville: The Tragedy of Mind* (Cambridge, Mass.: Harvard University Press, 1944); Howard Vincent, *The Trying-Out of Moby-Dick* (1949; Carbondale: Southern Illinois University Press, 1965); Charles Feidelson, Jr., "Melville," in *Symbolism in American Literature* (Chicago: University of Chicago Press, 1953), pp. 27-34; Paul Brodtkorb, Jr., *Ishmael's White World*; Edgar Dryden, *Melville's Thematics of Form*; and more recently, Warwick Wadlington, "Godly Gamesomeness: Selftaste in *Moby-Dick*," in *The Confidence Game in American Literature* (Princeton: Princeton University Press, 1975). See also Harrison Hayford, "'Loomings': Yarns and Figures in the Fabric," in *Artful Thunder: Versions of the Romantic Tradition in American Literature*, ed. Robert J. DeMott and Sanford E. Marovitz (Kent, Ohio: Kent State University Press, 1975), pp. 119-137.

of its properties. We receive knowledge from the entity itself, by allowing it to be what it is. Ishmael, as we have seen, voyages to see the world and to renew his faith in its essential meaningfulness. As he seeks to represent the "ungraspable phantom of life" (14), Ishmael makes language the servant of essences; he adjusts his words to make them fit the world. Ishmael's task therefore is a constative one: to narrate his encounter with knowledge.

The value of performance, in contrast, is signaled from the outset by Ahab's reliance on action. In portentous terms Ahab announces: "All visible objects, man, are but as pasteboard masks. But in each event—in the living act, the undoubted deed—there, some unknown but still reasoning thing puts forth the mouldings of its features from behind the unreasoning mask. If man will strike, strike through the mask! . . . [B]e the white whale agent, or be the white whale principal, I will wreak that hate upon him . . . I'd strike the sun if it insulted me. . . . Who's over me?" (144). Ahab's desire is always to stand alone, independent of mortal or immortal support, as a self-determined natural force. Thus, his hyperbolic language tries to be true, not to the acknowledged realities of the world or of the self's limitations, but to the absolute values he creates in his own soul. In passages such as this, therefore, the issues are not Ishmael's notions of delusion and disenchantment, nor his experiences of the loss or identification of the self. The issues which concern Ahab at least implicity are those of action and intentionality.

With Ahab we are faced with a complex verbal interaction between "truth" and "action." While he recognizes that truth resists constriction by the realms of knowledge, "Truth hath no confines" (144), Ahab supposes that action can fashion a world which can then be verified by truth. His utterances continually reflect this predilection for the active indicative mood: "What I've dared, I've willed; and what I've willed, I'll do!" (147.) This is as much to say that the performance of truth is contingent upon the individual's willful predication of its features. In contrast to Ishmael, who adjusts his words to the world, Ahab's linguistic acts are attempts to make the world fit his words. To the extent that the performative predicates the enactment of truth, it becomes a "living act," and an "undoubted deed" of significant proportions. Ahab conceives the idea of performativeness in language, and this reinforces his general belief in the ultimate value of action.

Early in the novel, as in a ritual from a mythic scene, Ahab succeeds in imposing his notion of the truth of action upon Ishmael and the rest of the *Pequod*'s crew by moving them to take a vow of vengeance upon Moby Dick: "Commend the murderous chalices! Bestow them, ye who are now made parties to this indissoluble league. . . . But the deed is done! Yon ratifying sun now waits to sit upon it. Drink, ye harpooneers! drink and swear, ye men that man the deathful whaleboat's bow—Death to Moby Dick!" (146.) The "ratifying sun" seems to vouchsafe their deed as the vow—"Death to Moby Dick"—becomes the primary act which precipitates the coming action. Ahab's vow represents the first step in his attempt to restore the economy of proper balance between the world and his own imperious will. But he proceeds under false authorization, for the sun ratifies nothing except in Ahab's proclamation that it does.

As speech act theorists have noted, the act of vowing is a curious one.[12] It is particularly suited to Ahab, for although it involves undertaking obligation to others, it is an obligation the speaker both creates and discharges in the fullest expression of agency conceivable. When one keeps a vow, that person is being true to his *own word*, not to the word of another. *Vowing* is a linguistic transaction that leaves the self inviolate, dependent only on its own moral and psychic resources. Ahab's vow does *not* implicate him in the reciprocal web of social intercourse

[12] Stanley Fish, "How to Do Things with Austin and Searle," *MLN* 91 (1976): 996.

that Ishmael's narrative wishes to initiate; rather, Ahab's words emphasize his willed autonomy.

While Ishmael admits that his attempts to predicate knowledge by constating it are certain to fail—his bibliographical classification of whales can "promise nothing complete" and will "infallibly be faulty . . . I know [the whale] not and never will" (118, 317)—Ahab's actions posit a natural relationship between willed action and comprehensive truth. In one of his sublimely tempestuous moods, Ahab, addressing the lightning that flashes around him, reveals this relationship:

> No fearless fool now fronts thee. I own thy speechless, placeless power; but . . . will dispute its unconditional, unintegral mastery in me. In the midst of the personified impersonal, a personality stands here. . . . Light though thou be, thou leapest out of darkness; but I am darkness leaping out of light, leaping out of thee! . . . Oh, thou magnanimous! now do I glory in my genealogy. But thou art but my fiery father; my sweet mother, I know not. Oh cruel! What hast thou done with her? There lies my puzzle; but thine is greater. . . . I know that of me, which thou knowest not of thyself, oh thou omnipotent . . . thou foundling fire, thou hermit immemorial, thou hast thy incommunicable riddle. . . . Here again with haughty agony, I read my sire. (417)

Ahab's words function as a flash of light in the darkness of his allegory. In this text, Ahab postulates the power of his own undying will on its ability to *know*. Even though nature may be more destructive than man, human sensibility is inherently superior because of man's ability to possess nature through knowledge. Dominance is proper to man because he *predicates* the unity of nature. Ahab thus thinks that because man predicates the unity of nature, then "action" (as the speech act of predication) and "knowledge" (as that which is eventually predicated) are indissoluble. But even here the possibility of action is qualified when conceived as verbal. When Ahab posits his future acts on his present ability to "read [his] sire," he implies that action is perhaps possible only against a background of interpretation. Future-oriented actions are thus dependent on prior acts of "reading," one's origin. In fact, the very acknowledgment of a genealogy which is presented not as something he declares but as something he recognizes qualifies his claim to autonomy at the very moment he makes it.

Nonetheless, this key act of reading designates the stability of Ahab's identity. His is not the personality of Ishmael's "water gazer," ready to lose himself in a Narcissistic plunge into "meditative water." Ahab's glance is set upon the blinding source of energy and life which eludes him. Later, faced with the mystery of reality, Ahab will ask, "What is it, what nameless, inscrutable, unearthly thing is it; what cozening, hidden lord and master, and cruel remorseless emperor commands me; . . . Is Ahab, Ahab?" (444-445). This fundamental question of Ahab's identity will be resolved ultimately only by the completion of the "living act, the undoubted deed," that is the vow to kill Moby Dick. But, already, armed as he is with the knowledge of his "genealogy," Ahab's answer is clear.

The most striking speech act in *Moby-Dick* is spoken as if in response to this question, "Is Ahab, Ahab?" and follows from the force of his vow of vengeance. Preparing for the climatic battle with Moby Dick, Ahab rejects Starbuck's final plea to leave off the chase. "Starbuck," says Ahab,

> of late I've felt strangely moved by thee. . . . But in this matter of the whale, be the front of thy face to me as the palm of this hand—a lipless, unfeatured blank. Ahab is for ever Ahab, man. This whole act's immutably decreed. . . . I act under orders. (459)

Obviously, Ahab means that Ahab can only act as Ahab. But under whose orders is not entirely clear. The simple statement that "Ahab is for ever Ahab" is momentous, because it implies that Ahab, with the certainty that he is who he says he is, is the one who orders. Following John Searle's "Taxonomy of Illocutionary Acts," I would label Ahab's statement a *declarative*, a kind of speech act with this major characteristic:

> The successful performance of one of its members brings about the correspondence between the propositional content and reality. . . . Declarations bring about some alteration in the status or condition of the referred object or objects solely in virtue of the fact that the declaration has been successfully performed.[13]

The force of the declarative can be captured in the phrase "saying makes it so."[14] While other speech acts are attempts to get words to match the state of the world, Ishmael's "bibliographical system," for instance, or to get the world to match

[13] Searle, "A Taxonomy of Illocutionary Acts," in *Language, Mind, and Knowledge*, ed. Keith Gunderson et al., *Minnesota Studies in the Philosophy of Science*, vol. 7 (Minneapolis: University of Minnesota Press, 1975), pp. 344-369. Searle offers these statements as examples of declaratives: "I resign," "I excommunicate you," "War is hereby declared," p. 358. Such declarations, Searle argues, involve "an extra-linguistic institution" in addition to the rules of language in order that the declaration may be successfully performed: "It is only given such institutions as the church, the law, private property, the state, and a special position of the speaker and hearer within these institutions that one can excommunicate, appoint, give and bequeath one's possessions, or declare war" (p. 359). He then adds that "The only exception to the principle that every declarative requires an extra-linguistic institution are those declarations that concern language itself, as for example when one says, 'I define, abbreviate, name, call, or dub' " (p. 360). Thus, Ahab does not need in conventional terms to hold a special position in an extra-linguistic institution to declare his autonomy, for his statement specifically concerns the act of *naming*. Ahab's entire speech is a model of performativeness: he is also *praying* (for the strength not to hear what Starbuck is saying); *beseeching* (Starbuck not to say more); and *declaring* (that Starbuck's face is no more to Ahab than a blank palm). It is also relevant that *Moby-Dick* begins with this very special class of the declarative speech act: "Call me Ishmael," thus announcing that we have entered a discursive system wholly independent of extra-linguistic (referential) institutions for its authority. Searle goes on to suggest that the most autonomous of declaratives is, of course, God's own divine self-naming, "I am I."

[14] Fish, "How to Do Things with Austin and Searle," p. 997, uses this phrase to describe a similar speech act situation in *Coriolanus*.

the words, such as Ahab's vow, the declarative works *both* ways: its words are made to fit the world at the same time as the world is made to fit the words. This is so, argues one speech-act theorist, because "declaratives *create* the conditions to which they refer. More obviously than any other class of speech acts, they testify to the power of language to constitute reality."[15] Ahab's declaration of independence, naming as it does the stability of his own identity, has, therefore, profound implications. His statement that "Ahab is for ever Ahab" does not mirror a state of subjective integrity; it *is* that state, which persists or falls to the extent that Ahab can continue to acknowledge it.[16] Ahab's reasoning implies that one can constitute a state of unqualified self-presence simply by affirming it. "Ahab is for ever Ahab," complete and sufficient unto himself, because his saying makes it so. This is crucial not because Ahab is concerned with identity but because he is concerned with the possibility of doing what he wants to do. The one depends on the other, even if the direction of the dependence between action and identity remains ambiguous. Within the logic of the declarative, the name of Ahab collapses into the entity which is its referent and provides, as a consequence, a unity of sense. But what exactly is the result of this declaration? What, in fact, does it perform?

❦ ❦ ❦

The physical act of Ahab's harpoon-thrust is significant only because it supplements the linguistic act which has already designated the presence of the willful self.[17] In effect, Ahab hunts

[15] Fish, p. 996; Searle points to the differences among various kinds of speech acts as a "difference in the direction of fit between words and world" ("A Taxonomy of Illocutionary Acts," p. 346).

[16] Searle, pp. 359-360, notes that for reason of their absolute autonomy, Austin had included declaratives (with vows and promises) as paradigms in the class of performative utterances.

[17] I am assuming, of course, that the determination of *absolute* presence is most readily constituted as *self*-presence, that is, as subjectivity. Ishmael's quest offers us a model of presence as presence-in-the mind, or, with qualifications, Descartes' *cogito ergo sum*. The realm of these cognitive statements is the

the White Whale not so much to deny the superiority of the natural world, as to identity himself.

At least since Aristotle, classical epistemology has maintained that the principle of identity is the most certain of all principles and that it is the ultimate ground upon which every demonstrative proof rests.[18] Only if we can depend on the stability of a statement such as "Ahab is Ahab" can the observable links of the natural, social, and psychological order be expressed. Each thing is that one single thing which it is. Lapses from this principle can lead only to irrationality and chaos. Indeed, the very order of rational discourse depends on this primary predication of the self-identity of things. "Only if a thing is unequivocally itself, internally," notes J. Hillis Miller, "can it correspond externally to other entities in an orderly series of displacements leading up to the 'I am I' of God."[19]

Coursing throughout Ahab's speeches are the key words "unity," "genealogy," "identity," "knowledge," "cause," "father," all of which rely on this stability of an inherited identity. In the passage quoted above, for example, Ahab bases his independence on the fact of his knowledge of a source: "I know that of me, which thou knowest not of thyself . . . thou foundling fire." With the security of the knowledge of his source, Ahab is confident of his own ability to be the determining agent of other effects, effects such as the fulfillment of his vow to kill

constative mode. Ahab's model of self-presence, in contrast, is a model of presence as presence-in-the act, offering the revised dictum of subjectivity: *ago ergo sum*. Its province is the performative mode. Ahab exists essentially only in the performance of intentional acts, which are bound together by the unity of causal meaning. As Melville realizes, there are still other models of self-presence available. For a discussion of the possible source of Melville's notions concerning Descartes, see Millicent Bell, "Pierre Bayle and *Moby-Dick*," *PMLA* 66 (1951): 626-628.

[18] See Paul de Man, concerning the principle of self-identity, in the essay "Action and Identity in Nietzsche," *Yale French Studies* 52 (1975): 16-30, reprinted as "Rhetoric of Performance (Nietzsche)," in *Allegories of Reading*, pp. 119-131.

[19] J. Hillis Miller, "Ariachne's Broken Woof," *Georgia Review* 30 (Spring 1977): 49.

Moby Dick. By the time he sets out for his final encounter with the whale, Ahab has resolved to his satisfaction the question of intentionality ("Is it I, God, or who that lifts this arm?"—445) by his assertion of undying defiance. But the fact of the source itself subverts absolute independence; and, in fact, Ahab wishes to have it both ways: he wants to declare autonomy (Ahab is Ahab) and at the same time perceive an institution (a genealogy) to serve as the basis for his declarations of immutable identity.

Sourceless action is precisely the absurdity Ahab rejects; his actions are performed to prove that the self can be its own vital source. In sharp contrast to Ishmael, who assumes that knowledge may be acquired (if not completely possessed) by "hypothesizing" (313), Ahab thus makes the identity principle the ground of all stability. Only if Ahab is truly Ahab can he control the world's destructive irrationality. Ishmael shows, however, that the stability of Ahab's identity is precisely that upon which we may not depend, when he describes for us the nature of Ahab's will:

> [E]ver since that almost fatal encounter, Ahab had cherished a wild vindictiveness against the whale, all the more fell for that in his frantic morbidness he at last came to identify with him, not only all his bodily woes, but all his intellectual and spiritual exasperations. The White Whale swam before him as the monomaniac incarnation of all those malicious agencies which some deep men feel eating in them. . . . [A]ll evil, to crazy Ahab, were visibly personified, and made practically assailable in Moby Dick. . . . [Ahab's] torn body and gashed soul bled into one another; and so interfusing, made him mad. . . . [E]ven then, when he bore that firm collected front, however pale and issued his calm orders once again; . . . even then, Ahab, in his hidden self, raved on. . . . Ahab's full lunacy subsided not, but deepeningly contracted. . . . But, as in his narrow-flowing monomania, not one jot of Ahab's broad madness

> had been left behind; so in that broad madness, not one jot of his great natural intellect had perished. That before living agent, now became the living instrument. If such a furious trope may stand, his special lunacy stormed his general sanity, and carried it, and turned all its concentred cannon upon its own mad mark. . . . (160-161)

The passage is a remarkable compendium of the special words that course throughout the text: *identify, personify, interfusing, self, agent, instrument, trope, mark,* and *end.* It designates the unities performed by and upon Ahab's tortured soul after his encounter with Moby Dick. But beyond the physical and psychological horrors that Ahab has experienced, in that combat the truth of identity has been seriously wounded, and madness arises as Ahab now becomes "a vacated thing . . . a blankness in itself" (175).

But while Moby Dick has disrupted the stability of Ahab's psyche, he has also initiated an equally destructive "interfusing" of body and soul. The metaphors of unity and disruption (fusion and fission) now give way to the hydraulics of sanity and insanity; as one ebbs, the other flows to fill the empty void of Ahab's inner self. It is as if Ishmael's narrative must overdetermine his meaning through a proliferation of metaphors in order to insure that at least part of his intended thought will be perceived and accepted by the reader. Moreover, the natural temporal movement of the passage from "then" to "now" serves to cushion the shock of the unnatural transformation of cause and effect, the general and the special, which Ishmael claims is the root of Ahab's madness: "That before living agent, now became the living instrument." Ishmael's "furious trope" makes intellect, which was an agent (a cause), now an instrument (an effected entity), and "general sanity" a property of "special lunacy." The entire passage thus points out that, in relation to Ahab's declaration of identity, our trust in the stabilizing power of cause and effect, and on the synecdochic dependence of the "special" upon the "general," is fundamentally misplaced. Whereas Aristotle can write with good sense that "A man is the originating cause of his actions,"[20] there is a clear sense in Ishmael's narrative that Aristotelean assumptions about coherence and order, particularly about coherence between will and act, in Ahab's case no longer hold. If they do not hold, if Ahab is not the originating cause of Ahab's actions, then it is possible that Ahab may not be Ahab. As a result of Ishmael's statements, which question the inviolability of the rules of logical and intentional order, the reader is now left free to wonder whether Ahab hunts Moby Dick and attempts to validate his existence because he is mad, or whether Ahab is mad because he hunts the whale and seeks his identity. If we are not outraged at this conclusion, we *should* be. Even Ishmael himself seems uncomfortable with his "furious trope" and questions whether "it may stand," for what he initiates here is no less than a deconstruction of the concepts of identity and cause.

Ishmael's statements on the enactment of Ahab's "undoubted deed" have always involved linking the notions of "origin," "cause," and "identity" with "action." The question of Ahab's identity, posed and left unanswered in the chapter entitled "The Symphony," receives, as we have seen, ostensibly definitive answers both in Chapter 119, "The Candles," where the lightning is Ahab's "fiery father," and in the penultimate chapter, where "Ahab is for ever Ahab." But the two answers are really quite different. The one is genealogical in that it confers identity upon Ahab by virtue of "origin": he knows who he is because he can "read [his] sire." The latter confers identity by action: Ahab is himself when he performs his intentions.[21] In presenting Ahab's identity as a genealogical recognition, the text

[20] *Nichomachean Ethics* (Penguin ed., 1958), p. 87; III, 1113b, 16-22.

[21] The performance of self, substantiated by the phrase, "Ahab is for ever Ahab," is even more tautological than this implies. If Ahab constitutes himself in the act of declaring his identity, then it may not be strictly correct to speak of an *intending* self, apart from a performing self, at all, since the self who intends exists truly only in the act of performing.

makes use of constative language. The second notion of identity is founded upon the performative function of language: it is a product of a declaration rather than a statement of fact. But the relationship between these two forms of identity is a discontinuous one. In fact, the performative disallows the identity principle and the constative concept of language grounded upon it, by denying that identity can be encountered in the present or given in reflection.

It would thus seem that Ahab both is and is no longer Ahab. This conclusion is of course absurd; it is madness, for it violates the very principle which serves as ground for all statements of knowledge. After this confusion of grounds for identity, we cannot now be certain whether Ahab's pronouncement, which by his own "sheer inveteracy of will," forces him into "a kind of self-assumed independent being" (175), asserts that Ahab *cannot* be anything other than Ahab, or whether Ahab *demands* that Ahab should be the creator of Ahab. The one reading makes Ahab's identity something capable of being *known*; the second makes of logic an *imperative*—the entity is not known in itself but rather is performed.

But now Ishmael has shown us that the statement "Ahab is for ever Ahab" cannot be regarded as a factual reporting of existing real conditions, for such statements are inherently problematic. Constatations of fact may be either true or false, but they cannot be proved *necessarily* true or false. What is more important, however, is that the sensible properties which made Ahab, Ahab, have now been "turned" by the "furious trope" of his monomaniac vow of vengeance. The convincing power of Ahab's statement of identity is due simply to the substitution of the *sensation* of the contingent properties of Ahab's fragmented self for the *knowledge* of his substantial essence: "Ahab never thinks; he only feels, feels, feels; *that's* tingling enough for mortal man!" Ahab admits (460). Fredric Jameson has argued that "phenomenology is the attempt to tell not what a thought is, so much as what it feels like."[22] After Ishmael's own reversal of "special" and "general" and of cause and effect, even the stability of Ahab's phenomenologically "felt" identity cannot be trusted.

Ishmael's narrative demonstrates that the act of conceptualization of Ahab's own identity is at least in part a verbal process, a trope based on the substitution of a semiotic for a substantial mode of reference. This is the process of assembling the clues of the foundling fire's "incommunicable riddle" into statements such as "I am darkness leaping out of light" (417), or less cryptically, "Ahab is for ever Ahab." But because this naming process is not rooted firmly on a base of ontological necessity, it can be reversed again and again, so that what was once "agent" may again become "instrument," while the "general" may become "special" with no decisive end in sight. At any moment in the cycle of rhetorical substitutions, Ishmael may designate that whirling process of signification, but he cannot stop it. And while the aberrant structure of Ahab's identity cannot be known absolutely, neither can it be entirely not known, for the narrative can name, at least, the outward manifestation of its substance. The best Ishmael can say then is that he must remain as undecided about Ahab as he is about the white whale because the processes of knowledge upon which he once thought he could depend have again been opened to suspicion.

But all these failures can be superseded: "Man's insanity is heaven's sense" (347). We have seen how Ahab's language of identity asserts itself in the performative mode and thus believes itself capable of positing a self and a world which are consistent with what in his soul he desires them to be. As such a "positional" statement, Ahab's speech act acquires a temporal dimension, for it posits as future what it is unable to do in the present: "Call me Ishmael" might thus be the future narrative equivalent of the present declarative "Ahab is for ever Ahab."

[22] *Marxism and Form*, p. 306.

But as we have also seen, temporal order has been transformed in Ahab's monomania: his "special lunacy" has turned his past "general sanity" into an instrument of present madness. Ishmael's trope thus proposes that we see Ahab's present inclination to future-oriented assertions as having determined the earlier catastrophe which made Ahab, the presumed agent of present effects, himself an effect of effects. Ishmael's deconstruction of Ahab's apparent self-knowledge into the metonymy of sensation is thus a surface feature of a more general deconstruction that reveals another reversal of the categories of "then" and "now." He shows us that the "truth" of identity, which was to be established in the future that would follow the statement "Ahab is for ever Ahab," already existed as the past unwarranted assumption that Ahab could "feel" and know his own identity.

But where does this deconstruction leave us?[23] It is one of those disheartening instances, as Ishmael in another context tells us, "where truth requires full as much bolstering as error" (177). The force of Ishmael's statement, that what was in Ahab before a "living agent" is now a "living instrument," has to do with its reduction of human identity to the level of a logical axiom:

where A = past Ahab
and A_1 = present Ahab
and a = agent
and i = instrument
Then if
$A = a$
and if $a = i$
and if $i = A_1$
then $A = A_1$.

[23] Cf. Paul de Man's "Rhetoric of Persuasion (Nietzsche)," pp. 119-131, for a compatible analysis of the constative/performative linguistic modes. I have drawn heavily from de Man's analysis in this essay.

The identity of past and present Ahab depends on the logical continuity of causal relations (the "if" statements). But, in these terms, the metaphysical issue of the identity of the subject, a humanistic concern, has been reduced to the level of logic, here, a rhetorical concern.[24] In renaming the novel's central issue as a substitution of corollary terms, Ishmael's deconstructive gesture reconceives the significant action of human subjects as the displacement of words by other words. And he seems to imply that by this sheer capacity for displacement, by this radical tendency to metaphoricity, the self-identical subject is constituted in the narrative line.

Narrative operates under the assumptions of causality and intelligibility.[25] By the persistent pressure of these ideas, temporal sequence is conflated with causal sequence: a series of events leads forward to other events, and backward to an intelligible source or cause. Narrative assumes that an action or event that can be recounted has a cause, since to account for something is to identify that cause.[26] When Ishmael's narrative questions the possibility of accounting for a present action by past events (by making it uncertain whether Ahab hunts because he is mad, or is mad because he hunts), and questions the possibility of establishing identity on the basis of "positional" logic, not only is he deconstructing the actions of cause and identity, but he is also putting in question the ability of narrative to represent the "reality" of the external world. Faced with the fantastic and awesome circumstances of the hunt for Moby Dick, Ishmael thus admits at one point that the entire situation was "so mystical and well nigh ineffable . . . that I almost despair of putting it in comprehensible form" (163).

The qualifying "almost" is crucial, of course. Ishmael is not

[24] I follow here Cynthia Chase's excellent discussion of a similar problem in her essay, "The Decomposition of Elephants: Double-Reading *Daniel Deronda*," *PMLA* 93 (1978): 215-227.

[25] Chase, "The Decomposition of Elephants," p. 217.

[26] Paul de Man, "Rhetoric of Persuasion (Nietzsche)," pp. 130-131.

denying the possibility of reference—if he were, then we would have no narrative at all. But what kind of "despair" is this then? And what kind of "comprehensible form" does Ishmael provide? At base, these questions involve not just the formal features of the work, but also put at stake the very enterprise of storytelling itself.[27] Ishmael cannot understand and communicate the meaning of those fabulous events without first naming the "ineffable" and taming the "mystical." This naming can only take place after the construction of a "syntax" to organize sentences, and to establish the most basic links between subjects and objects. Ishmael's originary task, therefore, is to formulate the very possibility of a grammar by which his mystical and ineffable visions might be communicated. Let us see what readers have expected of him and how he proceeds.

❦ ❦ ❦

While Ahab's performative function of language had been effectively removed as an instrument of truth, Ishmael's own constative attempts to circumscribe truth by enveloping it within a net of factual detail has proved equally ineffective. But, as we have noted, between the options of "saying" and "doing," readers within and without the text of *Moby-Dick* have chosen to see Ishmael's survival as justified on the basis of his transformation from spectator to performer of his own narrative. Paul Brodtkorb's excellent analysis thus centers on Ishmael's function as storyteller, as does that of Edgar Dryden. Of more recent studies, Walter Reed and Richard Brodhead too have seen Ishmael as hero on the basis of his existential transformation with his unleashing of the latent book metaphor into the patent text of *Moby-Dick*.[28]

[27] The formal aspects of the text are of course also involved. In fact, we might argue that the confounding morass of the plural self is controlled, at least in part, by the various registers of Ishmael's discourse: commentary, interpretation, analysis, and "fiction."

[28] Brodtkorb, pp. 123ff.; Dryden, pp. 104-113. Walter L. Reed, *Meditations on the Hero* (New Haven: Yale University Press, 1974), pp. 138-186; Richard

This transformation is taken as a clue of Ishmael's final discovery that, as Dryden puts it, his "creative gestures are a reminder to man that whatever seems stable in experience has been put there by himself. The hierarchical social structure aboard a well-ordered ship, the constructs of science and pseudoscience, pagan and Christian religious systems, even the concepts of space and time—all of the forms which man uses to assure himself that everything which happens follows certain laws—are revealed in *Moby-Dick* as 'passing fable.' " Dryden sees Ishmael's discovery as a movement toward Ahab's logical position. The world is not pre-existent and identifiable, but is rather a constructed system. It is also liable to the time-bound performative function of human declarations, pathetically, a "passing fable." Dryden concludes his valuable essay by then noting: "Ishmael's achievement . . . is the result of a victory of art over life. Finding the world a place which at first enchants, then confuses and terrifies, and recognizing that human constructs fail to explain or control it, he removes himself from both nature and society by retreating to a fanciful world of his own creation. . . . From this position he is able to face and describe safely the truth which the world's empty forms conceal."[29] This seems convincing because it allows Ishmael, inside narrative time, the wisdom which eludes him elsewhere. From this perspective, Ishmael may be said capable of viewing "truth," even if it is only a circumscribed "truth," because he has in fact become the author, the source of truth himself. Ishmael's act of writing might thus seem to perform the "undoubted deed" which Ahab's harpoon-thrust fails to do. It would take a full reading of Ishmael's statements about the nature of "reading" and "writing" to see whether such a conclusion is indeed warranted.

We have already seen, however, on the basis of Ishmael's

H. Brodhead, *Hawthorne, Melville, and the Novel* (Chicago: University of Chicago Press, 1976), pp. 134-162.

[29] Dryden, *Melville's Thematics of Form*, p. 83.

"furious trope" and of his interpretation of Ahab's will, that the performative function of language has been completely undone as a source of truth. If Ishmael is to transform himself into the "seer" that readers would have him be, he must therefore do so on the basis of an epistemologically sounder theory of expression than the one which makes *art* the "undoubted deed" of truth. Our observations might be reduced to the simple questions: What is the source of Ishmael's artistic truth? If experience has not revealed truth to him, then what is it that the writing of the text has taught Ishmael that enables him to perceive in the writing what was unseen in the experiencing? The answers might lie in the whiteness of the whale. This is the final point I would examine.

"It was the whiteness of the whale that above all things appalled me," says Ishmael (163). "But how can I hope to explain myself here; and yet, in some dim, random way, explain myself I must, else all these chapters might be naught." Faced with the seeming impossibility of a narrative about the incomprehensible, Ishmael begins by attempting, in accordance with the logic of positional knowledge, to understand the cause of the "vague, nameless horror" occasioned by Moby Dick. And as is his established procedure, he begins by cataloging historically the multiple ways in which "whiteness" has been understood by humanity. "Though in many natural objects, whiteness refiningly enhances beauty . . . yet for all these accumulated associations, with whatever is sweet, and honorable, and sublime, there yet lurks an elusive something in the innermost ideas of this hue, which strikes more of panic to the soul than that redness which affrights in blood" (163-164). Probing then toward "the innermost" recesses of the notion, Ishmael continues to ask "what but their smooth, flaky whiteness makes [the polar bear and white shark] the transcendent horrors they are?" (164). The consequence of this listing of white horror is the characteristic paradox: "Therefore, in his other moods, symbolize whatever grand or gracious thing he will by whiteness, no man can deny that in its *profoundest idealized significance* [my italics] it calls up a peculiar apparition to the soul" (166). The definition of whiteness is thus not to be accomplished empirically. "To analyze it, would seem impossible," says Ishmael, for the answer lies in a sphere unavailable to material sensation. "Can we, then by the citation of some of those instances wherein this thing of whiteness . . . is found to exert over us the same sorcery, however modified;—can we thus hope to light upon some chance clue to conduct us to the hidden cause we seek?" (166-167).

Since there is non-metaphoric language to apply to the "incantation of whiteness" (169) Ishmael continues to multiply his metaphors:

> Is it that by its indefiniteness, it shadows forth the heartless voids and immensities of the universe, and thus stabs us from behind with the thought of annihilation, when beholding the white depths of the milky way? Or is it, that as in essence whiteness is not so much a color as the visible absence of color, and at the same time the concrete of all colors; is it for these reasons that there is such a dumb blankness, full of meaning, in a wide landscape of snows—a colorless, all-color of atheism from which we shrink? And when we consider that other theory of the natural philosophers, that all other earthly hues . . . are but subtile deceits, not actually inherent in substances, but only laid on from without; so that all deified Nature absolutely paints like the harlot, whose allurements cover nothing but the charnel-house within; . . . pondering all this, the palsied universe lies before us a leper; and like willful travellers in Lapland, who refuse to wear colored and coloring glasses upon their eyes, so the wretched infidel gazes himself blind at the monumental white shroud that wraps all the prospect around him. (169-170)

Earlier, we saw how Melville's opposition of Ishmael's to Ahab's discursive habits anticipates with striking clarity the speech-act recognition of a difference between the propositional content and the illocutionary force of a statement. In passages such as this, Melville is now astonishingly close to up-staging the logic and methodology Nietzsche was to employ in a number of texts (as early as the notes to the projected *Das Philosophenbuch*, 1870-1872, through the *Birth of Tragedy*, 1875, and culminating in *The Will to Power*, 1882-1885) concerning the "phenomenalism of inner consciousness."

At the risk of oversimplifying this central problem of Nietzsche's in summarizing it, I will note that in these texts Nietzsche attacks what he sees as the aberrant authority granted to the *subject*. His deconstruction of the special significance of the "subject-stratum" (*Will to Power*, Section 477) leads in turn to other, wider, analyses of the nature of causal relations, action in general, consciousness, and finally, of epistemological authority itself. Before he comes to statements such as "'Thinking,' as epistemologists conceive it, simply does not occur: it is a quite arbitrary fiction, arrived at by selecting one element from the process and eliminating all the rest, an artificial arrangement for the purpose of intelligibility" (*Will to Power*, Section 477), Nietzsche puts into question, as Melville here does also, the dubious authority which allows the unwarranted totalization of surface appearance into the concept of substantial essence: "A nerve-stimulus, first transformed into a percept! First metaphor! The percept again copied into a sound! Second metaphor! And each time [we] leap completely out of one sphere right into the midst of an entirely different one."[30] In this manner, the metonymy of mere sensation is transformed inauthentically into the metaphor of substantial knowledge. I cite only one other related passage: "That which becomes conscious is involved in causal relations which are entirely withheld from us—the sequence of thoughts, feelings, ideas in consciousness

[30] From *Das Philosophenbuch*, tr. as "On Truth and Falsehood in Their Extra-Moral Sense," in *Complete Works*, ed. O. Levy (London, 1911), 2:178.

does not signify that this sequence is a causal sequence. . . . Upon this *appearance* we have founded our whole idea of spirit, reason, logic, etc. (none of these exist: they are fictitious syntheses and unities), and projected *into* things and *behind* things!" (*Will to Power*, Section 524.)

The passage I cite from *Moby-Dick* contains the clearest statement of Ishmael's view that the concept of "substance" might be simply a metaphor falsely derived from the pure metonymy of sensation: ". . . all earthly hues . . . are but subtile deceits, not actually inherent in substances, but only laid on from without." He speculates that with nothing more to go on than nerve stimuli, we create the categories of "essence" and "substance" to go along with the "subtile deceits" of surface appearance. Ishmael's faithless wanderer, in contrast, refuses to color the universe by looking at it through the darkening glass of faith. He will see the whiteness directly, even at the risk of all future sight. "And of all these things," adds Ishmael, "the Albino Whale was the symbol. Wonder ye then at the fiery hunt?" (170).

Now by its "indefiniteness," whiteness is said to "shadow forth" the "heartless void"; by its "dumb blankness," it speaks "full of meaning." The reason for the "fiery hunt" can only be given, it seems, in terms of the symbolic imagination and its vocabulary of contradiction, of oxymoron. But this language of oxymoron forms an impasse beyond which constative knowledge cannot proceed. What we are offered here is the notion of whiteness as of something like a free signifier—it does not itself refer, but forms the constative essence of signification. Upon its pure surface, imagination projects the possibility of meaning. "One is seal, and one is print," as Emerson puts it.[31] But to

[31] Ralph Waldo Emerson, "The American Scholar," in *The Norton Anthology of American Literature*, vol. 1, Francis Murphy and Hershel Parker, eds. (New York: Norton, 1979), p. 696. See Jacques Derrida, "White Mythology: Metaphor in the Text of Philosophy," p. 253 *passim*, for a full discussion of the use of "metaphor in order to give the 'idea' of metaphor."

avoid treating "whiteness" as mere surface, to consider whether it may in fact be an articulation of a truth natural to man, Ishmael also assigns it the roles of "shadowing forth the indefiniteness" and of serving as the "essence" of color. But these are all still metaphors. The very optical quality of the metaphor of whiteness opens up every theoretical point of view to question: ". . . all earthly hues . . . are but subtile deceits." It thus seems that the "monumental" and "essential" answers Ishmael seeks as ground for a stable epistemological structure are themselves a function of indefinite white knowledge. If the narrative is to signify at all, we must counteract this indefiniteness: the Albino whale is after all said to be the "symbol" of all these things. How may the indefinite be made definite?

There is a rhetoric to Ishmael's white discourse. First, the whiteness is *significant,* but it is so only to the extent that thought comes upon it. Of itself, the whiteness is latent and obscure; its sense emerges of itself, but in order to be understood, it must find the light of language. The sense of "whiteness" can be articulated only by way of language's indirections. We can know the essence of whiteness only metaphorically, by assigning quality to its "vague hue." This indirection necessarily carries the risk that the immediate truth of whiteness will be lost. Unless we take the risk of substitution, we remain in nonsense. But how can we be certain that we have taken a proper sense of whiteness?

The ideal of language, and of metaphoric substitution, is to allow the thing referred to by its sign to be known; an expression will be better the closer it brings us to its essential truth. Thus, while the symbol may indeed spawn a variety of sense, for a proper interpretation of its sense to take place, we must assume that its multiple meanings can be organized and be then differentiated in at least general terms, like planets around a ruling central sun. A "chance clue" to this "keystone sun" (359) of whiteness is what Ishmael seeks. Tropes of figural denomination always *imply* this sensible core, but allow it to remain absent.

Since, as Ishmael informs us, the source of light and whiteness is never properly present in its essential nature, but must be inferred from its contingent properties "laid on from without," we cannot be certain that the source of whiteness is ever present in the signs that name it. Around its sensible and contingent properties that "hidden cause" may be hypostatized—but if that is so, then we must call it an artificial essence not naturally present. Ishmael's appeals to criteria of "light" and "clarity" emphasize the fabulous nature of the human imagination. Contrary to readers' desires to make *art* the performative site of truthful discourse, a place from which we might "face and describe safely the truth which the world's empty forms conceal," Ishmael refuses to sanction even the creative imagination. In fact, for him, imagination functions solely through the processes of what Nietzsche will later term *idealization* and *appropriation*.[32] As a consequence, art may repeat and reveal the patterns of everyday "meaning," but it can create no necessary and absolute truth of its own, or substantiate any categorical claims. The specular metaphor inherent to all narrative art is thus for Ishmael yet another indication of the inconclusive movement toward an elusive source of self-presence. A step further, and what will be devalued is the will to truth itself.

The metaphor of "whiteness" thus has a readable syntax, but it is a syntax which leads us to no conclusive period. The presence of whiteness disappears behind its own whiteness, and if in the symbolic form of the white whale it is to provide us with a representation of the organic unity and wholeness of the world, that symbolic relation of part to whole is dissolved by the obliteration of definable causal relations between parts and wholes. The self-destruction of the text is prevented only by the fact that the process of metaphoric renaming tends to spread itself syntactically along the sentence into an extended metaphor—or, into *allegory*.

[32] Derrida, "White Mythology," pp. 246-253; see also Chapter One, n. 39 above.

In terms of rhetorical stability, perhaps no other term of the critic's vocabulary can equal the defineability of "allegory." Allegory is the temporal and spatial manifestation of a transcendent category; and the instrument of allegory is often the "symbolical" figure.[33] In *Moby-Dick,* however, we find that the very readability of the symbol is in doubt—its symbols do not illuminate but rather obscure transcendental categories. By revealing the fraudulent nature of "whiteness," Ishmael's discussion effectively removes it from the sphere of the symbolic, where the relations of symbol to symbolized are organic and natural. He degrades it instead into the level of metaphor. Metaphor, as we have seen, presumes no absolute relation between sign and signified, for in the very process of metaphorization, the natural link between an object and its proper name is dissolved and replaced by another relation or name. And it is because the metaphorical necessarily involves duplicity in sense that it cannot escape syntax: the "metaphorical" sense can come

[33] Richard A. Lanham, *A Handlist of Rhetorical Terms,* pp. 3-4, offers the classical definition of "allegory" as "Extending a metaphor through an entire speech or passage." See also Angus Fletcher's suggestion in *Allegory: Theory of a Symbolic Mode* (Cornell: Cornell University Press, 1964), p. 23, that allegories are "sequences of symbolic power struggles"; and Northrop Frye's discussion in *Anatomy of Criticism* (Princeton: Princeton University Press, 1957), pp. 89-92, of the degree to which all literature is in some degree "allegorical." One of the more impressive studies of allegory is that offered by Walter Benjamin in the section "Allegory and Trauerspiel" of *The Origin of German Tragic Drama,* trans. J. Osborne (1963; London: New Left Books, 1977), where he argues that "a genuine history of the romantic style could do no better than show . . . that even the fragment, and even irony are variants of the allegorical. . . . Allegory brings with it its own court . . . subject to the law of 'dispersal' and 'collectedness'" (p. 188). Paul de Man's essay, "The Rhetoric of Temporality," in *Interpretation: Theory and Practice,* pp. 173-209, can be seen as the logical development of Benjamin's statements on allegory. Given the multiple resonances of Melville's language, it is not surprising that readers have sought to stabilize its variety by recourse to allegorical reading. One of the most striking of allegorical readings is Alan Heimart's "*Moby-Dick* and American Political Symbolism," *American Quarterly* 15 (Winter 1963): 498-534. Together with Charles H. Foster in "Something in Emblems: A Reinterpretation," *New England Quarterly* 34 (1961), Heimart reads *Moby-Dick* in "the light of political fact and iconography," as "a fable of democratic protest."

into play only *after* the proper sense on the syntagmatic axis. And because metaphor cannot escape syntax, indeed must spread itself along the syntagmatic axis of the sentence, it always gives rise to a text, an extended, self-conceiving narrative, which is not exhausted by an account of its sense.[34] Furthermore, it is also a necessary process of metaphor that in its failure to envelop sense in syntax as the symbol purports to do, in setting syntax out in a labyrinthine wake of convoluted deviations, it carries itself away, loses itself, and indeed becomes itself by deconstructing and renewing itself, endlessly.[35]

The self-consumption of metaphor forbids it from returning us to the totality of accomplished meaning, as Ishmael properly realizes, when in the pathetic tones of the chapter entitled "The Gilder," he says: "There is no steady unretracing progress in this life; we do not advance through fixed gradations and at the last one pause. . . . But once gone through, we trace the round again; and are infants, boys, and men, and Ifs eternally. Where lies the final harbor, whence we unmoor no more? In what rapt ether sails the world, of which the weariest will never weary?

[34] Paul de Man, developing his complex theory of allegory, defines "text" in these terms in "Political Allegory in Rousseau," *Critical Inquiry* 2 (1976): 671-672; also available now as "Promises (*Social Contract*)," in *Allegories of Reading*, pp. 246-277.

[35] "Deconstruction" does not mean "destruction"; nor does it imply abandoning the structures (in this case, of identity and causality) that are being undone. Deconstruction is instead a disassembly of the old structure to show that its claim to unequivocal priority is a product of human labor and may thus be reconceived. Deconstruction cannot take effective aim at those prior structures without inhabiting them and borrowing all the strategic and economic resources for the analysis from the old structure. For this reason, the enterprise of deconstruction is only a provisional and strategic privileging of the moment of analysis. It does *not* presume its own finality. Instead, deconstruction is provisional and strategic in exact proportion to the amount of borrowing that has taken place. And it is *only* provisional and strategic to the extent that it must always fall victim to its own work. This cautionary note of course applies as well to my own proffered reading. It too must be seen as a moment in, rather than as an endpoint to the reading of Melville's novel. For a detailed discussion of the deconstructive act, see Jacques Derrida, *Of Grammatology*, pp. 24ff.

Where is the foundling's father hidden? Our souls are like those orphans whose unwedded mothers die in bearing them: the secret of our paternity lies in their grave, and we must there to learn it" (406). In opposition to both the young Ishmael's "joint-stock" corporate self and to Ahab's transcendentally free self, Ishmael now offers us a new, scattered or disseminated self. Its shifting and unstable elements in composite mass attempt to align into one sovereign subject. The return of the self to itself, however, effaces the self-identity of the subject as an independent and homogeneous entity. But in the world of yearning constituted by the desire for self-knowledge, metaphor is born to speak, to write, to name—to separate self from not-self and to make present what is absent. In fact, without metaphor to inscribe the dialectical non-presence of the other within the present, just as "whiteness" is the "visible absence" of color, the "self" as such could not be known. For Ishmael, the spirit of "whiteness" thus resembles that of the "self"; both seem to mark the enigmatic space of metaphor and to share its same empty structure. It is this endlessly generative capacity of metaphor, its ability to draw unwarranted surplus-value from the "dumb blankness, full of meaning," that Ishmael's narrative attempts to render explicit.

There is of course a pleasing structural symmetry between Ahab's and Ishmael's notions of identity. Each claims on the one hand the value of action, and on the other the importance of knowledge in establishing identity. And the temporality of the narrative does hypostatize the moment of unity between those two options. But as it turns out, for Ahab the performance is insufficient without the necessary constative moment; and for Ishmael, while the constative is valid in its own right, it is incomplete without the moment of performance as narrative.[36]

[36] See Paul de Man's discussion in "Rhetoric of Persuasion (Nietzsche)," p. 127: "Performative language is not less ambivalent than the language of constatation." Ahab's self-identity conceals itself unceasingly, I think, as does Ishmael's. In both the constative and the performative modes, the property of

In *Moby-Dick*, the referentiality of the issue of identity is thus suspended between two modes: the performative mode, which would define it as activity, and the constative mode, which would define it as a matter of knowledge. Both the affirmation of a performative and a constative concept of identity must stop short of asserting the fact or the act.[37] An affirmation of the performative mode would portray Ahab's self-identification as a real action, such as the successful defeat of Moby Dick and the subsequent denomination of nature's "dumb blankness" by the indomitable will. An affirmation of the constative mode would portray Ishmael's self-identification as real knowledge, as opposed to the acceptance of an assumed identity ("*Call* me Ishmael") and to the continuation of his orphan-hood. Both possibilities are excluded by Ishmael's account: neither certainty as to origin (paternity) nor as to end (knowledge) are validated by the narrative.

Ishmael is able to give those "well nigh ineffable" events, experienced inwardly in his soul and sanctioned outwardly by the awesome circumstances of the world, a coherent pattern only after he has produced a language, a discursive formation, by which to translate those conditions into conditions familiar to him (and to us, as sharers in his prejudices concerning the sociability of the self). But the reality thus perceived is in no way "real," for we cannot grasp the *essence* of anything pertaining to reality. Ishmael concludes that perception cannot offer us "knowledge," but only "interpretations." At the horizons of our knowledge, we institute words to denote truths which

identity allows the self to be itself ($A = A$, and other than itself ($A = A_1$). As a consequence, Ahab may not be simply Ahab, and Ishmael may only be called Ishmael. In either case, the property of the self is its inability to be absolutely proximate to itself. We might call this limitlessness of identity "whiteness," or "ambiguity." Whatever terminology we choose, however, the identified self ought now be understood, as Melville would have it, as an operative process and not as a state of being, as recurrent motion and not as stable structure.

[37] Here and in what follows, I rely on Cynthia Chase's argument in "The Decomposition of Elephants," pp. 223-224.

remain relative. This relativity applies as well to the self: it has no essence, no reality beyond its cultural and historical experience. In fact, the subject as Ishmael now views it is dispersed, forming a collectivity of "subjects," whose interactions and struggles are the basis of thought and consciousness. Far from eluding the determinants of action and identity outside language, Ishmael finds himself constituted by their clash. The product of this clash at the level of the individual is a metaphoric continuity of the self. Metaphor puts in place the heterogeneous subject, and allows the self a position of coherence and responsibility so that it may continue to act. As don Quijote discovered, with this initiation of action, and with the subject now appearing as the origin of its own activity, the possibility of identity is bolstered once again.

Thus the constatation of knowledge, even when considered a performative act, in its transformation into the narrative text, turns out to be as faulty as Ahab's attempt to establish the stability of the self by virtue of the identity principle. Ishmael's analysis points out that constative language, in its positing of metaphoric ground, is performative, but Ahab's project shows that the possibility of language to perform is just as fictional as the possibility for langauge to assert. Since this aporia between the performative and the constative lies at the heart of language, their interference forms a necessary impasse through which unmediated truth cannot penetrate.[38]

Yet that interference also serves as the surface upon which signification might take place. Ishmael does survive, and as a

[38] See Paul de Man, "Rhetoric of Persuasion (Nietzsche)," pp. 129-131, where de Man is partly concerned with displaying Nietzsche's anticipation both of the distinction between constatives as sayings and performatives as doings, and of the collapse of this distinction. Seizing upon the difference between representations and declarations of sovereign identity, Melville dramatizes the idea that making a descriptive statement is as much performing an illocutionary act as making a vow or declaring one's identity. The novel uses an initial binary structure, therefore, less to construct a felicitous synthesis than to mitigate the naive belief in synthesis as a logical necessity. It uses the paradigms of constatation and performance as intermediary positions in an ongoing negative dialectic.

survivor he must narrate what he has experienced, for in that narration he might recuperate himself, not as a positive presence but as the difference of conflicting forces. When he is sucked into the concentric circles forming the wake of the *Pequod's* plunge, the center Ishmael attains is not the Emersonian center of transcendental knowledge. If that center exists, it lies yet before us beyond the grave, "and we must there to learn it."[39]

[39] In this respect, it is useful to recall Melville's statements on "writing" in *Pierre*, which follow those of a long line of theoreticians of language from Plato, to Rousseau, Hegel, and Ferdinand de Saussure. Writing, they maintain, substitutes for the living flow of spoken words and everyday speech, the sterile forms and rigorous conventions of fixed rules. The dynamic immediacy of personal presence carried by the spoken word is reduced and distorted by the lifeless mediacy and second-level representation of the cryptic text: "The act of writing is nothing but a mediated representation or thought," argues Rousseau in *The Essay on the Origin of Language* (1781; New York, 1966). See also *Phaedrus* 278a; Hegel's *Enzyklopadie* 459; and Saussure's *Introduction to General Linguistics* for similar sentiments. Derrida's *Of Grammatology* provides the most comprehensive recent analysis of the nature of writing. Melville, too, I would suggest, enters into this traditional view of writing but extends it as he sets up an economy wherein the book comes to life only as the living presence of the author is diminished. In *Pierre*, the narrator tells us:

"Two books are being writ; of which the world shall see only one, and that the bungled one. The larger book, the infinitely better, is for Pierre's own private shelf. That it is, whose unfathomable craving drinks his blood; the other demands only ink. But circumstances have so decreed, that the one can not be composed on the paper, but only as the other is writ down in his soul. And the one of the soul is elephantinely sluggish, and will not budge at a breath. Thus Pierre is fastened on by two leeches; . . . He is learning to live, by rehearsing the part of death." (*Pierre, or The Ambiguities* [Evanston: Northwestern University Press and the Newberry Library, 1971], pp. 304-305.)

Writing destroys the vital being of the writer. It tyrannically substitutes the text for the self, as the writer accedes to the loss of his present and concrete existence in order to transfer himself into the ideality of textual truth and certainty. In effect, death by writing inaugurates life: "[Pierre] is learning to live by rehearsing the part of death." Within this system of economy, then, the writer's literary suicide creates a compensatory possibility (even though it must always be only "a bungled one") of access to true and unmediated identity. As substitute, however, the "bungled" text produces no relief but only marks the absence of the one "writ in the soul."

If we can still recognize the reality reproduced by the "bungled" text (the sensible copy of the one "writ in the soul"), then we must assume that the original text possessed a reproducible essence. Without this reproducibility, the

Ishmael remains the eccentric orphan looking for surrogate mothers and fathers, fated to encounter only substitute mothers like the *Rachel,* who weeps for her children because they were not.

While there can be no proper closure to the enterprise of constating/performing the truth of identity, Ishmael's continued uncertainty is not a symbol of the desolation of human existence. In the conclusion of his narrative, uncertainty as to the availability of clear and certain knowledge (even if only of the self) is not signified so much as much as it is displayed, as allegory. Since it is not possible to bring about a resolution of the drama of identity, even within the apotheosis of action in the finale, the solution takes place in allegorical fullness: as the allegory of rebirth. And this, I think, is the nature of narrative as Melville came to see it: that its ultimate objects, in which it can most fully secure for itself the signs of the self, turn into ambiguous allegories. These allegories in turn leap out, faithlessly, to fill and deny the very void in which they are represented.

"bungled" text could not be recognized as a representation at all. But by the same token, the original is enfeebled by subsequent reproductions. Imitation is therefore both the origin of art and its demise. Art and its death are comprised in the sphere of a necessarily impoverished representation.

This astonishing concept of writing as the radical absence of the self from life is of course also apparent in *Mardi,The Confidence Man,* and especially in "Bartleby, the Scrivener." It should now be apparent why Melville would be fascinated by the person of the copyist. The moment of transcription, more so than the moment of writing, is the moment of pure imitation. The good scrivener, reproducing the written signs of prior texts, must always resist the temptation to alter (and thus restore life to) the original text. He must eschew the life of letters in favor of their death.

❦ FIVE ❦

Reading the Letter of the Law: Thomas Hardy's *Jude the Obscure*

"Mark, the mark is of man's make
And the word of it Sacrificed."

Gerard Manley Hopkins
The Wreck of the Deutschland

Concern for the nature and response of an author's audience is, in some respects, one of the original tasks of literary criticism. Over the past decade, however, attempts to incorporate rhetorical, linguistic, and cognitive theories into literary criticism have led to the development of a formidable bibliography on the nature of the reader's role in the communication network of author, text, and reader. These reader-oriented studies stress, from their various philosophical perspectives, that the reader, as much as any character, contributes to the shaping of the novel's fictive world through his interpretive actions, which catalyze the immanent potential of the text to be understood.[1]

[1] See, as a sampling, the following studies which stress the need to recognize the reader's role and the process of reading as crucial aspects of the development of meaning in literature: Wayne Booth's *The Rhetoric of Fiction* (Chicago: University of Chicago Press, 1961) is still the most widely influential of these studies. After Booth, the topic develops in several directions. Cf. Martin Price, "The Fictional Contract," in *Literary Theory and Structure* (New Haven: Yale University Press, 1973); Georges Poulet, "Phenomenology of Reading," *New Literary History* 1 (1969-1970): 56-68; Roland Barthes, *S/Z* (Paris: Seuil, 1970); Wolfgang Iser, *The Implied Reader* (1974) and "Indeterminacy and the Reader's Response in Prose Fiction," in *Aspects of Narrative*, ed. J. Hillis Miller (New York: Columbia University Press, 1971), "The Reading Process: a Phenomenological Approach," *New Literary History* 3 (1972): 279-299, and *The Act of Reading* (1978). See also, Hans Robert Jauss, "Levels of Identification of Hero and Audience," *New Literary History* 5 (1973-1974): 283-317 on the "aesthetics of reception." These and other essays are collected by Jane Tompkins in *Reader-Response Criticism: From Formalism to Post-Structionalism* (Baltimore: Johns Hopkins University Press, 1980); and by Susan Suleiman and Inge Crosman, eds., *The Reader in the Text: Essays on Audience and Inter-*

If in *Moby-Dick* Melville is concerned with the possibility of composing comprehensible texts about the ineffable, in *Jude the Obscure* Thomas Hardy is concerned in major part with the ambiguous notion of "reading" and with the reader's role in the creation of meaningful texts. The critical value of this recent emphasis on the reader's role in the creation of meaningful literary texts and of "reception history" in general could thus well be rigorously tested by a text such as the author's "Postscript" to *Jude the Obscure*. There, the reading public is accused of "curing"[2] the novelist of all desire to write prose fiction. In this case Hardy would seem to have us question the reader's role in the *destruction* of texts, for in no uncertain terms, it is the reader, in his incapacity to read, who is made to bear the burden of guilt for Hardy's renunciation of the pleasures of novel-writing. Since we cannot read his meaning properly, even when there has been "no mincing of words" (Preface, p. viii) in its enunciation, complains the author, he will hereafter spare himself and the reader the infelicities of misinterpretation by simply ceasing to write novels.[3]

---

pretation (Princeton: Princeton University Press, 1980). Cf. the current efforts of language philosophers to apply speech act theory to literary discourse: John R. Searle, "The Logical Status of Fictional Discourse," *New Literary History* 4 (1972): 319-332; and Mary Louise Pratt, *Toward a Speech Act Theory of Literary Discourse* (1977). The most recent and engaging of contributions is Paul de Man's, "Reading (Proust)," in *Allegories of Reading*, pp. 57-78.

[2] Thomas Hardy, "Postscript" (added April 1912) to *Jude the Obscure* in *The Writings of Thomas Hardy in Prose and Verse*, The Anniversary Edition, III (New York and London: Harper & Brothers, Publ. [1920]), p. ix. All references are to this, the American, issue of the standard Wessex Edition, and will hereafter be identified by Part, Chapter, and page number in parentheses following the quotation.

[3] Hardy, "Preface to the First Edition," of *Jude the Obscure* (August 1895). For a more detailed summary of the reception of Hardy's novel, see Robert Cox, ed., *Thomas Hardy: The Critical Heritage* (London: Routledge & Kegan Paul; New York: Barnes & Noble, 1970), pp. 249-315, and especially, for its difference, the review by Edmund Gosse, which appeared in *Cosmopolis*, January 1896, i, 60-69. Cf. Lawrence Lerner and John Holmstrom, ed., *Thomas Hardy and His Readers* (New York: Barnes & Noble, 1968), pp. 103-152. See also the pertinent discussions in Albert Guerard, *Thomas Hardy* (New York:

Yet readers often find this and Hardy's later comment that he expected the novel to be read as "a moral work" (p. ix) somewhat disingenuous. We can hardly imagine after the reception of *Tess*, and after Hardy's attempt to cancel his contract with Harper & Brothers for *Jude*, that Hardy would not have anticipated the "shocked criticisms" and "execrations" (p. ix) which the publication of the novel incited. In fact, when Hardy announces in the "Preface to the First Edition" that the novel will "deal unaffectedly with the fret and fever, derision, and disaster, that may press in the wake of the strongest passion known to humanity" (p. viii), and then denies that "there is anything in the handling to which exception can be taken" (p. viii), he raises the very real possibility that the novel will be misread.

And it was misread. Angry reviewers and a solemn bishop saw in it, among other things, a cynical attack on the sacrament and institution of marriage. In a letter of November 1895 to Edmund Gosse, Hardy continued to express his concern for the proper reading of his text by indicating that *Jude* was not merely "a manifesto on 'the marriage question' (although, of course, it involves it)," but was more the story of the tragic result of two marriages because of "a doom or curse of hereditary temperament peculiar to the family of the parties."[4] The fact is, of course, as William R. Rutland has convincingly argued, that the novel *is* concerned with the marriage laws in more than just a casual way.[5] And Hardy himself points out that the plot of

New Directions, 1964); Ian Gregor, *The Great Web* (London: Faber and Faber, 1974); Michael Millgate, *Thomas Hardy: His Career as a Novelist* (New York: Random House, 1971), pp. 317-335; and J. Hillis Miller, *Thomas Hardy: Distance and Desire* (Cambridge, Mass.: Belknap Press, 1970), and *Fiction and Repetition* (Cambridge, Mass.: Harvard University Press, 1982). See also, Florence Emily Hardy, *The Life of Thomas Hardy 1840-1928* (1928 and 1930; rpt. New York: St. Martin's Press, 1962), pp. 262-275, which discusses Hardy's reactions to the negative reception of his novel.

[4] Letter to Gosse, cited in Florence Emily Hardy, *The Life of Thomas Hardy*, p. 271. Hardy writes Gosse to thank him for his favorable review of *Jude*.

[5] William R. Rutland, *Thomas Hardy: A Study of His Writings and Their Background* (Oxford: Blackwell, 1938), pp. 250-257.

Jude is "geometrically constructed"[6] around the marital realignments of the four principal characters. They repeatedly change their relationships through their alternately prospective and retrospective visions of one another and of the options society and nature allow them.

Poised between a desire for natural freedom and the need for a stabilizing social order, Hardy's characters try to act within their "geometrically constructed" system of marital and symbolic associations to accommodate their desires and needs. Hardy is clear about this. He tells us that *Jude the Obscure* dramatizes the sociological effects of the Victorian failure to reconcile the antithetical realms of culture and nature: "The marriage laws [are] used . . . to show that, in Diderot's words, the civil law should be only the enunciation of the law of nature" (Postscript, p. x). But the difficulty of reading *Jude* properly may well stem from the fact that the novel is more than a realistic analysis of the historical condition of marriage in late-Victorian England. I would like to suggest that the ambiguous status of the act of reading in the author's prefatory statements is only an indication, a sign, of a more radical investigation concerning reading and interpretation. By considering the interplay between "natural" and "civil" law, and by examining the nature of Hardy's "geometrically constructed" plot, we will be able to reflect on the possible relation of these issues to the apparent ease with which, according to Hardy, the novel can be misread. A reading of *Jude* which attempts to account for this cluster of formal and thematic elements can, I think, provide a new perspective on Hardy's conception of the realistic novel and how we might use it to read his final and most controversial novel.

A first difficulty in understanding the novel is thematic and stems from the portrayal in the text itself of numerous cases

[6] Letter to Gosse, cited in Florence Emily Hardy, *The Life*, p. 271. Hardy goes on to say: "I ought not to say *constructed*, for, beyond a certain point, the characters necessitated it, and I simply let it come." In a subsequent letter of January 1896, also to Gosse, Hardy elaborates: "The rectangular lines of the story were not premeditated, but came by chance: except, of course, that the involutions of four lives must necessarily be a sort of quadrille" (p. 273).

of misreading. From the beginning, for instance, Jude Fawley sees in Christminster and its university the image of an attainable ideal world. His desire for this ideal vision involves a rejection of reality. For his own sporadically controlled, partially understood world, he substitutes the image of a unified, stable, and understandable one. Beguiled by his desire for order, the young Jude thus turns initially to language-study both as a means of entering university life and as a possible source of stability:

> Ever since his first ecstasy or vision of Christminster and its possibilities, Jude had meditated much and curiously on the probable sort of process that was involved in turning the expressions of one language into those of another. He concluded that a grammar of the required tongue would contain, primarily, a rule, prescription, or clue of the nature of a secret cipher which, once known, would enable him, by merely applying it, to change at will all words of his own speech into those of the foreign one. . . . Thus he assumed that the words of the required language were always to be found somewhere latent in the words of the given language by those who had the art to uncover them, such art being furnished by the books aforesaid. (I, iv, 30-31)

Jude feels betrayed, consequently, when, attempting to learn Latin, he finds that "there was no law of transmutation, as in his innocence he had supposed" (31). Jude's desired "law of transmutation," the "secret cipher" to a system of translation, could exist only if a prior permanent code existed to allow a free substitution of signifiers for one, autonomous, permanently present signified. The metaphor of translation at this early point in the novel is doubly interesting. It both reveals Jude's desire for a serenely immobile text whose content might be transported without harm into the element of another language, and alludes to the relation Hardy establishes in the "Postscript" of 1912 between civil and natural law, making one the "enunciation" (p. x) of the other. These will continue to be decisive issues throughout the novel. At this point, Jude has no doubt that the voice of nature can, indeed, be read and translated, for when he "address[es] the breeze caressingly," it seems to respond: "Suddenly there came along this wind something towards him—a message . . . calling to him, 'We are happy here!' " (I, iii, 22.) By imposing single terms on the disparate variety of experience, we come to know and control our environment. Early on, however, Jude intuits that language is not a fixed system through which meaning can be "transmuted" from one system to another. Yet this is precisely the insight that Jude refuses to apply to his other readings of the world around him. Underlying the errors of both natural and textual translation is the illusion that reality is autonomous and stable, when it is really discontinuous and uncentered within the fictive world of Hardy's novel.

As he proceeds into the countryside, where the markings which hint at the limitations already imposed on his life stand to be deciphered, Jude's readings continue: "The only marks on the uniformity of the scene were a rick of last year's produce . . . and the path . . . by which he had come. . . . [To] every clod and stone there really attached associations enough and to spare—echoes of songs . . . of spoken words, and of sturdy deeds" (I, ii, 10). History, echoing across the generations, seems to focus in on Jude at the bottom of "this vast concave" field (I, ii, 9), but he does not yet understand its voice. The substance of this discourse latent within the countryside is the essential dimension of the tradition into which he has been born. These "marks" and "associations" in the landscape of Wessex are "signs" inscribed by that force motivating all events, which Hardy was in *The Dynasts* to name the "Immanent Will." Thus, long before his birth, long before the story of his family has been inscribed, this tradition has already traced the pattern of behavior within which are ordered the possible changes and exchanges which will occur in Jude's short life. Each crucial event in Jude's life seems to invite the reader to interpret Jude's actions as an attempted reading of the role ascribed to him in some determining book of fate.

Initially, the young Jude seems to see the schoolmaster, Phillotson, as another embodiment of his controlling "dreams" (I, iii, 20), and as a symbolic substitute for the absent "real" father.[7] This primary substitution of Phillotson for the absent father, at precisely the moment before Phillotson's own disappearance into the hazy realms beyond the actual experience of Jude's day to day world in Marygreen, is the first instance in a series of oscillations of disappearance and return of desired objects (people, ideals) which will constitute the novel's false center of ordered reality. Accordingly, when Phillotson does leave Marygreen, Jude replaces him with an ideal representation. This time Jude reads that ideal presence into the natural landscape of Wessex as Christminster, "that ecclesiastical romance in stone" (I, v, 36):

> Through the solid barrier of cold cretaceous upland to the northward he was always beholding a gorgeous city—the fancied place he likened to the new Jerusalem. . . . And the city acquired a tangibility, a permanence, a hold on his life, mainly from the one nucleus of fact that the man for

[7] I use the term in the sense that Jacques Lacan assigns to it in "The Function of Language in Psychoanalysis," trans. Anthony Wilden in *The Language of the Self* and in "D'une question préliminaire à tout traitement possible de la psychose," *Écrits* II (Paris: Seuil, 1970), pp. 43-102. Lacan speaks of the symbolic substitution of a father figure for an absent real procreator. This symbolic construct need not have a procreative function at all; it is sufficient that the symbolic figure stand for a guarantee of social order with which the child might identify. Although Jude's idealization of Phillotson is shattered at an early stage in the novel, the system of social formulas set up in relation to Phillotson retains its affective force, even after Jude discovers the illusory basis of his beliefs. This process of "idealization" is constant throughout the novel and even characterizes Jude's relations with Arabella: "His idea of her was the thing of most consequence, not Arabella herself, [Jude] sometimes said laconically" (I, ix, 65).

> whose knowledge and purposes he had so much reverence was actually living there. . . . (I, iii, 20)

In this ecstatic vision, Christminster, whose mark is "a halo or glow-fog" (I, iii, 21), seems to send "a message" (I, iii, 22), but, as we have seen, it is a message which must be translated from natural to human terms with all the inherent errors of language and its "figures" (I, iii, 25). In a moment of revelation, George Eliot's narrator in *Adam Bede* had commented: "Nature has her language, and she is not unveracious; but we don't know all the intricacies of her syntax just yet, and in a hasty reading we may happen to extract the very opposite of her real meaning."[8] Now, as Jude attempts to learn the "syntax" of nature's "message," Christminster, through Phillotson, becomes the organizing center of his life: "It had been the yearning of his heart to find something to anchor on, to cling to—for some place which he could call admirable. Should he find that place in this city if he could get there?" (I, iii, 24) The phrasing of his question in the rhetorical mode produces a grammatical structure that implies the existence of freedom of choice, when, in fact, the pattern of choices has already been ascribed for Jude by his own propensity for misreading. As he answers the questions posed in indirect discourse, beguiled by the transformation his mind has imposed on the scene through figurative language, Jude takes literally his own metaphors of the "new

[8] George Eliot, *Adam Bede*, Rinehart Editions (New York: Holt, Rinehart and Winston, 1948), Chapter XV, p. 155. In *A Pair of Blue Eyes*, Hardy's narrator had made a similar observation: "Nature seems to have moods in other than a poetical sense. . . . She is read as a person with a curious temper. . . . In her unfriendly moments there seems a feline fun in her tricks, begotten by a foretaste of her pleasure in swallowing the victim" (chap. xxii). See also, Charles May, "*Far From the Madding Crowd* and *The Woodlanders*: Hardy's Grotesque Pastorals," *English Literature in Transition*, 17 (1974): 147-158, who notes that "Hardy's central vision springs from the tension between his longing for a ground of meaning and value inherent in the natural world and his hard recognition that no such value or meaning exists there" (p. 150).

Jerusalem," "the city of light," and "the castle, manned by scholarship and religion" (I, iii, 24-25).

Sue Bridehead is also present in the metaphoric language which names Christminster. Jude has seen, for example, "the photograph of [her] pretty girlish face, in a broad hat, with radiating folds under the brim like the rays of a halo" (II, i, 90). In fact, the metaphoric process by which Sue will later replace both Christminster and Phillotson in Jude's dreams has been initiated and facilitated by the nature of Jude's language long before he is even conscious of Sue: earlier, he had become "so romantically attached to Christminster that, like a young lover alluding to his mistress, he felt bashful at mentioning its name . . ." (I, iii, 22). The transfer from Phillotson, to Christminster, and finally to Sue as metaphors of that sustaining vision is thus a simple, determined step. Jude's false reading of Sue at a chapel in Christminster as being "ensphered by the same harmonies as those which floated into his ears" (II, iii, 107) leads him to conclude that he has "at last found anchorage for his thoughts" (II, iii, 107), and he leaves the church "in a sustaining atmosphere of ecstasy" (II, iii, 107). When Jude finally meets Sue, he approaches her cautiously and speaks to her as he has of Christminster "with the bashfulness of a lover" (II, iv, 117). At each step in the evolution of his story, the controlling "dream" is a fiction which he has imposed on wayward circumstances. These dreams and visions are things which are not "actually" present in the landscape, but which Jude makes present through his language.[9]

[9] The problem of interpretation is complicated by the formal pattern of the narrative itself, which often ascribes speeches to Jude in the mode of indirect discourse. These *diegetic* instances, the narrative mode which Plato so deplores in Book III of *The Republic,* force the reader to shift attention from the question of the *meaning* of the characters' linguistic confusions, to that of deciding which *voice* is the source of ambiguity. In the passages discussed above, for example, some can be readily ascribed to Jude: I, iii, 20; I, iii, 24-25; IV, v, 243. Other passages, however, seem to be the narrator's interpretations of Jude's interpretations. This layering of interpreting minds dramatizes the difficulty in *Jude* of establishing absolute linguistic reference. Cf. John Sutherland, "A Note on

From the beginning, then, the object of desire is not "real" in any sense, but is a "phantasmal" (II, ii, 97) creation of Jude's own mind, as are the "ghosts" which haunt Christminster. For Jude, however, the ghosts of his desires disappearing into the "obscure alleys" (II, i, 92) of Christminster are as real as Arabella's "disappearance into space" (II, i, 92). Constituting himself as a whole subject by an identification with another who repeatedly disappears, "A hungry soul in pursuit of a full soul . . ." (III, x, 233), Jude is accordingly threatened by the possibility of disappearing too: "Jude began to be impressed with the isolation of his own personality, as with a self-spectre . . . seeming thus almost his own ghost . . ." (II, i, 92). Phillotson, Christminster, Arabella, and most strikingly, Sue, thus become the figures of an ideal paradise, which is fundamentally inaccessible, insofar as it is one more metaphor in a structuring system of substitutions and exchanges of phantasmal dreams. The displacement of desire among the various characters points out the existence of a symbolic order, which creates the idea of autonomy when, in fact, the characters exist determined by their propensity for interpretive error.

As an exegetic scholar, "divining rather than beholding the spirit" of his texts (I, v, 34), Jude can never resist the temptation to read deep meanings, the "assemblage of concurring and converging probabilities" of "truths" (II, i, 95) into a scene. Yet less "absolute certitude" (II, i, 95) lies hidden beneath the manifest content of human experience in the novel than a mystified, but nonetheless threatening, organization of that content. When Jude thereafter sees Sue and looks into her "untranslatable eyes" (II, ii, 104) and immediately begins to interpret her character, he is only repeating the established pattern of error. Despite the difference in the agency that produces it, Jude manifests again the desire for that earlier "law of transmutation." Here, *Sue* is the text to be translated; but, as with the Greek and Latin

---

the Teasing Narrator in *Jude the Obscure," English Literature in Transition* 17 (1974): 159-162.

grammars, no master code exists to guarantee the authority of the translation. The rules governing that metonymic transfer, the figure Latin rhetoric calls *transmutio*, belong to the same illusion of a metaphysics of presence in the word, and to the same hallucination of a language determined on the basis of a verbal representation.[10] Just as language is constituted through repetition, so too does Jude's life acquire a narratable consistency. But the symbolic "inscription" of Jude's desires upon the surface of Wessex as he travels its roads from Christminster to Shaston, to Aldbrickham and back again, constitutes only the provisional creation of meaning through deferment. As Jude's dreams are transmuted from Arabella to Christminster, and to Sue, the fantasy of stability creates an apparently meaningful and readable text. It is always only in retrospect, however, that Jude's perceptions of those illusions of totality and stability can be organized and lived as an aesthetically coherent *meaning*.

But it is more the inner tensions produced by the characters' shifting relations which shape the action than any haphazard or indifferent circumstance. Nor is it entirely coincidental that the act of reading surfaces again to indicate these changes in connection with the constant letters which reaffirm the importance of writings, signs, inscriptions, and marks in the lives of these characters.[11] Altogether there are at least thirty-two letters indicated or implied in the text, ranging from one-line

[10] See Jacques Derrida, "Freud et la scène de l'écriture," *L'Écriture et la différence* (Paris: Seuil, 1967), p. 316.

[11] It is of course appropriate that Jude reads St. Paul at several points in the novel since the Pauline text is itself concerned with the issue of a proper reading. Referring to the relationship of the Old Testament to the New, Paul in fact applies the linguistic metaphor of Christ as the Spirit inseparable from the letter of the Bible where It is expressed. As John Freccero pointed out in a seminar on Dante at Yale University in the Fall of 1975, Paul later suggests that the Word of God interprets the hearts of men, turning to stone the hearts of unbelievers, while the Spirit writes upon the fleshly tablets of the faithful. Hardy thus directs our attention to the nature of Jude's spiritual, but apocryphal, word. See also, R.P.C. Hanson, *II Corinthians* (London: SCM Press, 1954), p. 39, commenting on II Corinthians 3 and 4, from which, of course, derives the epigraph to *Jude the Obscure*.

suicide notes (''*Done because we are too menny*'') to full-sized, ''carefully considered epistle[s]'' (VI, iv, 433), directly or indirectly narrated, delivered or not delivered. The numerous instances of inscriptions and carvings reinforce the importance of the ''letter'' in the text as the emblem for the force of illusion.

The first of these letters between Jude and Sue had simply called for their initial meeting, but it was ''one of those documents which, simple and commonplace in themselves, are seen retrospectively to have been pregnant with impassioned consequences'' (II, iv, 115-116). By the time Sue is engaged to Phillotson, Jude is receiving sudden ''passionate'' letters (III, i, 153) from her which seem to close the psychic distance between the two in a way that they can never quite imitate in person. ''It is very odd—'' Jude says at one point, ''That you are often not so nice in your real presence as you are in your letters!'' ''Does it really seem so to you?'' asks Sue, who then replies, ''Well, that's strange; but I feel just the same about you, Jude'' (III, vi, 197). A letter is a medium which effectively separates the writer from the effects of the message, while the message received is often one created by the reader himself. Even in their coldest tones, Sue's letters, while banishing Jude, nevertheless constantly summon him to her by the very fact that they establish a link of communication between them. Similarly, Phillotson's letter relinquishing Sue paradoxically begins re-establishing his hold on her, for the ''shadowy third'' (IV, v, 288), like the substantial couple, is always primarily constituted by this act of communication. This discourse of renunciation in the letters alerts our attention to the constant difference between expression and signification in the lives of these characters.

Moreover, when Sue writes a letter, she simultaneously removes and retains her absence and distance. This simultaneity of absence and presence is primarily an outcome of written discourse and is indicative of Jude's more general mystification concerning the existence of a stabilizing meaning. Sue is an eminently desirable woman, but she also becomes a sign in Jude's mind for an absent source of meaning. Accordingly, the act of writing becomes a bolster for the illusion of presence and wholeness within a discourse which appears innocent and transparent. Sue's letter can never replace her, but her "real presence" is never identical with the original self promised in the letter. The written word never allows access to the thing in itself, but always creates a copy, a simulacrum of it which sometimes moves the reader of the word more strongly than can the actual presence of the represented thing. Thus, the curious result is that the graphic sign, rather than the actual presence, of the desired becomes the source of emotive energy. For Jude, the desire for this originary "anchoring point" becomes an indispensable and indestructible illusion situated in the syntax of a dream without origin.

The intersubjective complex which structures the novel *Jude the Obscure* offers us some version of the following schema:

(1) dreams that fail—Jude, Phillotson, Sue;
(2) marriages that fail—Jude and Arabella; Sue and Phillotson; Jude and Sue; Arabella and Cartlett; both sets of parents; the legendary ancestor (mentioned in V, iv, 340);
(3) returns to original failures—Jude and Arabella at Christminster; Sue and Phillotson at Marygreen.

We began with Jude and Arabella at Marygreen, and with Sue and Phillotson at Christminster. The intervening movements in the plot which lead to the present renewal of the characters' former relations thus trace the pattern that characterizes the narrative structure. It is a *chiasmus*, the cross-shaped substitution of properties: the original couples are reunited, but in reversed locales. Hardy had referred to this structure more obliquely as the "geometric construction" behind his novel, the "quadrille" which put in motion the opposing qualities of the four main characters. But it turns out that the very process of "construction" which the characters' actions enact is really one more reversal of earlier aberrant "constructions" already performed. Would it not follow, then, that this new turn should restore the characters to their "proper" places? If Jude and Sue have been improperly associated at Christminster, might we not recover a measure of truth by simply restoring her to Phillotson at Marygreen? Since this structure of reversal is not only at work on the thematic level of the story, within the marital relationships among the characters, but also animates the greater structure of the narrative, the plot itself, the de-construction of its pattern, has significant implications for the novel's concept of a readable, constructive, integrating process in general.

Jude's idea of a synthetic "anchoring point" of semantic stability originates as the effect of a prior requirement, the requirement that the elements of the synthesis can themselves be permanently fixed in relation to stable qualities. Failing to integrate the ideal and the real with Sue, Jude, is no more likely to do so with Arabella. Sue's situation with Phillotson and Jude is even more complex, for the two are versions of the same in different registers. Further reversals, consequently, promise only continued instability. And, I would say, it makes little difference in this novel whether one calls the trope governing the structure of the narrative metaphor, metonymy, chiasmus, or simply a "geometric construction," for, from the first, the characters' roles have been inscribed in the determining contextual system defined by the marriage laws.

In the Victorian novel, marriage is pre-eminently the foundation of social stability. As a quasi-contractual agreement, it sets up the participants as a center for other integrating relationships. These relationships are not simply necessary for society; they constitute it. And that larger social and historical life, the world of symbolic relationships, forms in dialectical turn the structure which orders individual behavior in Hardy's novels. In a moment of pure poetic insight Sue comments on the nature of those relations:

> I have been thinking . . . that the social moulds civilization fits us into have no more relation to our actual shapes than the conventional shapes of the constellations have to the real star-patterns. I am called Mrs. Richard Phillotson, living a calm wedded life with my counterpart of that name. But I am not really Mrs. Richard Phillotson, but a woman tossed about, all alone, with aberrant passions, and unaccountable antipathies. (IV, i, 246-247)

With remarkable clarity Sue recognizes that the social woman is a representation, a sign, transposed and supplemented by desire, of her real self. But the relation between her natural and social selves is like the relation between "real star-patterns" and traditional interpretations of the "conventional" constellation shapes, like that between a referent and its linguistic sign, that is, *aesthetic* and hence, *arbitrary*. The concept of the self is the product of an aberrant substitution of rhetorical properties. Sue here clearly understands that this rhetorical operation is at best a metaphorical, interpretive act—one which is necessarily open to a variety of figural misreadings.

We have seen that the law which regulates marriage ties in this novel superimposes the kingdom of *culture* on that of *nature*.[12] Following its dictates, Jude artificially imposes a vision of organic totality (figured at different times by Phillotson, Christminster, Sue, etc.) onto nature and accords it moral and epistemological privilege. In contrast, the narrator's ironic comments show Jude's substitutions and realignments within the marriage system and within the pattern of metaphors for his vision of an "anchoring point" to be purely formal, analogous only by contingency, and hence without privilege. When the value of those associations is questioned, when the notion of Sue as the representation of Jude's dreams is made problematic, the possibility of a simple relation between signified and signifier is also questioned.

[12] See Anthony Wilden's discussion of the relationship between social and linguistic systems in *The Language of the Self*, pp. 253-254.

That formerly unquestioned assumption is the original moment of illusion which the narrative demystifies. The narrator reveals to us that Jude and Sue's notion of a privileged system of law is an hypothesis, or fictional construct (a *doxa*) that makes the orderly conduct of human affairs possible. It is not a "true" and irrefutable axiom based on knowledge (an *episteme*).[13] Their tendency, as revealed by the metaphorical rhetoric of their desires, is always to abide by the lawful order of "natural" logic and unity: "It is," Sue says at one point, "none of the natural tragedies of love that's love's usual tragedy in civilized life, but a tragedy artificially manufactured for people who in a natural state would find relief in parting!" (IV, ii, 258.) But if the order of "natural" law is itself a hypothetical construct rather than a "natural" occurrence in the world, then there is no necessary reason to suppose that it can, in fact, provide "relief." And it is Sue once again who, after the tragic deaths of their children, perceives that possibility when she says to Jude:

> "We said . . . that we would make a virtue of joy. I said it was Nature's intention, Nature's law and *raison d'être* that we should be joyful in what instincts she afforded us—instincts which civilization had taken upon itself to thwart. . . . And now Fate has given us this stab in the back for being such fools as to take Nature at her word!" (VI, ii, 408-409)

Jude, who likes to think of himself "as an order-loving man" of an "unbiased nature" (IV, ii, 252), can only stand by help-

[13] Cf. Friedrich Nietzsche, "On Truth and Falsehood in Their Extra-Moral Sense," in *The Complete Works*, vol. 2, pp. 173-192. See also, the journal entry of August 5, 1890, cited by Florence Emily Hardy in *The Life*, where Hardy indicates that "Art is a changing of the actual proportions and order of things. . . . Art is a disproportioning—(i.e., distorting, throwing out of proportion)—of realities, to show more clearly the features that matter in these realities, which, if merely copied or reported inventorially, might possibly be observed, but would more probably be overlooked. Hence 'realism' is not Art" (pp. 228-229), and compare with Nietzsche's statements in Essay III, section 24 of *On the Genealogy of Morals*, concerning the nature of the interpretive act.

lessly as he hears Sue destroy the basis of their "natural" marriage.[14]

Hardy's novel situates itself explicitly within the context of the marriage laws which define the nature of exchange and communication which establish Victorian society. It portrays, as Hardy tells us, the attempted translation of the law of nature into civil terms. The characters, however, cannot legitimately perform this translation without confusing the names of two such divergent semantic fields as those covered by "natural law" and "civil law." Confusion arises because the terms designate contextual properties, patterns of integration and disintegration, and not absolute concepts. In Hardy's Wessex, the "law of nature" designates a stage of relational integration that precedes in degree the stage of "civil law" since civil law only "enunciates" what is already present in nature to be read. The undoing of a system of relations codified in "civil law" will always reveal, consequently, a more fragmented stage that can be called "natural." This prior stage does not possess moral or epistemological priority over the system that is being undone.[15] But Jude always does assign it priority.

Remembering that "his first aspiration—toward academical proficiency—had been checked by a woman, and that his second aspiration—toward apostleship—had also been checked by a woman," he asks himself " 'Is it . . . that the women are to blame; or is it the artificial system of things, under which the normal sex-impulses are turned into devilish domestic gins and

[14] See also, among the numerous and often contradictory allusions to "natural" and "civil" systems of law in Hardy's novel, the following passages: I, xi, 80; III, ii, 165; III, vii, 206; IV, ii, 258; V, viii, 384; VI, i, 396; VI, ii, 408-409; and VI, iii, 418 in addition to Postscript, x and the epigraphs to Part First from the Book of Esdras and Part Fourth from Milton's *The Doctrine and Discipline of Divorce*.

[15] Paul de Man, in the chapter "Promises (*Social Contract*)" of *Allegories of Reading*, points out the relation between textual and legal systems: "In the description of the structure of political society, the 'definition' of a text as the contradictory interference of the grammatical with the figural field emerges in its most systematic form" (p. 270).

springs to noose and hold back those who want to progress?' " (IV, iii, 261). The weight of the second clause of the question makes it simply rhetorical: the women are of course not to blame. Although the "natural" pattern which Jude and Sue attempt to substitute for the accepted "civil" one is itself one system of relations among others, they see it as the sole and true order of things, and not as an artifice like civil structure. But once the fragmentation of the apparently stable structure of civil law is initiated, endless other versions of "natural law" might be engendered in a repeating pattern of regression.

The decisive term characterizing Jude's and Sue's relationship, "natural law," thus presents itself to be read as a chiastic pattern also. Natural law de-constructs civil law; but natural law is then itself open to the process of its own analysis. Far from denoting a stable point of homogeneity, where they might enact the mythic integration of their "one person split in two" (IV, iv, 276), the "natural law" of Hardy's Wessex connotes the impossibility of integration and stability. Any of Hardy's texts that put such polarities as natural and civil law, desire and satisfaction, repetition and stability, into play will have to set up the fiction of a synthetic process that will function both as the deconstructive instrument and as the outcome of that deconstruction. For Hardy, dualisms are never absolute. Deconstruction, however, is the process which both reveals the deluded basis of the desire for the synthesis of dualisms, and also creates the elements necessary for a new and equally deluded desire for integration. *Jude the Obscure* thus both denies the validity of the metaphor that unites "natural" and "civil" law, and elaborates a new metaphor to fulfill the totalizing function of the original binary terms. This new metaphor of life as an organic and orderly process now allows the narrative to continue by providing a myth of a future moment when, as Phillotson's friend, Gillingham, says, Jude and Sue might make "their union legal . . . and all would be well, and decent, and in order" (IV, iv, 433). This mythic moment, however, never comes.

It is crucial, then, that the basic conflicts of the novel occur within the "give-and-take" of marriage, for it situates the issue directly in the referential contexts of ethics and legality. Civil law, in fact, can be conceived as the emblem of referentiality *par excellence* since its purpose is to codify the rules for proper social intercourse. But to abide by the law, we must be able to read its text; ignorance is, after all, in English common law no excuse. Attempting to read it, Jude concludes that "we are acting by the letter; and 'the letter killeth'!" (VI, viii, 469.) Jude thus interprets the Pauline dictum, "The letter killeth but the spirit giveth life," as an injunction against a *literal* reading of the codes governing ethical action. Yet his *figural* reading leads to no spiritual truth either. On the contrary, Jude's illusions result from a figurative language taken literally, as with Sue he takes "Nature at her word." For Jude and for Sue, then, there is no text present anywhere which is yet to be transmuted, yet to be translated from natural to civil terms. There is no *natural* truth written anywhere which might be read without being altered in the process. The text of associations Jude fabricates around him is already woven of interpretations and differences in which the meaning of dreams and the desire for illusions are unnaturally coupled. Everything in Wessex "begins" with repetition, with secondary images of a meaning which was never present but whose *signified presence* is reconstituted by the supplementary and belated word of Jude's desires.[16]

I am saying, of course, that the narrative of *Jude the Obscure*, while telling the story of Jude and Sue's unhappy marriages, also dispels the illusion of a readable truth; that the novel gains its narrative consistency by the repeated deconstruction of the metaphor of life as organic unity. But the story which tells why figurative denomination is an illusion is itself *readable* and *ref-*

[16] I use the word *supplementary* in Derrida's sense in *Of Grammatology*, p. 145: "But the supplement . . . adds only to replace. It intervenes or insinuates itself *in-the-place-of*; if it fills, it is as if one fills a void. If it represents and makes an image, it is by the anterior default of a presence."

erential to the negative truth that Jude never perceives, and the story thus relapses into the very figure it deconstructs. The structure of the narrative as chiasmus, the cross-shaped substitution of properties, also tells, therefore, another story in the form of allegory about the divergence between the literal and the figural dimensions of language. That the text reverts to doing what it has claimed impossible is not a sign of Hardy's weakness as a novelist, for the error is not with the text, nor with the reader who attempts to understand it. Rather, I would say that with Jude we find that language itself, to the extent that it attempts to be truthful, necessarily misleads about its own ability to take us outside its own structures in search of meaning.

The myth of a stabilizing natural or civil law, then, is actually the representation of our will to make society seem a unified and understandable organism. But Hardy's novel persists in showing society's laws as open to subversion by the actions of the individuals who make up society. In everyday life, there is an ever possible discontinuity between the Word of the law, its spirit, and the practice, the letter, of the law. And the necessary failure of the law to enforce its monologic interpretation of the infinite variety of human behavior can lead to the subversion of the entire relational system. This explains why Jude, by his actions, constantly and unintentionally subverts the Word which he figures in Sue and in his dreams of a university career.

In applying the accepted social law to themselves, Jude and Sue constitute a version of the law, but, in applying the general social law to their particular situation, they instantaneously alter it. Rather than serving as a source of universal order from which social relations might be unified and ordered within a social totality, the accepted social law exhibits its inability to constrain the heterogeneity of social relations. The law, then, is always shown to be grammatically structured, since it always engenders only a contingent, contextual meaning. But law is also constantly subverted in the application; it can legislate meaning only when it ceases to be legislative. Jude's revolutionary attempt to establish a ground for authentic meaning thus produces an anarchy of mutually exclusive readings of the one piece of language, "The letter killeth." This discontinuity between the "letter" and the "spirit" of the law, between a literal and a figural reading of its sign, is what constitutes Hardy's break with referentiality. Although the law indicates that "The letter killeth," Jude finds it impossible to decide what is the *letter* and what the *spirit* of the law. In each reading, whether within a "natural" or a "civil" system, the law is transposed, altered, and led to produce the conditions for its own undoing. Like Sue's ambiguous letters, law is consequently only a promise (which cannot be kept) of a future stability and is never adequate to deal with the instability of the present moment.

The repetitions in the novel put at stake not only the relation between Jude's present actions and his family's history, but also the very readability of the initial text of that history. Everywhere about him, history calls out to be read, but Jude consistently fails to do so properly. Because he cannot read it, his actions are never simply a representation of that past, but are an interpretation which has gone awry. Since the novel is itself a kind of history, it too is open to all the errors of interpretation of which it speaks. Hardy's "Postscript," which calls attention to the decisive issues of reading and interpretation, must thus be seen in retrospect as an ironic repetition of the situation dramatized in *Jude* concerning the impossibility of authoritative readings, for it accuses the reader of partaking in Jude's error. We cannot read the novel as Jude reads the motto of his life, that is, with expectation of encountering an ideally sanctioned stable Truth.

But how *are* we to read it, then? If the notion of representation is to be at all meaningful, we must presuppose the stability of subjects with stable names who are to be represented, and a rapport between the sign and the referent in the language of the representation. Yet both conditions are absent from this text (notoriously so in the allegorical figure of little Father Time). We can, of course, discern similarities among the characters' various actions. And, as we read, attempting, in Hardy's words, "to give shape and coherence to this series of seemings" (viii), we too must rely on Jude's example in constructing an interpretive model. But we cannot accept his model of metaphoric synthesis as an absolute.[17] Jude's model of metaphor (governing the patterns of idealization and substitution) is erroneous because it believes in its own referential meaning—it believes that the inwardly desired "anchoring point" can be concretely encountered in the external world as Phillotson, as Christminster, as Arabella, or as Sue. It assumes a world in which literal and figural properties can be isolated, exchanged, and substituted. For the reader and the narrator, metaphoric synthesis persists within the interpretive act, but not as the ground of ultimate reconciliations. Jude himself, however, remains caught in the error of metaphor. But it is an error without which reading could not take place.

One traditional reading of the novel attempts to place the responsibility for Jude's "unfulfilled aims" squarely on the author himself, who, with his notion of the "Immanent Will," has unfairly dictated the fate of his doomed characters. Such a reading can certainly be justified, for, as we have noted, the narrator does maintain a constant ironic distance from the characters' expressed delusions. Hardy's narrator stands above Jude's confusion of the "spirit" and the "letter" of the text of Wessex history and offers us his own authoritative version of the truth.[18]

[17] See Gérard Genette, "La rhétorique restrainte," and "Métonymie chez Proust," *Figures* III, pp. 21-40 and 41-66, respectively, for instances of the kinds of interpretations which use such a totalizing metaphorical model.

[18] See, for example, the readings proposed by John Sutherland, pp. 159-162; Patrick Braybrooke, *Thomas Hardy and His Philosophy* (London: C. W. Daniel Co., 1928), pp. 86-95, who argues that "in Jude . . . Hardy is 'using' a character" and that Jude is trapped within "wall[s] that [are] constructed by Hardy's fierce and uncompromising Determinism" (p. 92); Ernest Brennecke, Jr., *Thomas Hardy's Universe* (London: Fisher Unwin, 1924), who claims that Hardy "thinks that his view of life is the only possible one. . . . He looks forward with

And yet, as we also noted when we examined the geometric reversals in the plot of the novel, the narrator's own discourse seems frequently to resort to the very misapprehension of rhetorical order which he apparently ascribes to Jude. It seems, consequently, that we proceed in a fruitless detour by transferring the source of delusion from character to authorial voice, for both share in the error of metaphor. In any case, little is gained by pursuing the question of Hardy's fatality on the level of authorial intentions. When we attempt rather to discern the true nature of that "Immanent Will," which is the source of action in Wessex, we necessarily come to the recognition that "Immanent Will" is ultimately a pattern of language, which manifests itself in *Jude* as the repeatedly subversive power of the dialogic word both to say and not say what it means. As we trace out the implications of Hardy's own de-constructive discourse, then, we find that the problem of determinism is really a false problem. The same can be said of the characters' attempts to discern the true nature of the world around them and the people within it—their perceptions of the world and mind are governed by the aesthetic constructs of the human imagination, and their pathetic attempts to understand their fate in genetic, historical terms ("The world was not ripe for us") lead nowhere. Hardy's novel shows, on the contrary, that the dialogic by-play of those constructs cannot be eliminated simply by ascribing them either to historical, biological, or transcendental impulses.

We thus find that Hardy's narrative puts the assurance of the truth of the referent into question. But in making this

---

complacency, if not delight, to a future of endless unconsciousness whereby the harmony between human life and the unconsciously governed universe will be re-established" (p. 141); and Carl Weber, *Hardy of Wessex: His Life and Literary Career* (1940; New York: Columbia University Press, 1965), who says that "Hardy's aim was too sweeping, his skill too defective, and—it must be admitted—his artistic control too frenzied [in *Jude*]" (p. 206). Recent criticism has been, properly, kinder to Hardy than were his contemporaries and near contemporaries.

situation thematic, it does allow a meaning, the text, to exist. We are not dealing simply with an *absence* of meaning, for, if we were, then that very absence would itself constitute a referent. Instead, as an allegory of the breakdown of the referential system, *Jude the Obscure* continues to refer, to its own chiastic operations. This *new* referentiality is one bounded strictly by the margins of textuality. In our courses on the nineteenth-century novel we find it convenient to use *Jude* as a "transitional" text; it is either the last of the Victorians or the first of the Moderns.[19] Morten Zabel has written, for instance, that Hardy was "a realist developing toward allegory . . . who brought the nineteenth century novel out of its slavery to fact."[20] This seems to me fine, as far as it goes. But I would add that this allegorical pattern manifests itself in *Jude* primarily through the subversive power of the dialogic word, which refuses to be reduced to the single "anchoring point" of a transcendent and determining Will, Immanent or otherwise.

As Hardy came to see early on, the function of realistic fiction was to show that "*nothing* is as it appears."[21] It is no wonder, then, that Hardy's last novel was misread. The suggestive and

[19] Irving Howe, *Thomas Hardy* (New York: Macmillan; London: Collier, 1967), argues for a similar reading when he notes that if "modernist" literature works "on the premise that there is no secure meaning in the portrayed action, or that while the action can hold our attention and rouse our feelings, we cannot be certain, indeed must remain uncertain, as to the possibilities of meaning," then *Jude the Obscure* "does not go nearly as far along the path of modernism" (p. 144) as do Kafka's, Joyce's, or Faulkner's novels. In my reading, Hardy's refusal to posit the absolute *absence* of meaning, but only its unverifiability, is, in some respects, a more profoundly "modern" act than would be the simple negation of "meaning." See also, Lawrence O. Jones, "Imitation and Expression in Thomas Hardy's Theory of Fiction," *Studies in the Novel* 7 (1975): 507-525; and J. Hillis Miller, "Fiction and Repetition: *Tess of the d'Urbervilles*," in *Forms of Modern British Fiction*, ed. Alan Warren Friedman (Austin: University of Texas Press, 1975), pp. 43-71; and also, the discussion by Edward Said, *Beginnings*, pp. 137-139.

[20] "Hardy in Defense of His Art: The Aesthetics of Incongruity," in *Thomas Hardy*, ed. Albert Guerard, p. 43.

[21] Florence Emily Hardy, *The Life*, Journal entry for December 21, 1885, p. 176.

poetic force of *Jude* arises less from its positive attempt to represent appearance than from its rejection of any vision pretending to convey the totality and complexity of life. Accordingly, in *Jude* Hardy repudiates the notion that fiction can ever be Truth, that it can ever "reproduc[e] in its entirety the phantasmagoria of experience with infinite and atomic truth, without shadow, relevancy, or subordination."[22] He dramatizes, instead, the recognition that in narrative "Nothing but the illusion of truth can permanently please, and when the old illusions begin to be penetrated, a more natural magic has to be supplied."[23] To be realistic, the text must proceed as if its representing systems correspond to those in the world; it must create a new illusion of reference to replace the old of representation.

But this transmutation of illusions modifies the original considerably. Like Sue's "real presence," perpetually deviating from the ideal figure of Jude's dreams, the letter of the text, "*translat[ing]* the qualities that are already there" in the world,[24] contains after all only the inadequate ciphers of the spirit of meaning, not the "thing" itself. The deconstruction of the metaphorical model of substitution and translation (operating in Jude's various desires for Christminster, Sue, natural law, etc.) is performed by the rhetorical structure of chiasmus, whose own figural logic both asserts and denies referential authority. From the reader's point of view, the results of each of these figural movements can then be termed "meanings." These figural movements and systems of reference and their resulting sociological, ethical, legal, or sexual categories become historically constituted, coercive contexts for meanings that claim for themselves universality to the extent that they make us forget that they are undone by the very process that creates them.

It may well be, therefore, that Hardy's final novel does not

22 Hardy, "The Science of Fiction" (1891), in *Thomas Hardy's Personal Writings*, ed. Harold Orel (Lawrence: University of Kansas Press, 1966), p. 135.

23 "The Science of Fiction," p. 135.

24 Florence Emily Hardy, *The Life*, Journal entry for January 1887, p. 185.

"mean"; but it does signify to a redoubtable degree. It signifies the laws of language over which neither Hardy nor his readers can exercise complete control. To read those laws is to undermine their intent. This is why Hardy, like Jude who adds to the textual allegory of Wessex and generates its history while marking its closure, is bound to allegorical narratives: he creates the fiction of an ideal reader while he constructs a narrative about the illusion of privileged readings. On this level of rhetorical self-consciousness, prose fiction is on the verge of becoming poetry.

❦ SIX ❦

The Flowers of Speech: James Joyce's *A Portrait of the Artist as a Young Man* and *Ulysses*

> The "right perception" . . . is a nonentity full of contradictions: for between two utterly different spheres, as between subject and object, there is no causality, no accuracy, no expression, but at the utmost an *aesthetical* relation, . . . a stammering translation into quite a distinct foreign language.
>
> FRIEDRICH NIETZSCHE.
> "On Truth and Falsehood in Their Extra-Moral Sense"

> We have hanged our hearts in her trees; and we list, as she bibs us, by the waters of babalong.
>
> JOYCE.
> *Finnegans Wake*

Jude's misfortunes in seeking a worldly "anchoring point" for his transcendental desires are the thematic ruse by which Hardy undoes the myth of a stable and intelligible natural order. And yet, as Hardy realizes, no "de-construction" can ever entirely compromise the complexity of the myth or eliminate its usefulness. The very possibility of any personal history seems to be grounded on the belief in life's narratable consistency. In recognizing that such a belief is a defensive verbal strategy by which the inconsistent world is given fictional order, Hardy's final novel leads us to the limits of fictional discourse. From Hardy, the move toward the rhetorically self-conscious texts of the modernist era was not a complicated one.

Hardy's notions that "Nothing but the illusion of truth can permanently please," that "when the old illusions begin to be penetrated, a more natural magic has to be supplied," become with James Joyce the very principles by which narratives are born. Joyce begins with the recognition that narratives are like elaborately crafted mosaics, painstakingly assembled to portray the complexity and seeming unity of life's fragmentary moments. For Joyce, however, these finished mosaics also remain intractable reminders of the artificial quality of all perceived and constructed unities. The aesthetic theory outlined in *Stephen Hero* and completed in *A Portrait of the Artist as a Young Man* and *Ulysses* is a statement about the construction of such artistic unities. It can also stand as a paradigm of their seductivity. In Joyce, the conceptual language novelists up to Hardy had trusted to represent life becomes itself one other fictional construct by which life's inconsistencies may be signified.

❦ ❦ ❦

> There was a special class for English composition and it was in this class that Stephen first made his name. . . . Stephen laid down his doctrine very positively and insisted on the importance of what he called the literary tradition. Words, he said, have a certain value in the market-place—a debased value. Words are simply receptacles for human thought: in the literary tradition they receive more valuable thoughts than they receive in the market-place.[1]

This passage from the beginning of the surviving pages of the manuscript of *Stephen Hero*, the rejected early version of *A Portrait*, marks out two key issues in Stephen's aesthetic doctrine. First, it shows a naive speculation about the nature of words and their place in the "literary tradition." Second, it characterizes linguistic transactions as similar to economic exchanges. Words gain and retain value in that exchange by virtue

[1] James Joyce, *Stephen Hero*, ed. John J. Slocum and Herbert Cahoon, rev. ed. (New York: New Directions Pub. Co., 1963), p. 27. Hereafter cited in parentheses as *SH*, followed by page numbers. The manuscript of *Stephen Hero* begins in mid-sentence at MS page 519 and runs, with minor gaps, to page 902. This segment corresponds approximately to what was to become Chapter V of *A Portrait*.

of the solvency of the bank of the subjective mind.[2] For Stephen, language is an empty "receptacle"; it has no autonomous force apart from the willed intentional action of a performing subject. The narrative continues:

> As Stephen walked . . . through the ways of the city he had his ears and eyes ever prompt to receive impressions. It was not only in Skeat that he found words for his treasure-house, he found them also at haphazard in the shops, on advertisements, in the mouths of the plodding public. He kept repeating them to himself till they lost all instantaneous meaning for him and became wonderful vocables. . . . He would return home with a deliberate, unflagging step piecing together meaningless words and phrases with deliberate unflagging seriousness. (*SH*, 30-31)

In the context of an aborted narrative, this seems impressionistic and innocent. But it is here, with this initial insight into the contingency of the signifying "vocable" (as being susceptible to distortion and reconstitution in infinite variation) that we can first discern the organizing structure which was to become the form and theme of the later novels.

As he walks through Dublin, Stephen finds "heaps of dead language" (*A Portrait of the Artist*, 179) all around him. Language is dead to Stephen because it has been devalued by constant, uncritical circulation. He now makes it his task to revive language, to reconstruct its systematically debased edifice of meaning. In the early sections of *Stephen Hero*, "meaning" then does not exist as a property of words. It is rather a product to be provisionally fashioned by the aesthetically sensitive mind. In order to begin that narrative fashioning, however, the artist

[2] Theodore Spencer notes in the new "Introduction" to *Stephen Hero* that the date of the manuscript is ambiguous. The documentary evidence seems to favor the period between 1904 and 1906 as that most likely for the writing of this early text. In *A Portrait* Stephen's present notion of linguistic value is parodied by the image of the "great cash register" in the heavens.

must assume that the linguistic elements at his disposal *are* significant and capable of communicating meaning. It will become the task of Joyce's future texts to remember that their initial acceptance of the "market-place value" of words is only a provisional acceptance and that *true* meaning is something still to be created by the artist.

With this emphasis on the *teckne* of *poesis* in *Stephen Hero,* Stephen posits an ideal, immanent "beauty" and "essence" in the heart of things. The role of the artist is to penetrate to this inner core and express its significance in the poetic word. The narrator's vocabulary describing the artist's attempts to apprehend, read, and reform reality thus emphasizes the constructive nature of the act of perception: "Stephen . . . strove to pierce to the significant heart of everything. . . . And over all this chaos of history and legend, of fact and superstition, he strove to draw out a line of order, to reduce the abysses of the past to order by a diagram" (*SH* 33). But, while the narrator defines the artist as one "who could disentangle the subtle soul of the image from its mesh of defining circumstances" (*SH* 78), and claims that the artistic imagination "has contemplated intensely the truth of being of the visible world" and that "beauty, the splendour of truth, has been born" (*SH* 80), he is also careful to imply that this "beauty" and "truth of being" which Stephen beholds did not exist prior to the artist's perception of them. The narrator's description of Stephen's attempt "to reduce the abysses of the past to order by a diagram" suggests that the source of those "rude scrawls" is Stephen's own contemplating mind.

In *Stephen Hero,* the recognition of "beauty" is thus predicated upon the discovery of an intelligible language in nature. The meaning of that language, however, is always one which the mind of the perceiver has imposed upon nature. Together with the opening scenes of *A Portrait,* these initial scenes document the first encounter between the artist's inner world and the external world, as mediated by language. They are also the occasion when the individual, touched by the signs of the external world, comes into his own for the first time, for the discovery of words as plastic entities will lead him to experience emotions previously unknown. When confronted hereafter by new experiences, the disharmony elicited in Stephen will lead him to recall the disharmony he had felt before a new word. Stephen will remember then the charming fluidity of the word and use it to fit a name to the emotion before him. As a budding artist, Stephen becomes practiced in shaping language to take care of experience. Thus he will later come to know all things linguistically.

At one time or another, every reader of modern literature has probably been tempted to apply Joyce's aesthetic insights to the criticism of Joyce's own novels.[3] Thus, one can find such categorical, and contradictory, statements about those theories in the Joycean secondary literature. Edward Morin, for example, has argued that Joyce misrepresented Aquinas, for "God's universal beauty is an end in itself, connoting no further desire because it fulfills all desire. To make a final end of earthly beauty or the seeking thereof is a mistake. . . ."[4] Haskell M. Block, however, writes: "The theoretical formulation of Joyce's aesthetic rigidly follows Thomistic principles. It does not distort Thomistic doctrine to shape a personal aesthetic, but Joyce's critical theory does represent a rationalization of contemporary literary tenets as scholastic principles."[5] William York Tindall, in contrast, asserts that Joyce diverged from Aquinas, "who, liberally interpreted and applied, is made to serve ends other than his own."[6] In a later development, Maurice Beebe has

[3] Joyce's statements on Aesthetics in his Paris and Pola notebooks are available as "Aesthetics," in *The Critical Writings of James Joyce*, ed. Ellsworth Mason and Richard Ellmann (1959; rpt. New York: The Viking Press, 1970), pp. 143-148.

[4] "Joyce as Thomist," *Renascence* 9 (Spring 1957): 129.

[5] "The Critical Theory of James Joyce," *Journal of Aesthetics and Art Criticism* 8 (1949-50): 178-179.

[6] *James Joyce: His Way of Interpreting the Modern World* (New York: Scribner's, 1950), p. 20.

added that ". . . the theory of art presented by Stephen Dedalus in *A Portrait* . . . is both a key to the novel in which it appears and a programme for Joyce's later writings. . . . A point by point comparison of Joyce's theory with the Thomist sources from which it derives, will reveal that Joyce follows the form of certain scholastic principles, but by denying the premises upon which they are based, distorts the meaning. . . . Joyce's conclusions . . . would be the despair of neo-Thomists."[7]

My own discussion of the aesthetic theory in Joyce's novels will not go over ground already minutely covered in the first six decades since the publication of *Ulysses* in 1922. It does not attempt to provide the final word on the relationship between Joyce's own theories of art and those presented by Stephen Dedalus. My purpose is rather to understand how those theories function in the production of narrative. The aesthetic theory is a statement about literary language and about the way in which narratives create meaning; both *A Portrait* and *Ulysses* allegorize the procedures of meaning-creation throughout their narrated stories. But in order to see this allegorical pattern, we must first study the structure of the theory of language latent in these two novels. That larger theory, already indicated in *Stephen Hero*, is the basis of Dedalus's aesthetic principles,

[7] "Joyce and Aquinas: The Theory of Aesthetics," *Philological Quarterly* 36 (1957): 20-21. See also William T. Noon, *Joyce and Aquinas* (New Haven: Yale University Press, 1957), p. 17; David E. Jones, "The Essence of Beauty in James Joyce's Aesthetics," *James Joyce Quarterly* 10 (1972-73): 291; David Hayman, *Ulysses: The Mechanics of Meaning* (Englewood Cliffs: Prentice-Hall, 1970), pp. 51-68; Jerry Allen Dibble, "Stephen's Esthetics and Joyce's Art: Theory and Practice of Genre in *A Portrait of the Artist as a Young Man*," *Journal of Narrative Technique* 6 (1976): 29-40; Nathan Halper, "The Aesthetics of Joyce: James Joyce and His Fingernails," in Kathleen McGrory and John Unterecker, eds., *Yeats, Joyce, and Beckett: New Light on Three Modern Irish Writers* (Lewisburg: Bucknell University Press, 1976), pp. 105-109; Jacques Aubert, *Introduction à l'esthetique de James Joyce* Etudes Anglaises 46 (Paris: Didier, 1973); Dolf Sörensen, *James Joyce's Aesthetic Theory: Its Development and Application* (Amsterdam: Rodopi, 1977); Richard Ellmann, *The Consciousness of Joyce* (London: Faber & Faber, 1977), pp. 73-95; Robert Boyle, S.J., *James Joyce's Pauline Vision: A Catholic Exposition* (Carbondale: Southern Illinois University Press, 1978), pp. 42-58; and Wolfgang Iser, "Patterns of Communication in Joyce's *Ulysses*," in *The Implied Reader*, pp. 196-233.

which express his deluded belief in a myth of the proper reading of the essential layer of truth present within reality.

❦ ❦ ❦

In *A Portrait of the Artist,* Stephen explains that this subsistent layer of truth is the quality which allows a thing to be "that thing which it is and no other thing."[8] The "radiance" of which Aquinas speaks, claims Stephen, "is the scholastic *quidditas,* the *whatness* of a thing. This supreme quality is felt by the artist when the esthetic image is first conceived in the imagination . . ." (*P* 213).

Earlier, Stephen had subsumed the very possibility of the discovery of *quidditas* to a prior "first phase of apprehension," during which "a boundary line was drawn about the object to be apprehended": "An esthetic image is presented to us either in space or in time. But, temporal or spatial, the esthetic image is first luminously apprehended as selfbounded and selfcontained upon the immeasurable background of space or time which is not it" (*P* 212). The conceived "esthetic image" is thus not the *quidditas* of the thing itself, nor is it something entirely different. It is rather a kind of objective correlative, or a sign, for the "selfbounded" essence of the object. Words, then, are images which represent the physical object and which preserve its *quidditas* by replicating the representational nature of the "esthetic image." The *whatness* of an object is simply a correlation that the perceiver forms through the acts of repetition which name its presence. As a logical result, the *quidditas* of an "esthetic" object, its presence and ideality, cannot be immediately known; it can be perceived only by virtue of the creative force of the artist's representational discourse which exists necessarily at a double remove from essential *quiddity.*

[8] Joyce, *A Portrait of the Artist as a Young Man,* The Viking Critical Library Edition, ed. Chester G. Anderson (1916; New York: Viking Press, 1968), p. 213. All references are to this edition of the novel, henceforth identified by the abbreviation *P,* and page number.

Thus Stephen's aesthetic, at base really a theory of perception, also describes the necessary mediation of language as the medium for the play of presence and absence (in repetition) which gives rise to the notion of "essence" as a linguistic hypothesis. But in this sequence of statements, Stephen has conflated aesthetic notions with linguistic principles, and these in turn have become epistemological categories. His theoretical maneuvering is not without consequences, however, for in the transposition of the object in space from a phenomenal to a perceptual event, its extrinsic character has been essentially altered. In phenomenological terms, we might say that Stephen "reduces" the objective existence of real (empirical) entities by converting them into subjective (mental) categories. This apparently innocent transfer, taken by Stephen as of neutral quality and as negating the possibility of seeing the "esthetic image" as a symbol of substantial essences, is in fact crucial. As Joyce realizes, it represents the true moment of aesthetic conception.

Stephen rightly understands that the tenor of his phrasing might lead us to suppose that his theory leads in a transcendental direction:

> The connotation of the word [*claritas*] . . . would lead you to believe that [Aquinas] had in mind symbolism or idealism, the supreme quality of beauty being a light from another world, the idea of which the matter is but the symbol. I thought he might mean that *claritas* is the artistic discovery and representation of the divine purpose in anything or a force of generalisation which would make the esthetic image a universal one, makes it outshine its proper conditions. (*P* 212-213)

He goes on to explain, however, that his own interpretation of the Thomistic *claritas* denies the possibility of a transcendental phenomenology: *Claritas* is simply the signifier of the essential core of the esthetic image, which signifier the core uses to "project" itself into the world through the light of an ideal form, paradigm, or parable of signification—the artistic word. This rejection of idealism is important because Stephen wishes to establish the essentiality of all objects, that is to say, their *quidditas*, as an immanent property of the material world, rather than as a gift from the divine. With every apprehended "radiance," Stephen assumes, the god-like artist comes nearer to the sublime moment when he might "disentangle the subtle soul of the image from its mesh of defining circumstances" and liberate it into phenomenal and material beauty (*SH* 78).

In Stephen's sense, artistic creation would thus be delivered from all dependence on the perfect cohesion between transcendental meanings and temporal forms and would come to existence solely by virtue of the performative function of the human imagination.

According to the Dedalan doctrine, Truth and Beauty can be authoritatively expressed. Aquinas postulates that the essence of a thing is derived from its participation in the essence of God, and that one can know God through the discovery of the essences of things.[9] Stephen's theory, in contrast, denies the existence of vertical links to an ideal, transcendental world, yet accepts the possibility of ideal, formal relationships within the world. As Stephen argues: ". . . all people who admire a beautiful object find in it certain relations which satisfy and coincide with the stages themselves of all esthetic apprehension. These relations of the sensible, visible to you through one form and to me through another, must be therefore the necessary qualities of beauty" (*P* 209).

The artist establishes these "relations of the sensible" through his perception of *claritas* in the "esthetic image," which itself

[9] Jacques Maritain has argued the scholastic position that: "Every form . . . is a remnant or a ray of the creative Mind impressed upon the heart of the being created. . . . The beautiful is in close dependence upon what is metaphysically true, in the sense that every splendour of intelligence in things presupposes some degree of conformity with that Intelligence which is the cause of things . . ." (*Art and Scholasticism*, trans. J. F. Scanlon [London: Sheed and Ward, 1939], pp. 25-26).

stands as a sign of an object's *quidditas*. Thus, while knowledge of essences may not lead to God, it may at least lead, through the fluid circuit of language, to the "supreme quality of beauty." In Stephen's theory, the artistic word does not conduce toward the "splendour of beauty" because of a transcendental imperative; its flow toward beauty is rather the result of the circular referential movement of signification. Hence, as we can readily see, despite Stephen's expressed desire to avoid "idealism," the aesthetic theory does not eliminate "idealism"; it merely redirects its forces and lends to referential language a categorical privilege which in daily use it cannot readily justify. Stephen's theory is thus simultaneously a heroic attempt to recover a naturally poetic language, an expression of his naive faith in a proper way of indicating the relationship between human and ideal worlds, and a misguided attempt to formalize that relationship into a universal poetics, a grammar of archetypes for the proper reading of the sensible world. It is the process which might finally allow the artist to escape from the imprisoning "nets" of the world's literal differences into the transcendental universe of Beauty's assimilated unities: "When the soul of a man is born in this country there are nets flung at it to hold it back from flight. You talk to me of nationality, language, religion. I shall try to fly by those nets" (*P* 203).

It is also a part of *A Portrait*'s ironic drama, however, that Stephen's theory fails to recognize the possibility that the artistic word floating before the reader in the "fluid and lambent narrative" of "dramatic form" (*P* 215) might have no reality but that provisionally marked out for it by the artist's arbitrary reduction of the entire confusing play of signification surrounding its "market-place value." Although Stephen feels that the process he describes allows the heroic creation of a "purified" image of truth, he describes a romantic confusion of transcendental and phenomenal attributes, arbitrarily reduced to one function by the very figural logic of the words he uses to express his theory. As in the discussion of *quidditas*, the present instances which seem to celebrate Stephen's belief that the artist can effect a self-willed union between worldly and ideal essences in fact show that the repetitive, mechanical patterns of the language expressing those supposed moments of refined perception are not genuine visions of the esthetic image, but only of metaphoric transpositions derived from randomly associated phenomenal events.

Joyce, who would certainly have agreed to the assimilation of phenomenal experience and literary creation, will strive to keep signification outside the self-presence of transcendental life.[10] The rhetoric of his texts, however, always seems to posit the existence of a transcendental referent, which might serve as the organizing point for all valuative, ethical, and aesthetic judgments. Accordingly, Stephen's aesthetic theory implies that it is the artist's heroic task to seek access to direct and unmediated awareness of the present moment and its content as a timeless and context-free phenomenon. His entire work is thus caught up in the linguistic web of the indicative sign attempting to establish verifiable reference to such transcendental visions, and it is the elaboration of this attempted verification, in the form of an extended metaphor, that constitutes the body of his fictional performance.

❦ ❦ ❦

Immediately after the theorizing, Stephen awakens from a dream which has seemed to offer a vision of such unity in the "ecstasy of seraphic life": "O what sweet music! His soul was all dewy wet. . . . He lay still, as if his soul lay amid cool waters, con-

[10] Richard Ellmann reports a conversation between Joyce and Louis Gillet on the difficulties of the autobiographical novel in which Joyce said: "When your work and your life make one, when they are interwoven in the same fabric . . ." and then hesitated, as if overcome by the difficulty of naming those problems. Joyce was consciously, Ellmann notes, "turning his life into a fiction for the purposes of his book" (*James Joyce* [1959; London: Oxford University Press, 1965], p. 154). See also Ellmann's *the Consciousness of Joyce*, pp. 73-74.

scious of faint sweet music. . . . A spirit filled him, pure as the purest water, sweet as dew, moving as music. . . . It was that windless hour of dawn when madness wakes and strange plants open to the light and the moth flies silently forth. An enchantment of the heart!" (*P* 217). The phrase, "An enchantment of the heart," identifies the dream as an example of those aesthetic moments described earlier when the "supreme quality of beauty" and "clear radiance" (*P* 213) are apprehended by the mind. Since the function of art is the expression of this pre-existing, hidden layer of meaning, Stephen, as a budding artist, proceeds dutifully to translate that moment of the "ecstasy of life" into language.

As in the perception of *quidditas,* the latent experience of that ecstatic moment must be communicated in order for it to achieve its full potential of meaning: "The instant flashed forth like a point of light and now from cloud on cloud of vague circumstance confused form was veiling softly its afterglow" (*P* 217). This is the moment of representation when static self-communication is carried over into the kinetic flow of language. Stephen's prior notions, which seemed to annul the value of linguistic signs by making them mere receptacles for ideas, are now rejected in favor of a new notion which makes signs, the bodies of words, modifications of (and derivations from) an ideal presence, now departed: "O! In the virgin womb of the imagination the word was made flesh. Gabriel the seraph had come to the virgin's chamber. An afterglow deepened within his spirit, whence the white flame had passed, deepening to a rose and ardent light" (*P* 217). Here as elsewhere in the novel, artistic creation takes place only after the empirical impulses of sexual arousal are transformed into an allegory of spiritual ecstasy.

Now as Stephen lies in his bed recalling his amorous failures with Emma, the "temptress of his villanelle" (*P* 223), his desires are renewed and again seek expression in language: "A glow of desire kindled again his soul and fired and fulfilled all his body. . . . Her eyes, dark and with a look of languor, were opening to his eyes. Her nakedness yielded to him, radiant, warm, odorous and lavishlimbed, enfolded him like a shining cloud, enfolded him like water with a liquid life: and like a cloud of vapour or like waters circumfluent in space the liquid letters of speech, symbols of the elements of mystery, flowed forth over his brain" (*P* 223). In these as in many other passages, the liquid metaphors naming the essential ideality, or "radiance," of the soul also name Stephen's erotic desires. But Stephen remains unmindful of how the rhetorical mode of his own words relates to the meanings he wishes to express.

Stephen's metaphors, announcing the moment of the immaculate artistic conception of an ideal *quidditas*, of a moment of pure experience, fully understandable without reference to transient circumstances or empirical concerns, continue to name the obverse of ideality and thus repeat the notions he has previously denounced. His words shift from a religious to an ethical and to an erotic connotation with no underlying constraint. In fact, there is finally very little in Stephen's relationship to the "esthetic image" which does not parallel his former relationship to God, or his anticipated relationship with Emma or any other woman, for in each case the sense of Stephen's words exists in time, determined as he fears by very real historical and linguistic factors—"History . . . is a nightmare from which I am trying to awake" (*U* 34). His poetic expressions acquire meaning, however, less in terms of their relation to any transcendental essence than in terms of their role in human activities, that is to say, in terms of their rhetorical force. As a consequence, the timeless realm postulated by the aesthetic theory can be understood only as an aspect of, an abstraction from, decidedly temporal occasions, which the young artist is constantly at pains to conceal. Thus, far from allowing him to escape the "nets" of "nationality, language, religion," Stephen's artistry functions as yet another subtler version of those enveloping nets.

We have seen Stephen experience this confusion of rhetorical modes at least once before: "A girl stood before him in midstream, alone and still, gazing out to sea. She seemed like one whom magic had changed into the likeness of a strange and beautiful seabird. Her long slender bare legs were delicate as a crane's and pure save where an emerald trail of seaweed had fashioned itself as a sign upon the flesh" (*P* 171). The "magic" effecting this epiphanic transformation too, however, is Stephen's own unbridled metaphoric word, rather than anything mystically pure and simple, which might serve as the foundation for the direct, unmediated understanding of the present moment and its ideal *quidditas*.

Phrases and periods continue to flood Stephen's mind with words as in succeeding passages he appears willing to drown in a polymorphous linguistic sea: "A soft liquid joy like the noise of many waters flowed over his memory and he felt in his heart the soft peace of silent spaces of fading tenuous sky above the waters, of oceanic silence . . ." (*P* 225-226). As "a priest of eternal imagination, transmuting the daily bread of experience into the radiant body of everliving life" (*P* 221), Stephen thus views his task as one guided by the metaphorical impulse of *transmutio*—the process which in the Roman Catholic mass effects the hypostatic union of consubstantiality. Stephen's intoxication with the beauty of language, with the sensual body of the material signifier, and with his presuppositions about art as an access to the absolute simplicity of the material world, allow him first to transfer his erotic desires into expressions of piety, and then to translate these into signs of artistic inspiration. Each of these priestly transformations is facilitated by the marked tendency of his ideas toward the creation of idealizing metaphors.

In attempting to "express" the transformations, however, Stephen continues to sense the possibility that any "expressive" language will be something supervenient upon "the soft peace of silent spaces," the "oceanic silence" of absolute self-knowledge: "He wanted to meet in the real world the unsubstantial image which his soul so constantly beheld. He did not know where to seek it or how: but a premonition which led him on told him that this image would, without any overt act of his, encounter him. They would meet quietly as if they had known each other and had made their tryst. . . . They would be alone, surrounded by darkness and silence: and in that moment of supreme tenderness he would be transfigured" (*P* 65). The youthful delusion of a possible "transfiguration" is the constant target of the narrator's irony throughout *A Portrait*. This is not to say that Joyce's portrait fails to show the growth of artistic consciousness. In a negative way, it succeeds brilliantly. But Joyce realized that this portrait could not be direct or literal; it could only work through figuration. Consequently, nowhere is the separation between the portraying and the portrayed artists greater than in those moments when Stephen claims to have plumbed the mysteries of literary creation.

❦ ❦ ❦

It is now time to look more closely at the figural processes operating in the representation of that artistic consciousness. One example in particular might clarify the nature of Stephen's artistic conceptions and also pattern the narrative mode to be exploited later in the more radical chapters of *Ulysses*. Toward the end of Chapter III of *A Portrait*, the reader encounters the simple repetition of a relatively meaningless phrase, "hither and thither," in the course of the narration of a dream sequence. At that point in the novel, Stephen has been driven by his fear of eternal damnation to confess his precocious sexual activity. His guilt and fear cause this nightmare:

> A field of stiff weeds and thistles and tufted nettlebunches. Thick among the tufts of rank stiff growth lay battered canisters and clots and coils of solid excrement. . . . Creatures were in the field; one, three, six: creatures were moving in the field, hither and thither. Goatish creatures with human faces. . . . The malice of evil glittered in their

> hard eyes, as they moved hither and thither. . . . Soft language issued from their spittleless lips as they swished in slow circles round and round the field, winding hither and thither through the weeds . . . soft language issuing from their lips, their long swishing tails besmeared with stale shite. . . . (*P* 137-138)

The emphatic repetition of the phrase "hither and thither" is of no significance unless the reader recalls its one earlier use. Hidden by the very transparency of its innocuous, meaningless value, the phrase there was easily passed over in the course of reading. Now, however, in retrospect the innocent words at the beginning of Chapter III acquire a "goatish" if not an excremental significance: "Forms passed this way and that through the dull light. And that was life. The letters of the name of Dublin lay heavily upon his mind, pushing one another surlily hither and thither with slow boorish insistence" (*P* 111).

The neutral phrase reappears in an entirely different context. In Chapter IV Stephen is asked to consider whether he might not have a calling to the priesthood. He enters the director's office, having already guessed the "meaning of the summons," but "an unresting doubt flew hither and thither before his mind. . . . The echoes of certain expressions . . . sounded in remote caves of his mind" (*P* 157). A few pages later, musing over the director's portentous words that the "sacrament of Holy Orders is one of those which can be received only once because it imprints on the soul an indelible spiritual mark which can never be effaced" (*P* 160), Stephen's mind is suddenly invaded by "a din of meaningless words [which] drove his reasoned thoughts hither and thither confusedly" (*P* 161).

The pattern continues but with a difference. Near the end of Chapter IV, Stephen, walking along Sandymount strand, seems to experience a moment of spiritual ecstasy, and the entangling rhetoric of "religion" and "nationality" fall away in favor of the liberating influence of art. A girl glimpsed in midstream, who "seemed like one whom magic had changed into the likeness of a strange and beautiful seabird," suffers his intent gaze, and then draws her eyes from his, all the while "stirring the water with her foot hither and thither." The narrative continues: "The first faint noise of gently moving water broke the silence, low and faint and whispering, faint as the bells of sleep; hither and thither, hither and thither: and a faint flame trembled on her cheek" (*P* 171). The phrase, "hither and thither," with its faint and ambiguous echoes of moral and veridical transgressions, has now changed entirely from a simple adverbial modifier to a vehicle of a developing sub-narrative. Variously developed in the preceding "hither and thither" passages, the topics of guilt, sexuality, language, temptation, and redemption are here brought together by a phrase which of itself has little significant valuc.

One last use of the phrase "hither and thither" occurs in the text, after the delineation of the aesthetic theory and after the writing of the villanelle. By that point in the novel, the simple phrase carries with it charged allusions to the most important categories of life and art. On the steps of the library of the National University in Dublin, Stephen pauses to gaze upon a flock of birds. The aesthetic theory, it should be recalled, had postulated such moments of apprehension as the means by which one could pierce through to the essential meanings of things: "He watched their flight; bird after bird: a dark flash, a swerve, a flash again, a dart aside, a curve, a flutter of wings. . . . Why was he gazing . . . watching their flight? For an augury of good or evil? A phrase of Cornelius Agrippa flew through his mind and then there flew hither and thither shapeless thoughts from Swedenborg on the correspondence of birds to things of the intellect and of how the creatures of the air have their knowledge and . . . unlike man . . . have not perverted that order by reason" (*P* 224-225). The progression of Stephen's thoughts from the empirical birds swirling through the air, to the memory of a literary text, to the creation of a "correspondence" between "birds and things of the intellect," is a *metastatic* movement which veils with subtle rhetorical strands the sleight-of-hand creation of a false identity by virtue of metaphor. This is of course another instance of the quixotic process which we have detailed from Cervantes to Hardy by which narratives transform figural similarities into literal identities. But Stephen's deft metastasis, uniting true knowledge and metaphorical flight, is only the first moment of a still more complicated figural operation.

While the phrase "hither and thither" is in itself neutral and exerts no modification of the surrounding elements of the sentence within which it occurs, the prior, equally neutral, instances of that expression across the pages of the text allow it an accumulation of reference which gradually builds into definable sense. If at any future instance one were to encounter the phrase "hither and thither" in the Joycean text, one could rightly expect that the weight of the accumulated allusions to sensuality, guilt, redemption, and language would immediately come to bear upon that new sentence.[11] For this is the process by which the narrative continually unfolds. A metonymical chain of contingent associations creates a recognizable metaphoric semantic field which can be coded and deciphered, altered and transposed, to gain status as an independently meaningful sign.

Therefore Stephen's theories to the contrary notwithstanding, artistic creation in *A Portrait* does not arise from the perception of essential *quidditas*. Rather, the contamination of the axis of similarity by that of contiguity creates a narrative that testifies to the malaise of the rhetorical episteme of Stephen's aesthetic as it registers such anamolous phenomena that threaten

[11] The phrase appears only rarely in Joyce's later novels. Appropriately enough, it does appear in the "Nausicaa" episode of *Ulysses* (363). There, the interplay of guilt, sensuality, and language are explicitly present as Gertie McDowell prepares to expose herself to Bloom. These themes are discussed by Fritz Senn, "Nausicaa," in *James Joyce's Ulysses: Critical Essays*, ed. Clive Hart and David Hayman (Berkeley: University of California Press, 1974), pp. 277-311. Cf. *Finnegans Wake*, p. 216: "Beside the rivering waters of, hitherandthithering waters of. Night!" (1939; New York: The Viking Press, 1959).

to explode its limits altogether. Joyce's narratives are examples instead of a global semantic field produced by the juxtaposition of the simple elements of everyday linguistic material. Moreover, they are allegories of the seductive power of the meaningless and insubstantial body of the signifier, divorced from a transcendental referent.[12]

On the positive side, as a product of contingent semantic values metonymically associated and extended to form a text grammar, the Joycean metaphor does designate a semantic combination unforeseen by the existing code. The aesthetic quality of this metaphor is produced by contextual elements and by the articulation of paradigmatic traits. As in the "hither and thither" example, each semiotic term is explicable by other terms, and each, in turn, by an infinite chain of interpretations, is potentially interpretable by all other terms. The narrative thus engenders a universal system of reference by stressing the apparent interdependence of contiguous relationships, when, in reality, those relationships have no basis for semantic authority but that of their purely spatial association. One critic has argued that in *Finnegans Wake* ". . . we should try to remain conscious of the dual function of every word. There is a linear function, a contribution to the syntactic complex in which the word stands. . . . Secondly there is a systemic function, a contribution to the tone of the section."[13] This network of contiguous relationships

[12] Phillip Herring observes that "The difficulties in reading *Ulysses* and *Finnegans Wake* are the direct result of Joyce's creative process, which Joyceans, and Joyce himself, have described as that of a mosaic craftsman. . . . Joyce's method was meticulous and exacting; he could never be completely satisfied with anything he wrote. The piecing together of ideas and phrases through the various drafts of *Ulysses*, though his goal was always to give both unity and depth to his mosaic design, resulted from an almost psychotic compulsion" [*Joyce's Ulysses Notesheets in the British Museum* (Charlottesville: Published for the Bibliographical Society of the University of Virginia by the University of Virginia Press, 1972), p. 1]. This mosaic quality of Joyce's later novels is of course evident in *A Portrait of the Artist* too. See also, Umberto Eco, *Le Poetiche di Joyce, Dalla "Summa" al "Finnegans Wake,"* 2nd ed. (Milan: Bompiani, 1971).

[13] Roland McHugh, *The Sigla of Finnegans Wake* (Austin: University of Texas Press, 1976), p. 2.

creates just such a systemic tone in *A Portrait.* It offers a fiction of an authoritative meaning at the center of the labyrinth of language. But this meaning arises from the syntagmatic axis of the narrative line and not from any paradigmatic relations of essential *quiddity.* As it turns out, Stephen's aesthetic theory simply rationalizes the construction of a figural maze which at its center contains a semantic void.

What is achieved by this network of linguistic associations is thus essentially a demystification of the process of creation itself, an implicit rejection of the valorization of metaphor, which since Aristotle has been regarded as "the sign of genius." The metonymies linked by the repeating "hither and thither" phrase initiate a fundamental subversion of Stephen's organic aesthetic theory for which the very essence of the poetic process consists in the perception, and in fact the invention, of essential relations and analogies. Fredric Jameson points out that "the primacy of metaphor is the projection of a literary hierarchy for which poetry and poetic inspiration are felt to be loftier and more noble than the humdrum referential activity of prose."[14] As Roman Jakobson argues, however, the fundamental mechanism of realistic prose is in fact not metaphor but metonymy:

> Following the path of contiguous relationships, the realistic author metonymically digresses from the plot to the atmosphere and from the characters to the setting in space and time. He is fond of synecdochic details. In the scene of Anna Karenina's suicide Tolstoy's artistic attention is focussed on the heroine's handbag; and in *War and Peace* the synecdoches "hair on the upper lip" or "bare shoulders" are used by the same writer to stand for the female characters to whom these features belong.[15]

[14] Jameson, *Fables of Aggression: Wyndham Lewis, the Modernist as Fascist* (Berkeley and Los Angeles: University of California Press, 1979), p. 29.

[15] Jakobson and Morris Halle, *Fundamentals of Language* (The Hague: Mouton, 1956), p. 78. Cited by Jameson.

In Joyce, however, metonymy is placed against metaphor, as its determinate negation: ". . . it thus becomes a sign of the devaluation of inspiration itself and of the art-sentence as a composed, subjectively ripe melodic unit in its own right."[16] This aggressive deconstruction of metaphor and its valorization of organic form and the symbol is just one part of Joyce's assault on Romantic and *fin de siècle* theories of art. His modernity projects the symbolic value of an anti-transcendental text grammar whose capacity for sheer production of sentences stands against the mysteries of poetic creation and the organic primacy of the "beautiful" or the "essential."

In our "hither and thither" example, for instance, the zero-degree phrase is invested with semantic value by virtue of repetition in the context of thematically significant notions such as language, sensuality, and redemption and is itself made a connotative vehicle. The increasing semantic value at each successive repetition in the text occasions the fiction of authoritative meaning. At all times, however, the transformations named in those passages are shown to be derived from a system of neutral associations taken as being correspondences of one another by a mystified consciousness which has forgotten the conceptual nature of his own artifactual productions.

This weave of contiguous relationships is, in effect, the narrative fabric of *A Portrait of the Artist* and finally, explicitly, links all the variant homologues of the novel's themes, each of which appears initially as a useless supplement but is in fact saturated with "pseudo-logical" links and knots. In this narrative weave, the dissemination of artful figures is "not the random scattering of musings toward the infinity of language but a simple—temporary—suspension of affinitive, already magnetized elements."[17] Thus, immediately after Stephen begins to write the villanelle which is to free him from his desire for Emma, Emma reappears in a half-dream and Stephen recalls

[16] Jameson, *Fables of Aggression*, p. 30.
[17] Roland Barthes, *S/Z*, p. 182.

Sunday afternoons long past, visiting in her parlor: "She passed now dancing lightly across his memory as she had been that night at the carnival ball, her white dress a little lifted, a white spray nodding in her hair. She danced lightly in the round. . . . At the pause in the chain of hands her hand had lain in his an instant. . . . [S]he had danced away from him along the chain of hands, dancing lightly and discreetly, giving herself to none" (*P* 219). Emma's dance can stand as an emblem of the rhythmic play of the signifier, repeating along the chain of the linear text, denying a necessary allegiance to any particular referent, and as a symbol of Stephen's allegorical search for the elusive word of essential meaning.[18] The writing of the villanelle is the unversed artist's attempt to hypostatize the play of the signifier and signified, of the desirer and the desired. At this point in the fable, Stephen Dedalus is indeed an artificer, but he is caught in the act of constructing the labyrinth of his discontent. He attempts to create an image of stability, figured as beauty, the image of truth, which will veil the indifferent chaos he senses at all times everywhere around him. But that stability does not exist in the world; it resides only in his imagination, which attempts to draw linear, that is to say, grammatical, diagrams to order and define the world.

Earlier in the text, as Stephen had stood on the Sandymount beach, experiencing one of his mythic moments of spiritual insight into the truth and beauty of things, the narrator had informed us of the direction of Stephen's thoughts. The effect of that moment of static aesthetic pleasure is described in a curious metaphoric progression which speaks of the process I have examined: "His soul was swooning into some new world, fantastic, dim, uncertain as under sea, traversed by cloudy shapes and beings. A world, a glimmer, or a flower? Glimmering and trembling, trembling and unfolding, a breaking light, an open-

[18] Emma, with a "glow in her cheek," is another version of the girl epiphanized on Sandymount strand: cf., "A faint flame trembled on her cheek" (*P* 171).

ing flower, it spread in endless succession to itself, breaking in full crimson and unfolding and fading to palest rose, leaf by leaf and wave of light by wave of light, flooding all the heavens with its soft flushes . . ." (*P* 172). The bodacious transport into "another world" of super-consciousness and perception is characterized as being "spread in endless succession to itself," and thus repeats the structure of syntagmatic accumulations across space which seem to engender significance as in the "hither and thither" passages. Here, however, the chain of contingent successions creates now a metaphoric flower as a vision of orderly organic growth. The rhetorical flower, a mystic bloom unfolding and spreading in response to the light of understanding, too is a product of the seductive physical pleasure of pure linguistic creation. The flowers of Stephen's rhetoric thus continue to exude an intoxicating influence which numbs him and leads him to believe that his own exuberant illusions are privileged expressions of an immanent universal truth.

That self-delusion always makes the young artist think himself to be the ideal interpreter of the universe. Leading up to and contributing to the false image of unity, the reader always encounters the metonymic elements which form the basis for that illusion. Not the least of these chance contingencies exploited into becoming an originating point for the chain of unfounded reference is Stephen Dedalus's own name:

> Now, as never before, his strange name seemed to him a prophecy. . . . Now, at the name of the fabulous artificer, he seemed to hear the noise of dim waves and to see a winged form flying above the waves and slowly climbing the air. What did it mean? Was it a quaint device opening a page of some medieval book of prophecies and symbols, a hawklike man flying sunward above the sea, a prophecy of the end he had been born to serve and had been following through the mists of childhood and boyhood, a symbol of the artist forging anew in his workshop out of the sluggish

matter of the earth a new soaring impalpable imperishable being? (*P* 168-169)

No rare providence has named him after the mythical artificer par excellence, Daedalus, the builder of the Cretan labyrinth. Joyce's choice of name for his character is but one more example, admittedly of a different category, of the fabrication of metaphoric systems which purport to unify the disparate elements of the universe under one totalizing aesthetic vision but which are really mosaics of independent parts.[19] In this passage Stephen is caught in the act of mosaic-building. The dizzying heights to which his discourse impels him, into the upper regions of poetic ecstasy, ever nearer to the flaming point of rhetorical ardor, are extremely dangerous. A fall is always imminent, as the text affirms in the guise of the background voices of the swimming youths: "O, cripes, I'm drowned!" (*P* 169). But the artist has lost himself in himself and does not hear their demystifying cry. The impetus to the preordained fall has always been Stephen's own mind reading "prophecies" where there are but contingent events, and his own words forging "symbols" out of the indifferent "sluggish matter of the earth."

No doubt there is a portent here, and the portent is surely, as Stephen recognizes, that of writing. Thus, when the narrative returns, as it always returns, to the false metaphor of unity, it is specifically in the context of the theme of writing. Whereas the ecstasy of epiphany along the strand, the revelation of the hidden divine principle, had disappeared with the breath that had named it, the second instance of ecstasy is captured in the writing of the villanelle. With that act, writing comes explicitly to the fore as a means of remedying the loss of the substantiating presence of the visions of beauty.

[19] In a letter of 7 October 1921, to Harriet Shaw Weaver, Joyce wrote that "*Ulysses* will be finished in about 3 weeks . . . (if the French printers don't all leap into the Rhone in despair at the mosaics I send them back)" (*Letters of James Joyce*, vol. 1, ed. Stuart Gilbert [New York: Viking Press, 1957], p. 172).

❦ ❦ ❦

Immediately after he has written his villanelle, Stephen pauses, in a passage cited above in reference to the creation of metonymic chains, to reflect on the nature of his newly accepted vocation as an artist: "A sense of fear of the unknown moved in the heart of his weariness, a fear of symbols and portents, of the hawklike man whose name he bore soaring out of his captivity on osierwoven wings, of Thoth, the god of writers, writing with a reed upon a tablet and bearing on his narrow ibis head the cusped moon" (*P* 225). From the complexity of features which form the myth of Thoth, Stephen has drawn but one characteristic, that of Thoth's function as the "god of writing."

Egyptian mythology orders around the figure of Thoth a series of oppositions: speech/writing, life/death, father/son, soul/body, legitimate son/illegitimate orphan, night/day, sun/moon, which are treated along with the myth of the origin of writing.[20] Stephen does not describe the personage of Thoth nor establish his own resemblance to the mythic god of writing. It would be useful to examine this interesting figure more closely.

In the classic study *The Gods of the Egyptians*, E. A. Wallis Budge writes that although the *Book of the Dead* states that Thoth was the companion of Ra, the Sun God, from the very beginning of the time when Ra sprang up from the abyss of Nu, and while the Pyramid Texts establish Thoth as a funereal god, "there is no description in those early works of the functions of the god."[21] For that information one must turn to inscriptions from the later Dynastic Period which name Thoth as "Lord of Khemennu, self-created, to whom none hath given

[20] Jacques Derrida, "La pharmacie de Platon," *La dissémination* (Paris: Seuil, 1972), p. 96; trans. Barbara Johnson, *Dissemination* (Chicago: University of Chicago Press, 1981), p. 84.

[21] *The Gods of the Egyptians* (Chicago: The Open Court Pub. Co.; London: Methuen and Co., 1904), p. 400.

birth, god One," as "he who reckons in heaven, the counter of the stars" and is the "heart of Rā who cometh forth in the form of Thoth." He is the "Lord of divine words."[22] His shrine was in Hermopolis, where one also finds the god called "Thrice great." From this last was derived the epithet "Trismegistos" of the classical writers. Other passages tell that he was the "inventor and god of all the arts and sciences, that he was the *lord of books* and the *scribe of the gods* and *mighty in speech.*"[23]

Another eminent Egyptologist notes that the inscriptions referring to Thoth provide one of the "extremely rare examples in Egyptian texts . . . whereby the God introduces himself in the first person singular: 'I am Thoth, the eldest son of Ra'."[24] Ra, the Sun God of Heliopolis, who coalesces with the supreme deity Ammon to form Ammon-Ra, is the creator who engenders Being directly through the mediation of the word: Ammon-Ra "had but to *speak* in order to create; all beings and all things evoked were born at the sound of his voice."[25] Scholars have also noted that the name of Ammon can be translated to denote a characteristic feature of the god: he is the "Hidden One."[26] As the heart of Ra and the mediating form through which the hidden god is incarnate, Thoth stands close to the source of power.

In Socrates's enchanting version of the myth as related in the *Phaedrus*, Thoth is the demi-god who first discovers or invents the sciences of numerical calculation and the characters of written script. Upon his momentous invention, Thoth, as dutiful vassal to his king and father, offers his treasures in homage to Ammon. In his role as divine arbiter of universal

[22] Budge, pp. 400-401. "Rā" and "Re" are variant transliterations of the same hieroglyphic sign.

[23] Budge, p. 401.

[24] Siegfried Morenz, *Egyptian Religion*, trans. Ann E. Keep (Ithaca: Cornell University Press, 1973), p. 33.

[25] S. Sauneron, *Les Prêtres de l'ancienne Egypte*, p. 123. Cited by Derrida, *Dissemination*, p. 87.

[26] Morenz, *Egyptian Religion*, p. 21.

value, Ammon appraises Thoth's gifts and, after detailed consideration of their positive and negative potential, assigns them value. It is thus the solar deity who consecrates the virtue of Thoth's marvelous inventions and who in accepting or rejecting them constitutes their worth. Writing thus has value only to the extent that Ammon grants it—and he grants it very little:

> When they came to letters, Theuth began: "This invention, O king, will make the Egyptians wiser, and better able to remember, it being a medicine which I have discovered both for memory and wisdom." The king replied: "Most ingenious Theuth, one man is capable of giving birth to an art, another of estimating the amount of good or harm it will do to those who are intended to use it. And so now you, as being the father of letters, have ascribed to them, in your fondness, exactly the reverse of their real effects. For this invention of yours will produce forgetfulness in the minds of those who learn it, by calling them to neglect their memory, inasmuch as, from their confidence in writing, they will recollect by the external aid of foreign symbols, and not by the internal use of their own faculties. Your discovery, therefore, is a medicine not for memory, but for recollection,—for recalling to, not for keeping in mind. And you are providing for your disciples a show of wisdom without the reality. For, acquiring by your means much information unaided by instruction, they will appear to possess much knowledge, while, in fact, they will, for the most part, be disagreeable people to deal with, as having become wise in their own conceit, instead of truly wise."[27]

I quote at length from Socrates's story because it dramatizes so charmingly a scene from the family romance, the instruction

[27] *Phaedrus*, 274-275. I cite the Everyman's Library Edition by Ernest Rhys, *Five Dialogues of Plato Bearing on Poetic Inspiration: Ion, Symposium, Meno, Phaedo, Phaedrus* (1910; London: J. M. Dent; New York: E. P. Dutton, 1913), pp. 270-271. This was Joyce's personal copy and, with Joyce's Trieste Library as a whole, is now in the collection of the Humanities Research Center at the University of Texas at Austin.

by the knowing father of his innocent son. God the father may indeed be a primal illiterate, but his divine ignorance testifies to his sovereign independence, for he has no need of symbolical script. He speaks, he utters, he dictates and his word suffices. Whether or not a scribe in his service supplies a supplementary transcription of his speech acts is a matter of secondary importance. From the Socratic version of the myth, Ammon, god the father who speaks, accepts the homage of his son, even while he deprecates the gift of script.

As Jacques Derrida has pointed out in his masterful discussion of the myth of the origin of writing, Socrates's retelling of the myth is an excellent example of the typical Platonic scheme which ascribes both the origin and the vitality of language, that is of the *logos*, to a *paternal* position. The *logos* is not simply associated with the father; the very origin of the *logos* is the father. "One could say anachronously that the 'speaking subject' is the *father* of his speech. . . . *Logos* is a son, then, a son that would be destroyed in his very *presence* without the present *attendance* of his father. His father who answers. His father who speaks for him and answers for him. Without his father, he would be nothing but, in fact, writing. . . . The specificity of writing would thus be intimately bound to the absence of the father."[28]

Such an absence can of course come to pass in various ways:

[28] Derrida, *Dissemination*, p. 77. In *Of Grammatology*, Derrida also notes that Thoth "occupied the function of the secretary/substitute who usurped first place; of the king, the father, the sun, of their eyes" (p. 328, n. 31). Derrida then cites Jacques Vendier to the effect that "As a general rule, Horus' eye became the lunar eye. The moon, like everything that touched the astral world, intrigued the Egyptians greatly. According to one legend, the moon was created by the Sun-god to replace itself at night: it was Thoth whom Rê designated for the exercise of this high function of substitution. Another myth tried to explain the vicissitudes of the moon by a periodic battle whose protagonists were Horus and Seth. During the combat, Horus' eye was wrenched out, but Seth, finally vanquished, was obliged to return to his victorious opponent the eye that he had lifted; according to another version, the eye returned on its own, or was brought back by Thoth" (*La religion égyptienne* [Paris: P.U.F., 1944], pp. 39-40). These myths of substitution can be related to Stephen's concerns with representation, paternity, and authority.

the son may lose his father to a natural or to a violent death. Socrates insists, in any case, on the pitiable orphan's role which writing always plays with respect to the living spoken word: ". . . it always needs its parent to come to its help, being unable to defend or help itself."[29] The meaning and force of the living *logos* is contingent upon the presence of the father who speaks. Written words, however, at a tertiary remove from the father, are like Dickens's poorest orphans, doomed to wander the world without expectations of paternal support. In Socrates's metaphors, then, Thoth's attempt to return writing to the father is an allegorical attempt to reunite the orphaned supplement of script with its rightful, present, living source.

According to another legend, Thoth's ability to fill in for Ammon's essential absence is the origin of the moon as a substitute for the son: "One day while Ra was in the sky, he said: '*Bring me Thoth,*' and Thoth was straightway brought to him. The Majesty of this god said to Thoth: '*Be in the sky in my place. . . . You are . . . my replacement, and you will be called thus: Thoth, he who replaces Ra.*' "[30]

We can thus sum up the traits of Thoth as the medium of divine speech, the manifestation of supernatural power, and as the representation of the divine Logos. Thoth is god of signification. Through Thoth's mediation of the divine word, the hidden sun is represented to humanity in symbolic script. Yet the message which he delivers is itself derivative from the absolute power of creation figured in the divine speech act of Ammon-Ra; the god of writing is himself a subordinate technocrat without the father's power to create. But as negligible as Thoth's powers may seem in universal terms, he remains nonetheless a significant deity in his role as the manifest performance of his "hidden" father's creating word. With Horus, who stands for Ammon's conceiving mind, Thoth, who repre-

[29] *Phaedrus*, 275e.

[30] Derrida, *Dissemination*, p. 89, citing A. Erman, *La Religion des egyptiens* (Paris, Payot), p. 118.

sents the performative power of language, is always a mediatory presence at the moment of absolute creation. As the god of language, Thoth himself can become an originary force only through a metonymic substitution which displaces the moment of creation from Ammon's enunciatory speech act—*Fiat lucem*—to its belated representation in the word of Thoth. And as in the aesthetic theory where *quidditas* cannot be immediately present but can be perceived only by virtue of the artist's representational discourse, so here the essential source of being can only be signified by Thoth's mediating representation of the divine Logos.

I hope that the reason for our digression to the myth of Thoth will now be apparent. As the "Lord of divine words," a supplement capable of standing in the place of the primary sun-king, and Logos, Thoth contingently appropriates the properties of the Father, who is the supreme origin of the authoritative word. In Joyce's narrative the character equal to that task of replacement and usurpation is Stephen Dedalus. His property, like that of Thoth, is contingency. He himself is the product of that floating indetermination which permits substitution and free play. The paralyzing opposites of art and life, speech and writing, spirituality and sensuality, which the narrative names are merged and made to disappear by the resolution which proclaims Stephen Dedalus the authority who is to "forge . . . the uncreated conscience of [his] race" (*P* 253).

As the substitute for the absent light of day, Thoth, the figure of the spectral moon, is said to represent the possibility of the assimilation of polarities. When Stephen Dedalus aligns himself with this figure, the complex and various strands which the narrative has interwoven finally knot. Dedalus, the "hawklike man," substitutes himself for the "ibis headed god" as a statement of his coming rejection of the authority of the Father (figured variously by Irish art, church, and state) whose word has determined the nature of the Son's linguistic performance.

Like a fallen angel, Stephen thus boldly claims: "I will not serve that in which I no longer believe whether it call itself my home, my fatherland or my church" (*P* 246-247). But that rejection is occasioned by the subtle play of rhetoric which by metastasis shifts the suspicion about the efficacy of the paternal word as a medium of truth into a deluded intuition as to the possibility of escape from the determining structures of language. In *A Portrait of the Artist* the figure of Thoth represents the mythical possibility of the creation of a universal language which would communicate the Word of truth and which would be sanctioned by divine, supreme authority. The delusion about the existence of such a Word is exploded in *Ulysses*, to which we now turn.

❦ ❦ ❦

Joyce's text poses its own unreadability in the continuous ambivalences which affect its very creation. Far from affirming Stephen's project of energizing the insensitively debased value of everyday language by transposing it into ecstatic poetic realms, the rhetorical pattern of the language of Joyce's narrative foregrounds the working of the word in its myriad differential relationships. Stephen's aesthetic theory posed the possibility of "creating imaginary worlds from the revelation of things in themselves, made radiant in a moment of epiphany,"[31] as the *quidditas* of a signified object was allowed to shine through to the perceiver's consciousness. The rhetoric of substitutions of metonymically related differences, however, continually worked against the intention of that project. Stephen continually fails to see that the signifier is not a transparent and neutral form by means of which the artist can pierce through to the "significant heart of things" (*SH* 33). Instead, the linguistic sign continues to resist its own annihilation and insists on its own status as an object in itself, capable of bearing traces of possible

[31] Suzette Henke, *Joyce's Moraculous Sindbook: A Study of Ulysses* (Columbus: Ohio State University Press, 1978), p. 6.

relations with other signs which will affect the accumulation of meaning.

Jonathan Culler has noted that the multiplicity of such relationships "makes meaning not something already accomplished and waiting to be expressed but a horizon, a perspective of semiotic production."[32] Stephen Dedalus's *Portrait* is done in a language which does not "express, press out again, from the gross earth" a communicable, pre-existent sense. Rather, it presents what one critic has rightly described as "*une écriture-science*, a work of language in which the limits of communication are largely undone, exposed, and fractured in a play of the signifier which allows us to see the 'impulse of meaning.' "[33] Gone is the "prefall paradise peace" (*FW* 30) of language. In Joyce's antitranscendental texts, the independent play of the signifier produces an illusion of meaning where in fact there is but a possible meaning (and that haphazardly manufactured); it also subjects any pre-existing ideas which may seem to lie beyond language ready to be translated into human speech to the indeterminacy of chance substitutions and necessary contradictions.[34]

Stephen's aesthetic categories and his fancied notions concerning the creation of meaning in language inform his illusory dreams of a world in which meaning exists ready to be recovered as a "sudden spiritual manifestation" (*SH* 211) rather than as a project to be completed. These categories and deluded notions are continuously deconstructed in and form the narrative of *A Portrait of the Artist as a Young Man*. In an article on *Finnegans Wake*, Stephen Heath claims that the *Wake* is "the construction of a writing that courses through language, causing the signified to slip ceaselessly within the signifier, in order to discover the

[32] *Structuralist Poetics*, p. 106.
[33] Stephen Heath, "Ambiviolences," *Tel Quel* 50 (1972): 65, quoting Philippe Sollers, *Logiques* (Paris: Seuil, 1968), p. 148.
[34] Culler, *Structuralist Poetics*, pp. 106-107.

drama of language, its production."[35] One does not have to turn to *Finnegans Wake*, however, to see the enactment of this semiotic drama. As we have seen, these dramatizations are already explicit in the earlier works, *Stephen Hero* and *A Portrait of the Artist as a Young Man*. However, that drama is most clearly present in *Ulysses*.

To read *Ulysses* is to participate in the production of the text. The reader must collect, collate, cut and reassemble traces of possible meanings and rebind them into a readable text.[36] Reading becomes an enterprise of the creation of meaning. It is an act supplementary to the writing of the text and supplants the unavailable "real" intention of meaning. Joyce forces the reader into total participation in the act of interpretation as he joins the distinct planes of reading and writing into one similar act which is never closed but left open even beyond the final term of the text.

Each successive section of the novel *Ulysses* reveals a new path toward the attainment of the goal of meaning, but that path always leads to other paths which cross and recross at every word of every sentence in paradigmatic juncture. Allusions to prior and succeeding events, repetitions of words and themes, puns, and puns upon puns, half-answered riddles, fragmented parables, and multi-perspectival narratives creates an illusion of a solid presence deep within the linguistic maze.[37] The thread

[35] Heath, *op. cit.*, p. 71. For a related discussion, see also Margot Norris, *The Decentered Universe of Finnegans Wake: A Structuralist Analysis* (Baltimore: Johns Hopkins University Press, 1977).

[36] Ellmann notes that the construction was carried over into the creation of language itself. Joyce, having been asked once whether there were not words enough for him in English, is reported to have replied, "Yes, there are enough, but they aren't the right ones. . . . I'd like a language which is above all language" (*James Joyce*, p. 410). See also the letter of 3 January 1931 to George Antheil: "I am quite content to go down to posterity as a scissors and paste man for that seems to me a harsh but not unjust description" (*Letters*, vol. 1, p. 297).

[37] Ellmann reports that in a conversation with Edmond Jaloux Joyce insisted that *Finnegans Wake* would be written to suit "the esthetic of the dream, where forms prolong and multiply themselves, . . . where the brain uses the roots

which would guide the reader through the labyrinth to the center and back again has always yet to be spun, as the reader is left alone to find his way through the maze of the text.

To read *Ulysses* is thus to enter into the labyrinth and to fabricate a structure from which one can emerge to read again what will always be another text with the same title. *Ulysses* poses itself as a permanent replying of linguistic folds, a constant refolding upon itself, with repose, as of an interstellar flower, ever-opening to reveal not a budding stamen of truth, but an infinitely expandable and reducible non-center.[38] The text is never complete; the "ideal reader suffering from an ideal insomnia" (*FW* 120) is one who responds to that incomplete text not by attempting to master its meaning but by becoming a party to the creation. The reader cannot assume that a creative reading of the novel will attempt to unify the disparate elements of the text, for the text always remains discontinuous; it allegorizes the fragmentation of meaning by posing it as a category permanently deferred.

Joyce's works run the gamut of style available to English language prose, accepting no one style in particular. The multiplicity of styles, however, continually fails to constitute the artist as subject of a narrative of plenitude. On the contrary, in that never-ending process of fabulation the personality of the artist seems to be lost. The reconstitution of his personality thus becomes one of the themes of his narratives. But reconstitution is precisely what is not charted in his stories. Rather, what we see is the creation of a tissue of interrelated words naming and renaming an artificial construct which is provisionally accepted as a deposit of sense. That disappearance and reconstruction of a subject who can define the world is dram-

---

of vocables to make others from them which will be capable of naming its phantasms, its allegories, its allusions . . ." (*James Joyce*, p. 559). This description aptly refers to the function of language throughout great portions of *Ulysses* also.

[38] This is the metaphor the text uses to express the notion of organic totality. See, for instance, *P*, pp. 148 and 172.

atized by the recurrent structure of narratival pastiche, discontinuity, and fragmentation.[39] The "Proteus" episode of *Ulysses* is one instance of the repetition of differences which creates an illusion of continuity despite overt narrative breaks, reinstatements into discarded systems, mutations of signs, and unmotivated detours in search of the proper word which might order the world.

❦ ❦ ❦

In "Telemachus," the initial episode of *Ulysses*, Stephen had found himself chastened by his abortive flight to Paris but still ensnared by the symbolic order which structures Irish society. Its nightmare of historical forces—nationality, language, religion, unconsciously reified by its citizenry to the status of socially symbolic acts which form a seemingly untranscendable horizon—continue to paralyze Stephen's creative imagination. In the "Proteus" episode of the novel we thus find Stephen once again walking on the beach at Sandymount, the scene of important earlier "epiphanies." Stephen begins to muse on the nature of his relationship to the fragmentary external world:

> Ineluctable modality of the visible: At least that if no more, thought through my eyes. Signatures of all things I am here to read, seaspawn and seawrack, the nearing tide, that

[39] This disappearance of the subject often takes place within the context of fluid metaphors. See, for example: "The personality of the artist, at first a cry or a cadence or a mood and then a fluid and lambent narrative, finally refines itself out of existence" (*P* 215). Bloom, "waterlover," dissolves also in a rhetoric of fluidity: he admires "its infallibility as paradigm and paragon: its metamorphoses as vapour, mist, cloud, rain, sleet, snow, hail" (*U* 672). It is also pertinent to note that Nietzsche uses water metaphors to describe the processes of metaphor. See, for instance, "On Truth and Falsehood in Their Extra-moral Sense," *The Complete Works*: man is said to have erected conceptual structures "on a movable foundation and as it were on running water" (2:182). The original metaphoric world was, according to Nietzsche, "an original mass of similes and percepts pouring forth as a fiery liquid out of the primal faculty of human fancy" (p. 184). According to Ellmann, Joyce became familiar with the works of Nietzsche during the period 1903-1904 (*James Joyce*, p. 147).

> rusty boot. Snotgreen, bluesilver, rust: coloured signs. Limits of the diaphane. . . . Stephen closed his eyes to hear his boots crush crackling wrack and shells. . . . I am, a stride at a time. A very short space of time through very short times of space. Five, six: the *nacheinander*. . . . If I fell over a cliff that beetles o'er his base, fell through the *nebeneinander* ineluctably. . . . My two feet in his boots are at the end of his legs, *nebeneinander*. . . . Am I walking into eternity along Sandymount strand?[40]

Stephen still believes his purpose is to "read" the world around him, as he toys with Aristotelean metaphysics to provide the grammar for the proper reading of the book of nature. The "shells" he walks on ("Wild sea money") flash us back to the previous episode, "Nestor," where Stephen, in Mr. Deasy's office, had run his hand over shells "heaped in the cold stone mortar: whelks and money . . . the scallop of St. James . . . dead treasure, hollow shells. . . . Symbols soiled by greed and misery" (*U* 29-30), constructing a weave of semiotic allusions. The shells, like the gold sovereigns in his pocket, are elements of an all-encompassing symbolic network which binds Stephen to the distracting real world.

As he walks on, he encounters two midwives ("*Frauenzimmer*"), and he wonders what one carries in her bag: "A misbirth with a trailing navelcord, hushed in ruddy wool. The cords of all link back, strandentwining cable of all flesh."[41] His meditation creates a vision of humanity linked umbilically to an original source: "Gaze in your omphalos. Hello. Kinch here. Put me on to Edenville. Aleph, alpha: nought, nought, one" (*U* 38). Eve, the mother without a naval, represents the primal

[40] *Ulysses* (1934; New York: Random House, 1961), p. 37. All quotations are from the 1961 corrected New Random House Edition and will be identified hereafter in the body of the text.

[41] *U* 37-38. The phrase "ruddy wool" could well prefigure Bloom's later thoughts of his deceased son, Rudy, wrapped in lamb's wool in "Oxen of the Sun."

source which might offer Stephen relief from the weight of guilt occasioned by his disobedience of his own mother's, his Church's, and his nation's words. Attempting to find a substitute artistic word to supplant the rejected determining codes of "nationality, language, religion," he finds signs all around him, but not the required expiatory one: "Morose delectation Aquinas tunbelly calls this. . . . Language no whit worse than his. Monkwords . . . roguewords . . ." (*U* 47).

A gipsy woman passes him along the shore, and she too seems a prophetic cipher: "Across the sand of all the world, followed by the sun's flaming sword, to the west, trekking to evening lands. . . . Tides, myriad-islanded, within her, blood not mine, *oinopa ponton*, a wine-dark sea. Behold the handmaid of the moon" (*U* 47). She proceeds as if in search of the light which will reveal all true presence, but, significantly, also toward the darkening "evening lands." The procession nonetheless inspires Stephen: "Turning his back to the sun he bent over far to a table of rock and scribbled words" (*U* 48), and he too becomes as a sign amidst the readable universe: "His shadow lay over the rocks as he bent, ending. Why not endless till the farthest star? Darkly they are there behind this light, darkness shining in the brightness, delta of Cassiopeia, worlds. Me sits . . . by day beside a livid sea, unbeheld, in violet night walking beneath a reign of uncouth stars. I throw this ended shadow from me, manshape ineluctable, call it back. . . . Who watches me here? Who ever anywhere will read these written words? Signs on a white field" (*U* 48).

The inseparable projects of reading and writing form the grid of complex associations between the "ineluctable modality of the visible" and the "ineluctable modality of the visuality" (*U* 48) which serves to constitute Stephen as a subjective protean consciousness. What is constituted in the play of signs of the readable world and the perceiving (writing) consciousness is a discontinuity in progress. Consciousness perceives, reshapes, distorts, that is to say, interprets present reality. But the result of that perception is not a unified center of transcendental egotism, a godlike presence capable of "disentangling the subtle soul of the image from its mesh of defining circumstances." Such mythic creative powers elude Stephen even while his search for them provides the matter for Joyce's flamboyant creation.

Searching for the proper word which might fill the abyss between the discontinuities of a physical world and consciousness which can approach that world only through language—"What is that word known to all men?" (*U* 49)—Stephen micturates, as if to join his waters with those of the seas, as if attempting to forge a link to the source of some natural language: "Listen: a fourworded wavespeech: seesoo, hrss, rsseeiss, ooos. . . . It flows purling, widely flowing, floating foampool, flower unfurling" (*U* 49). Wittgenstein writes: "To imagine a language means to imagine a form of life." In these early scenes, Stephen imagines himself a linguistic outcast, the only one among all humanity to whom an integrating imagined language and form of life remain unavailable, as the vital "wavespeech," translated by onomatopoeia into human speech, offers no meaningful sign to solace him.

Stephen's aesthetic had posited a hidden essence, a deeper "immanent" allegorical quiddity or master narrative which might allow itself to be represented by a "universal language, the gift of tongues" (*U* 432). Here, his initial substitution of an immanent radiance for the transcendent radiance which Thomistic ontology had predicated, still operates, but as a play of traces, "signatures," and supplementary interpretations of the natural world. The master signifier that might translate the soul of things into human speech is, however, always lacking, and, as Stephen imagines, still to be found. Nonetheless, the substitution does provide the pattern for other metonymic associations so that the arbitrarily associated elements of the visible spatial world *nebeneinander* seem to coalesce into an authoritatively ordered temporal sequence *nacheinander*, which order in turn then becomes the formal grammar of the visible world. Mere contingency is informed with the Aristotelean necessity of a plotted beginning, middle, and end. This ordering of random events into a meaningful flow now creates the deluding metaphor of the "readable" world. An artificial chain of causal relationships charged with meaning derived from their relation to both origin and end thus seems to emerge from multiple, isolated interpretations, offering Stephen the comfort of a genealogical tie to a primary source. He could scarce continue to speak of the link by "anastomosis" to a primal Eve, for instance, had he come to comprehend that his notion of the revelation of the immanent truth of being is a linguistic construct and therefore, an arbitrary fiction, produced by a seemingly inoffensive play of words: *nebeneinander* becoming *nacheinander*.[42]

This pattern continues to be well established as the determining structure of Stephen Dedalus's reading of the world. In the "Telemachus" episode, for example, he reads the natural rhythm of the sea in a manner which turns an innocent metaphor into another bit of evidence implying a causal force behind nature: "Woodshadows floated silently by through the morning peace from the stairhead seaward where he gazed. Inshore and farther out the mirror of water whitened, spurned by lightshod hurrying feet. White breast of the dim sea. The twining stresses, two by two. A hand plucking the harpstrings merging their twining chords. Wavewhite wedded words shimmering on the dim tide" (*U* 9). From the beginning of the passage we would expect no radical adjustments of the conceived notions of relationships between the natural world and consciousness. The eye gazing out into the external world ascribes to the sea serenity, which exists within the self, as a property of the external world.

From that innocent turn of phrase the narrator ascribes to Stephen another cliché: the sea as a "mirror of water." With

[42] See Henke, *Joyce's Moraculous Sindbook*, pp. 53-65, for a discussion of Gotthold Lessing's definition in *Laocöon* of time as *nacheinander* and of space as *nebeneinander*.

this phrase we move toward more explicit metaphoric patterns that substitute human attributes for sunlight by the figure of personification: ". . . spurned by lightshod hurrying feet. White breast of the dim sea." Inner tranquility is transposed to the external world by the act of "reading," creating the beautifully seductive image of sunlight and sea in human form. With that transference of attributes, the final movement which allows the mute world to express its immutability in the mode of poetic rhythm seems a necessary step: "The twining stresses, two by two."

This metaphoric sequence is of course a deliberate parody on Stephen's part of earlier literary performances of the same sequence of tropes. In fact, "*Epi oinopa ponton*" (*U* 5) suggests a Homeric source. What is significant to note, however, is that the apprehension of the world always implies in Stephen's mind, by analogy, the act of reading which joins the discontinuous elements of mind and external world through the shared property of language: "Wavewhite wedded words." What the one utters in a natural tongue, the other can read and understand, thus creating a span between the material world and consciousness, and allowing for the play of substitutes by means of which later claims of totalization can be made. In the wake of those "wavewhite wedded words" all later transformations of metonymies into metaphors are authorized.

Throughout the early parts of *Ulysses*, Joyce thus extends the social and psychological nets which hold Stephen's soul in bondage. The "nightmare of history" is now represented as a universal problem, not simply as a provincial Irish one. But Stephen clings to his vision of himself as the artist-god determined to transform his world into imperishable art.[43] To effect this transformation, Stephen seeks the symbolic word, the totalizing metaphor, whereby his soul might "express itself in unfettered freedom" (*P* 246). Full seduction by this totalizing

[43] E. L. Epstein discusses the problems of history in "Nestor," *James Joyce's Ulysses: Critical Essays*, ed. Clive Hart and David Hayman, pp. 17-28.

metaphor can occur only when the initial transfer of properties from consciousness to external world is formalized by the narcissistic identification of world with mind: ". . . in my mind's darkness a sloth of the underworld, reluctant, shy of brightness, shifting her dragon scaly folds. Thought is the thought of thought. Tranquil brightness. The soul is in a manner all that is: the soul is the form of forms. Tranquility sudden, vast, candescent: form of forms" (*U* 26). As is so often the case in Joyce, the transfer is carried out by the beam of light which radiates from the source of understanding. The mind in darkness, "a sloth of the underworld," is illumined by the "candescent tranquility" created by the perception of the *quidditas* of any other external entity, be it object or another mind.

This brightness on darkness, it will be remembered, is the primary characteristic in Stephen's description of the nature of writing and of his own existence: the poem begun on Sandymount strand was a pattern of dark "Signs on a white field" (*U* 48), while his "shadow . . . [which] lay over the rocks as he bent writing" (*U* 48) was another darkness on brightness. The association also causes him to recall his own signature inscribed in the heavens, "delta in Cassiopeia" (*U* 48), and finally leads to the complete unification of the notions of light and dark, soul and matter, male and female which in the binary logic of Stephen's aesthetic are associated with the inward, imaginary world of reading and writing: "You find my words dark. . . . Our souls, shamewounded by our sins, cling to us yet more, a woman to her lover clinging . . ." (*U* 48). This transfer is carried out by the analogies which result from the primary association of soul with radiance and femininity.[44]

The transfer follows an established pattern of substitution: light on dark, man on woman, all tinged, however, by the remnant of guilt carried over from Stephen's earlier combinations of the rhetoric of piety with that of sensuality. From the

[44] Here, as in *A Portrait* ("his soul . . . she sank"), the grammatical gender of *soul* (f., *anima*) forms the basis of the personifying metaphor.

moment that self can unite with world through the act of reading, the fragmented experience of reality can be made continuous by the wholesale application of metaphor to describe what are really metonymic associations. Stephen must constantly force himself to turn away from the seductive rhetoric of church, state, and family for it is formed by abuses as threatening as those of his own discourse.[45] In *Ulysses* as in *A Portrait*, Stephen has yet to emerge from the mystified belief that his metaphorical constructs are authoritative expressions of the nature of things; the text continually points out rather that it is in the chain of these constructions that meaning insists, for none of its individual elements as such consists in meaning.

❦ ❦ ❦

Stephen's Shakespeare lecture in the National Library in the "Scylla and Charybdis" episode is one more manifestation of his preoccupation with language as the scene for the discovery of the hidden word which might order all reality. From *A Portrait* we know that Stephen has accepted the mission implied by his mythological name. "Now as never before his strange name seemed to him a prophecy," we are told, and Stephen identifies himself with the "fabulous artificer," the "hawk-like man" as a "symbol of the artist forging anew in his workshop out of the sluggish matter of the earth a new soaring impalable imperishable being." His recognition of his mythopoeic role, notes Ellmann, "is accomplished like a late puberty"; for Stephen, "To mature is to become archetypal, to recognize one's place in the role of entrepreneurs of the spirit."[46] Putting his biological father and fatherland aside, Stephen seems at the end of *A Portrait* free to choose "a mythical fatherland in the land

[45] Cf. *P* 244: "The soft beauty of the Latin word touched with an enchanting touch the dark of the evening, with a touch fainter and more persuading than the touch of music or of a woman's hand."

[46] Ellmann, *Consciousness of Joyce*, p. 16.

of the spirit."[47] The linguistic nets ("Weave, weaver of the wind"—*U* 25) strung across *A Portrait* and carried over to *Ulysses* gradually seek to gather the divergent categories of linguistics and paternity under one metaphysical system. Hence, it is not surprising to encounter once again Stephen's mind returning to the multiform myths which structured his previous flights into the heights of rhetorical ardor.

Recalling the last words of *A Portrait*, "Old father, old artificer, stand me now and ever in good stead" (*P* 253), Stephen now chides himself with self-sarcasm: "Fabulous artificer, the hawklike man. You flew. Whereto? Newhaven-Dieppe, steerage passenger. Paris and back. Lapwing. Icarus. *Pater, ait.* Seabedabbled, fallen, weltering. Lapwing you are" (*U* 210). The "vital sea" of *A Portrait* has become the scene of "salt green death" (*U* 243). Stephen seems now to pass easily between the roles of father and son, capable of playing both Daedalus and Icarus at once. In *Ulysses* the possibilities of mythical union seem almost endless, all real and imaginary fathers and sons being eligible for fusion.[48] After the fall, however, the artist is no wiser than before. His project remains the grand one of determining the existence of an immutable world to give impetus, order, and meaning to linguistic creation. It is in the context of the family romance that Stephen now narrates his interpretation of Shakespeare's *Hamlet*, for he sees Shakespeare as he who accomplished the seemingly impossible task of fathering a narrative to smooth over the incoherences of personal experience.

That accomplishment is, however, not without its price, a price which Stephen is more than willing to pay in exchange for the release from literary impotence. According to Stephen's interpretation, the price of Shakespeare's creativity was banishment, as symbolized by his role as ghost in *Hamlet*: ". . . banishment from the heart, banishment from home. . . . It

[47] Ibid., p. 18.
[48] Ellmann, *Consciousness of Joyce*, pp. 18-19.

doubles itself in the middle of his life, reflects itself in another, repeats itself, protasis, epitasis, catastasis, catastrophe" (*U* 212). Stephen feels much in common with both figures, the ghost of King Hamlet as played by Shakespeare, and the young Prince Hamlet, one the spectral absence within presence, the other a formal presence without essence.[49] King Hamlet is said to be "a ghost, a shadow now . . . the sea's voice, a voice heard only in the heart of him who is the substance of his shadow, the son consubstantial with the father" (*U* 197).

The theory thus becomes another version, a transformation, of Stephen's original structuring myth of the transcendental signified, of the primary logos of a universal language which would allow the assimilation of differentials in a coherent and aesthetically meaningful narrative. The *figure* of the father, as a symbol of the primary signifier, is the element which might regulate the function of all other elements within the system. The *name* of the father constitutes the system of substitutions, set up by the father, from which all other signifiers can proceed and to which all can be linked to form a genealogical point of origin. This notion of fatherhood, however, as in all previous versions of Stephen's myth, is a fanciful construct, filling the gap left by the recession of the original Word. The father comes to stand, according to Stephen, in the place of the absent fixed point from which all existential categories (love, desire, guilt,

[49] For a detailed discussion of the correspondences between Stephen Dedalus and Shakespeare in Stephen's reading of *Hamlet*, see William M. Schutte, *Joyce and Shakespeare* (New Haven: Yale University Press, 1957), esp. pp. 90ff. See also the compatible discussion by Colin MacCabe, *James Joyce and the Revolution of the Word* (New York: Barnes & Noble, 1979), pp. 69-132, and "The Voice of Esau: Stephen in the Library," in *James Joyce: New Perspectives*, Colin MacCabe, ed. (Brighton: The Harvester Press; Bloomington: Indiana University Press, 1982), pp. 111-128. Hugh Kenner points out that the *Portrait* "is unified by Stephen's twenty years' effort to substitute one father for another. . . . Fatherhood is rather a role than an estate; to shift fathers is for the son, too, to shift roles, to be no longer the son of a drunken bankrupt but heir to the vocation of the fabulous artificer" (*Ulysses* [London: George Allen & Unwin Ltd., 1980], pp. 10-11).

etc.) proceed in necessary order as the primary rule of syntax which governs the metonymic movement of signs in a sentence.

Stephen realizes the fictional status of this symbolic father (he has, after all, rejected traditional ontology, which poses a transcendental God as the defining entity), but he surreptitiously puts that transcendence back into a diacritical system with the ruse of the metaphor of immanent radiance. *Quidditas* has always been Stephen's referent for the lost point of origin. The fiction of presence marks the circle of meaning which arbitrarily relates signification to reality while, in fact, if a signifier can be said to refer to a signified, it is only through the mediation of the entire system of other signifiers: ". . . there is no signifier that doesn't refer to the absence of others and that is not defined by its position in the system [of signifiers]."[50] "Paternity," says Stephen at one point, "may be a legal fiction. Who is the father of any son that any son should love him or he any son?" (*U* 207.) In the "market-place," the name of the father is the signifier for the function performed by the procreator. But the legal definition of paternity is "a mystical estate . . . founded, like the world, macro- and microcosm, upon the void. Upon incertitude, upon unlikelihood" (*U* 207). The circularity and apparent autonomy of language lead to the postulation of a necessary presence to fill the void. Meaning, in the form of a fictive father ("a necessary evil"), is constructed to organize the void. As Stephen also understands, that fiction founded on the void is the most stable of fictions because it cannot be revealed as fiction without putting the entire system of signification into question: "No later undoing will undo the first undoing" (*U* 196).

It is this ruse, the filling of the primordial gap by the fiction of fatherhood, which allows causal substitution to take place where in reality there exists only a tenuous link," "an instant of blind rut" (*U* 208), between father and mother to link father

[50] Jean Laplanche and Serge Leclaire, "The Unconscious," *Yale French Studies* 48 (1972): 154.

and son. "*Amor matris*, subjective and objective genitive, may be the only true thing in life" says Stephen (*U* 207), but even that relationship is one created by the grammatical metaphor of possession. The constituting paternal metaphor is of course open to numerous transformations, as Stephen notes. "Sabellius, the African, subtlest heresiarch of all the beasts of the field, held that the Father was Himself His Own Son" (*U* 208), thereby positing the closure of the distance between the Word and the Word made Flesh, between God the Father and God the Son, who comes to humanity to be in His Father's stead as a sign of eternal salvation. While traditional church doctrine since Augustine has viewed a person's soul as an image of the Trinity, the Sabellian statement makes the Son, the manifestation, a perfect repetition of God in the outer world.[51]

Aquinas opposes this interpretation in order to establish the case that procession in God implies a relationship of *origin* between Father and Son. William Noon explains that "when Aquinas says there are processions in God he means simply that there are real relations of origin in God."[52] The origin of the Son is therefore in the manner of semantic generation: He is the consubstantial image of the divine intellect—a sign of the differential without discontinuity or subordination. Father and Son thus form a perfect relationship in which the speech act of the Father is manifested instantaneously in the substantial form of the Son. Through the Incarnation, Christ becomes the phenomenal sign of transcendental self-presence, both messenger and message of divine self-sufficiency and unity. The import of Christ's life is that it provides the one, aesthetically complete, instance when sign and signified obtain in perfect cohesion, the one instance when sign and signified are anchored firmly to one another in an authentic relationship of unity. In *A Portrait*, Stephen's vision of himself as a "fosterchild" (*P* 101) had hinted at his secret desire for the appearance of a mythical father who,

[51] Noon, p. 110.
[52] Ibid., p. 111.

in embodying the name of Dedalus, might also have served to fix the identity of the son as different from but sharing in the creating father. Now, Stephen wishes to appropriate for and attribute to Shakespeare, the fictional hero of his parable of fatherhood, these same qualities.

In the Shakespearean word, the play *Hamlet*, for instance, the discontinuities which block the expression of the creative word are assimilated within the sign of the Father, who constitutes the possibility of creation and who utters the "universal language" which makes truth available to all humanity and guarantees their mutual understanding: "When Rutlandbaconsouthamptonshakespeare or another poet of the same name in the comedy of errors wrote *Hamlet* he was not the father of his own son merely but, being no more a son, he was and felt himself the father of all his race, the father of his own grandfather, the father of his unborn grandson who, by the same token, never was born . . ." (*U* 208). Stephen thus creates a triple-tiered parallel among God the Father, who constitutes instantaneous meaning by the very fact of His existence and who can represent the Word to humanity in the figure of His Son; Shakespeare, who is, like Thoth, a "lord of language" (*U* 196); and himself, a father-seeking stand-in son.[53] The literary faculty invents a fictional theology, which analogically justifies the secondary creation of a myth about authentic creativity, which finally imparts the possibility of an aesthetic ideology to guarantee the proper expression of reality.

This conceptualization of fatherhood as the possibility of substituting one sign for another (with the Son as a representation of organic continuity), on the basis of a resemblance which hides differences, is the theory which Stephen by analogy uses to concoct his model for artistic creation.

And since Stephen takes fatherhood as the conceptualization of relationships, fatherhood actually becomes a sign of those

[53] Cf. *P* 253. Stephen there defines his role as that of the exiled Son who will recreate the "conscience of his race."

relationships and not their cause. It literalizes the referential indetermination of the statement which poses a desire for a verifiable genealogy into a specific unit of reference. The name of the father refers to the proper mode of relationships between distinct but similar entities. As such, fatherhood is the Dedalan paradigm for the process of linguistic creation and self-integration. And by raising his need for the denseness of artistic being implied by Shakespeare's presence to the level of symbolization, Stephen discharges his need for a literal father. In this action, Stephen also sublimates the name, that is to say, the sign, of the father to the function of a signifier and reality to the sophistication of signification, all the while constructing the symbolic gridwork on his own ego.[54] Searching for the other, he thus constitutes himself: "We walk through ourselves, meeting robbers, ghosts, giants, old men, young men, wives, widows, brothers-in-love. But always meeting ourselves" (*U* 213), says Stephen. As regards the integrity of the conceiving ego, Stephen assumes that the self is constituted on the basis of the image of the speculary other. The imaginary relationship of the subject to his own ego is thus basically narcissistic: subjectivity presents itself to itself through a stand-in. But Stephen seems willing to go one step further than any banal Freudianism. The ego is not *simply* narcissistic—the idea of the self based on the image of the other can exist only by virtue of the fact that the self *is* the other. Having earlier seen himself as a unified image, Stephen now begins to suspect that in seeing his being in relation to others, he also sees the fragmentary quality of his existence.[55]

[54] On the heterogeneous creation of the language-using subject, see Jacques Lacan, "Subversion du sujet et dialectique du désir," *Écrits* 2 (Paris: Seuil, 1971), pp. 151-191. See also the discussion "On the Subject of Lacan" by Rosalind Coward and John Ellis in *Language and Materialism: Developments in Semiology and the Theory of the Subject* (London: Routledge & Kegan Paul, 1977), pp. 93-121.

[55] Lacan, "The Function of Language in Psychoanalysis," Wilden, ed., pp. 39-45. Ellmann mentions that Joyce had in his possession in Trieste Jung's *The Significance of the Father in the Destiny of the Individual* (1909), Freud's *A Childhood Memory of Leonardo da Vinci* (1910), where the relation of early

Actual language does not use the name of the "son" as the conceptual term—it uses the name of the other. But this other, which for Stephen is always his own reflection, is a being created by one's own conceptualization.

It goes without saying, of course, that in turn and as in a confederacy of wills, the father also conceives himself by his conception of the son, a being who is himself at best a possible suspension of the real differences between fathers and sons. Stephen well knows that in the beginning was the Word. Now from the trace of the father's literal absence Stephen constructs a spiritual presence in the production of the symbolic universe. Hence in a very real psychological sense Stephen is correct to accord to the son a symbolic paternity and to see him, in his multifarious forms, as the father of his own father, able to reconceive him in the mind as a symbol, for the totality of the referential father can be controlled and manipulated through the representation of a stand-in: the linguistic sign.[56] The order imposed on the world by linguistic manipulation of differences is mirrored by the spectral self-creation of human relationships and demonstrates an insistent verbal defense against the chaotic phenomenal field of everyday existence by the creation of an illusion which is capable of maintaining the consistency of fiction. Thus, even while piercing the nature of the metaphysical construct, Stephen continues to have faith in its efficacy for authentic truth expression.

---

memories to works of art is displayed, and the earliest version of Ernest Jones's, *The Problem of Hamlet and the Oedipus Complex* (1911). The library also includes *On the Psychopathology of Everyday Life* (1917). His possession of the pamphlets, argues Ellmann, "strongly suggests that he [Joyce] knew about psychoanalysis" several years before his stay in Zurich. Ellmann adds that "The relevance to Joyce of this new way of thinking about the mind can hardly be overstressed. The three essays 'burst in upon his porcelain revery' with their transformations, combinations, and divisions of the self, their picture of its abasements and suppressed appetites and ambivalences, which were as yet largely untapped for conscious literature" (*Consciousness of Joyce*, p. 54).

[56] Coward and Ellis explain in these terms the subject's attempt "to master the symbolic function" (*Language and Materialism*, p. 105).

It is, consequently, no surprise to find in this context that Stephen's mind returns to myths which had structured his previous flights into the heights of rhetorical self-delusion: "Coffined thoughts around me, in mummycases, embalmed in spice of words. Thoth, god of libraries, a birdgod, moonycrowned. And I heard the voice of that Egyptian priest. *In painted chambers loaded with tilebooks*" (*U* 193). Thoth, it will be remembered, was to be the stand-in of Ra, the hidden sun god, the absent father of all things. The unity of configurations proposed by the "Scylla and Charybdis" episode is based on the efficacy of a representative word such as that of Thoth, the creation of being and all life, paternity and filiation. Thoth is the son who usurps the place of the absent father and establishes himself as a sign of autonomy.[57] Father-tending, heliotropic Thoth bears the sign of Ammon-Ra, the hidden, sun father, and interprets it. His word, consequently, is derivative from and subordinate to the primal word of the absolute Creator. But Thoth cannot be a perfect mediator, a mythologically pure channel in a system of divine telecommunications. On the contrary, he introduces into human history the plurality of different languages.[58] It is thus far more correct to see Thoth as the author of difference. With his mediating word, he supplants the father, the holy word, while being his annunciatory sign.

Jacques Derrida thus notes in "Plato's Pharmacy" that "the figure of Thoth is opposed to its other (father, sun, life, speech, origin or orient, etc.), but as that which at once supplements and supplants it. . . . But it thereby opposes *itself*, passes into its other, and this messenger-god is truly a god of the absolute passage between opposites. . . . The god of writing is thus at

[57] Stephen has called Shakespeare "a ghost by absence, and in the vesture of buried Denmark, a ghost by death" (*U* 189). While Thoth constitutes himself by assuming the place of the Father, Stephen's Shakespeare constitutes himself by assuming the place of a Father-creating Son. The myths are thus mirror reflections of one another. By this point in *Ulysses* Joyce clearly had recognized the limitations of proceeding single-mythedly.

[58] Morenz, *Egyptian Religion*, pp. 25-26.

once his father, his son, and himself. He cannot be assigned a fixed spot in the play of differences. . . . Thoth is never present. Nowhere does he appear in person. No being-there can properly be *his own*."[59] Thoth is never present as himself because he always appears instead of another: as such, he is the emblem par excellence of the linguistic sign. The significant metaphor which associates Stephen Dedalus, "the hawklike man," with Thoth, "the ibis-headed god," represses the force of difference behind the innocent acceptance of the possibility of an integrating representation.

In both *A Portrait of the Artist as a Young Man* and *Ulysses* Stephen is associated with a figure who supplants another figure of unmediated presence. The ideal "fluid and lambent narrative" into which the personality of the artist could be assimilated had represented for Stephen the scene of a possible subjective self-integration. It created the metaphor of a genealogical link to a hidden totalizing source of truth and beauty. By inspiring life into the world in the form of a vital narrative, the artist could then properly think of himself as simultaneously his own creator, the product of that creation, and as himself in himself. He could feel himself "the father of all his race, the father of his own grandfather, the father of his unborn grandson" (*U* 208). That movement, however, fails to constitute him as one, definable entity. Rather, by representing always another, he is never himself. This displacement of differences is the movement by which the narrative of *Ulysses* constitutes itself as a history, but in that movement of displacement the notions of a simple origin, of a source, of an unmediated presence is completely subverted.

Stephen Dedalus is the figure of Joyce's allegory of the mystified search for the Word which will serve as the foundation for a universal language. With the figure of Leopold Bloom, the text makes the parable of the search for a missing son the

[59] Derrida, *Dissemination*, pp. 92-93.

vehicle for the deconstruction of Stephen's mystified project. Bloom does not possess a more privileged word than that of Stephen; he simply utters its homologue. The juxtaposition of his word with that of Stephen, however, does create the sublime pathos of the novel *Ulysses*.

❦ ❦ ❦

Language is among the several of Leopold's preoccupations as he emerges into the sunlight on Bloomsday. In the act of confronting the world Bloom too confronts only his own reflection in the act of interpreting the world: "Wander along all day. Might meet a robber or two" says Bloom (*U* 57), as he anticipates Stephen's statement in "Scylla and Charybdis" that "we walk through ourselves, meeting robbers, ghosts, giants. . . . But always meeting ourselves" (*U* 213) and his own later thought that "Think you're escaping and run into yourself" (*U* 377). As he steps into the sunlight, he begins to muse: "Somewhere in the east: early morning: set off at dawn, travel round in front of the sun, steal a day's march on him. Keep it up for ever never grow a day older technically. . . . Kind of stuff you read: in the track of the sun. Sunburst on the title page" (*U* 57). Dublin, bathed in radiance, becomes for Bloom a scene of writing and interpretation, as if the sun "Wants to stamp his trademark on everything" (*U* 378).

Marked on its walks, shop advertisements, bookstalls and emitted from the mouths of the people of Dublin, the "trademark of the sun" imprints itself on Bloom and finally transforms, in this scene from "Calypso," humanity into its own image: "Quick warm sunlight came running from Berkeley Road, swiftly, in slim sandals, along the brightening footpath. Runs, she runs to meet me, a girl with gold hair on the wind" (*U* 61). This metonymic desubstantialization of human form into "sunlight," together with the previously established association between the images of the "sun" and "sunlight" with the theme of language, point out the parallel between Stephen's and Bloom's metaphor-creating tendencies. From the fragmented, discontinuous phenomena of the world, they construct multiple associations whose intersections produce the appearance of solidity and continuity. With Bloom, consequently, we remain in a narrative movement which seems to progress from a definable origin toward a definitive goal, a meaningful point at the end of the totality of individual sentences which refer to his actions.

In the "Lotus Eaters" episode, the text shifts from solar to floral metaphors as Leopold blossoms into "Henry Flower." Reacting against the frustrations of his nonexistent sexual life, he has begun an affair with Martha Clifford, an affair, however, that exists only on paper. The improper "anonymous letters" (*U* 465) which become the signs of his guilt and humiliation later in the nightmares of the "Circe" episode ("He implored me to soil his letters in an unspeakable manner, to chastise him as he richly deserves"—*U* 467) here create a Bloom where there is none. This proxy flower represents a nonexistent figure, for Bloom, even in his own *persona,* is always someone other than himself: cuckolded husband of Molly, usurped protector of Milly, dupe of Dublin's Irish citizenry, son-seeking father of Rudy.

Walking along, he opens a letter newly arrived from Martha to find a flower enclosed. He tears the flower from its pinhold and smells its "almost no smell" and thinks: "Language of flowers. They like it because no-one can hear." He reads the letter again: "Angry tulips with you darling manflower punish your cactus if you don't please poor forgetmenot how I long violets to dear roses when we soon anemone meet all naughty nightstalk wife Martha's perfume" (*U* 78). A few pages later, at the end of the chapter, Bloom thinks of taking a bath and foresees his own body becoming a flower: "He saw his trunk and limbs riprippled over and sustained, buoyed lightly upward, lemonyellow: his naval, bud of flesh: and saw the dark tangled curls of his bush floating, floating hair of the stream around the limp father of thousands, a languid floating flower" (*U* 86).

Both Bloom's severe parody of Martha's letter and his more luxurious vision of his own body transforming into a flower are manifestations in the "language of flowers" of a thought which remains to be deciphered from the text. As a puissant rhetorician, Joyce would know that "flowers of speech" is a traditional designation for the metaphors and figurative language that characterize literary discourse and distinguish it from referential or more scientific kinds of writing. Joyce now links figurative language, or flowers of speech, with the "language of flowers," or the principle of euphemistic or courtly diction.[60] He depicts what are in the eyes of Dublin's bourgeois society Bloom's perverse and unspeakable desires by a flowery style. When unspeakable thoughts do emerge into the light of language, metaphor too of necessity arises, for it is precisely the work of metaphor to disguise the impropriety of the literal signified behind the transforming mask of the figural signifier. So Bloom's expressions of sexual desire, of love for a departed son, of nostalgia for a past time of sensual wholeness can only be spoken through an indirection which names something else as a preoccupation of the mind. The indirection of the language of flowers is not, however, with Bloom, as it is with Stephen, a result of delusion. Rather, the origin of metaphor is for Bloom the condition of sense. Metaphor has become the only manner of expressing his "unspeakable" desires. Any expression which resists the "Flower to console me . . . language of flow" (*U* 263) will as a consequence remain foreign and inexpressible on Bloomsday.

In "Nausicaa," Bloom's language of flowers becomes a lit-

[60] In *Finnegans Wake* Joyce will refer to it as "the languish of flowers" (*FW* 96) and as a "florilingua" (*FW* 117). The *Dictionnaire de l'Academie Française* (1694 edition) offers this definition for the language of flowers: "Langage symbolique dans lequel les fleurs, soit isolées, soit assemblées, suivant un certain choix, servent à exprimer une pensée, un sentiment secret." Cited by Geoffrey Hartman in *Saving the Text: Literature/Derrida/Philosophy* (Baltimore: Johns Hopkins University Press, 1981), p. 94. See also p. 125 on the "flowers of speech." To paraphrase Hartman, we might say that Joyce uses the language of flowers not to inform but to evoke; as the guardian of the symbolic and differential realms, it is always *dia-logos*.

erally flowery rhetoric, but even there metaphoric flowers arise to name indirectly the notions of sensuality, desire, and language. After her self-exposure (a "wondrous revealment half offered"—*U* 366) Gertie McDowell meets Bloom's glance with her own full "sweet flowerlike face" (*U* 367). As she turns to leave, she wafts her handkerchief in the breeze. Slowly, across seven pages of text, the scent of her perfume floats toward Bloom, a synaesthesia of the silent sexual language that had passed between them: "Wait. Hm. Hm. Yes. That's her perfume. Why she waved her hand," and Bloom proceeds to read its import. "I leave you this to think of me when I'm far away on the pillow. What is it? Heliotrope? No, Hyacinth? Hm. Roses, I think. . . . Molly likes opoponax . . . with a little jessamine mixed. Her high notes and her low notes" (*U* 374). The language of flowers, itself a figural displacement of sexual deprivation, fills the space between Gertie and Bloom, as if promising to fill the void of her absence. That displacement is itself immediately displaced by metaphors which lead to Molly as emblem of plentitude and self-sufficiency. Gertie is mere *simulacrum* of Molly, as her perfume is a poor imitation of Molly's scent, which is also her voice.[61]

The interesting flower in this garden is the heliotrope. Formerly, heliotrope was the name applied to the sunflower, marigold, or any plant the flowers of which turn toward the sun.

[61] Molly is of course herself a flower. See *U* 176 ("Flowers her eyes were"), 284 (Molly's "crocus dress"), 652 (she is "in the full bloom of womanhood"), 759 (Molly imagines one "Don Miguel de la Flora" and recalls that "there is a flower that bloometh"), and 783 (she is a "mountain flower"). In the *Odyssey*, Ulysses is given as amulet by Hermes, the Greek analogue of Thoth, a "magic plant . . . black root and milky flower—a *molü* in the language of the gods—" (Book X, 286-314, trans. Robert Fitzgerald [New York: Doubleday, 1961]) to ward off the temptations of Circe. Ellmann quotes Joyce: "Hermes . . . is an accident of providence. In this special case his plant may be said to have many leaves, indifference due to masturbation, pessimism congenital, a sense of the ridiculous . . ." (*James Joyce*, p. 511). Randolph Splitter points out the shared floral imagery in Joyce and Proust in *Proust's Recherche: A Psychoanalytic Interpretation* (Boston: Routledge & Kegan Paul, 1981), pp. 63-76.

Now, it names a plant with small clustered, purple flowers commonly cultivated for fragrance.[62] Bloom has both meanings of the word in mind, for as he stands on the beach, the sun begins to set and his mind begins weaving together the previous strands of thought into a single pattern. He remembers that the "Best time to spray plants [is] in the shade after the sun" (*U* 376) and then returns to the idea of the heliotrope: woman are described as "Open[ing] like flowers, know their hours, sunflowers" (*U* 376). His sunward-turning flowers are the metaphors of the single over-riding obsession on his mind today—the possibility of stamping his mark (as the sun "Wants to stamp his trademark on everything") on the fluid phenomena of ever-changing differences by the conception of a son to be in the place of the one he has lost. But the possibility that such a script will come to pass seems now impossibly remote.

In succession, then, the solar and floral metaphors which name the intersection of the other concepts (sexuality, paternity, and even language) increasingly create a weave of metaphoric inter-reference. Bloom becomes more and more the sun-tending heliotrope, while Stephen comes increasingly to stand for that lost son (sun)[63] until, in the "Oxen of the Sun" episode, the association is made virtually explicit.[64]

[62] *OED*, s. v. "heliotrope." Walter W. Skeat's *Concise Etymological Dictionary of the English Language* (1882; Oxford: The Clarendon Press, 1911), Joyce's dictionary of choice, offers: *heliotrope*—a flower. lit. 'sun-turner'; from its turning to the sun. (F.-L.-Gk.).

[63] The son-sun pun becomes especially plausible if one compares *Ulysses* (1934 edition), "The *son* unborn mars beauty" (p. 205), with *Ulysses* (1961 edition), "The *sun* unborn mars beauty" (p. 207), where the context seems to call for *son*. Neither the facsimile placards nor page proofs show emendations of the 1934 version. See *The James Joyce Archive* facsimile of page proofs for *Ulysses* Episodes 7-9, Michael Groden, ed. (New York and London: Garland Publishing, 1978), p. 316. See also *U* 637: "washed in the blood of the sun," which metastasizes 'blood of the *lamb*' into 'blood of the *son*,' which finally becomes 'blood of the *sun*.'

[64] Bloom is continually portrayed gazing at the sun, standing in the sun, reading the stars, and in situations generally associated with the heavens. Some examples: *U* 61, 71, 164, 166, 345 (Bloom, "having raiment as of the sun"),

In the maternity hospital, "Leopold that had of his body no manchild for an heir looked upon him [Stephen] his friend's son and was shut up in sorrow for his forepassed happiness and as sad . . . that him failed a son of such gentle courage . . ." (*U* 390). Stephen, as has always been prefigured by the prior associations with the figure of Thoth, here becomes the representation for Bloom of the departed son. Further on, Bloom again in reverie ("a mirror within a mirror"—*U* 413) becomes amid the boisterous students "paternal" and imagines that "these about him might be his sons." "Who can say?" the narrator asks, for "The wise father knows his own child" (*U* 413). Memory and daydream recede and Bloom is left with neither son nor woman to "bear the sunnygolden babe of day": "No, Leopold! Name and memory solace thee not. . . . No son of thy loins is by thee. There is none now to be for Leopold, what Leopold was for Rudolph" (*U* 413-414). Metaphors, an effect of substitution and displacement and a manifestation of analogy, will thus be a means of satisfying desire until that proper son can be re-conceived. However, Bloom cannot be content with mere metaphor and continues to seek a form of discourse which will lead to truth in all its fullness. Rather than finding truth, however, Bloom continues to find only other metaphors which in an impossible combination attempt to describe the fact of paternity.

Since Molly is unavailable to bear the son, Bloom creates replacements, metempsychotic Mollies, and metaphors to take the place of the real source of life. As he does so, a totalizing vision seems to arise before Bloom:

377, 378, 495 (Bloom "eclipses the sun by extending his little finger"). This stellar association becomes explicit in the "Ithaca" section. See also *FW* 349: "In the heliotropical noughttime. . . ." Avrom Fleishman discusses astronomical imagery in "Science in 'Ithaca,' " *Fiction and the Ways of Knowing* (Austin: University of Texas Press, 1978), pp. 136-148; as do Mark E. Littmann and Charles A. Schweighauser in "Astronomical Allusions, Their Meaning and Purpose in *Ulysses*," *James Joyce Quarterly* 2 (1965): 231-246.

> And, lo, wonder of metempsychosis, it is she, the everlasting bride, harbinger of the daystar, the bride, ever virgin. It is she, Martha, thou lost one, Millicent, the young, the dear, the radiant. How serene does she now arise, a queen among the Pleiades, in the penultimate antelucan hour, shod in sandals of bright gold, coifed with a veil of what do you call it gossamer! It floats, it flows about her starborn flesh and loose it streams emerald, sapphire, mauve and heliotrope, sustained on currents of cold interstellar wind, winding, coiling, simply swirling, writhing in the skies a mysterious writing till after a myriad metamorphoses of symbol, it blazes, Alpha, a ruby and triangled sign upon the forehead of Taurus. (*U* 414)

This radiant presence which arises to fill Bloom's longing for authoritative determinability of reference is the locus of intersection of several prior metaphoric systems and, if it is to provide a vision of transcendent truth, it does so at the risk of immediate deconstruction by the underlying rhetorical structure. Martha, insubstantial lover, and Millicent, the departed daughter, merge into one figure who traces an interstellar script which seems to refer to the source of all meaning, Alpha.

The feminine form is thus simultaneously lover and daughter, sun-seeking heliotrope and author of revealing signs. The ruby sign of Alpha is a paranomasia for both the deceased son Rudy and his substitute presence, Stephen (whose own signature in the heavens is "delta in Cassiopeia").[65] But the veiled stellar script of "sapphire, mauve and heliotrope," which is to provide the sign of salvation from the meaningless language of flowers, itself bears the illusions which have coursed through previous attempts to pin down the slide of the signifier to an expression of authentic meaning. After the heavenly writing fades there remain only the repetition and elaboration of other versions of

[65] *U* 210, 700, and 712. The myths refer to Thoth as "Bull [Taurus] among the stars," Derrida, *Dissemination*, p. 92.

each of these metaphors in isolation, in new configurations, in new permutations always, however, expressing the same lack.

In their chiasmic exchange of desires (Stephen, the father-seeker, soaring sunward) and Leopold (a son-compelled flower) the pair seem to align along an axis of paradigmatic compatibility.[66] Yet even Stephen, who "likes dialectic, the universal language" (*U* 600), is free enough from illusion in "Ithaca" to see that the ideal synthesis of antitheses is still but a remote possibility. Reduced to their simple reciprocal forms, and substituted by chiasmic exchange, "Stephen for Bloom Stoom" and "Bloom for Stephen Blephen" (*U* 682), each represents only a composite, asymmetrical image which cannot endure as a meaningful personality. The omniscient narrative voice of "Ithaca"[67] foresees that the reduction of Bloom by such cross substitution could render him "a negligible negative irrational unreal quantity" (*U* 725).

As soon as either Dedalus or Bloom begin to think that totalization is accessible, they discover that all the terms of the analogizing statement are individually set in metaphorical relations. Bloom the "suncompelled" figure "obey[ing] the summons of recall" (*U* 728) and Dedalus, the hawklike man "soaring sunward" (*P* 169), find their sun to be not a source of truth but rather a *simulacrum* of it. If a proper sun does exist, it remains

[66] The solar metaphors, along with the punnings on "sun" and "son," are the figural strategies by which the thematic father and son relationship between Stephen and Bloom is created. See the dramatic aside "*Was Jesus a Sun myth?*" (*U* 485), and the passage beginning "God, the sun, Shakespeare . . ." (*U* 505). See also, Maud Ellmann, "Polytropic Man: Paternity, Identity and Naming in *The Odyssey* and *A Portrait of the Artist as a Young Man*," in MacCabe, *James Joyce: New Perspectives*, pp. 73-104.

[67] Joyce to Frank Budgen, End February 1921: "I am writing Ithaca in the form of a mathematical catechism. All events are resolved into their cosmic, physical, psychical etc. equivalents . . . so that the reader will know everything and know it in the baldest and coldest way, but Bloom and Stephen thereby become heavenly bodies, wanderers like the stars at which they gaze" (*Letters*, vol. 1, pp. 159-160).

invisible, veiled by darkness and eclipsed by linguistic illusions. Its traces, "Holy Writ," as the narrator informs us, are always found to be but "genuine forgeries."[68]

If Bloom's story is not a tragic one, and certainly it seems more comic than tragic, it is because he manages in his innocence to create a manner of self-integration by his equanimity before the meaninglessness of his cuckolded, son-less existence. The narrator of "Ithaca" poses the possibility that Bloom might smile as he crawls back into the "bed of conception and of birth, of consummation of marriage and of breach of marriage, of sleep and of death":

> If he had smiled why would he have smiled?
>
> To reflect that each one who enters [the bed of marriage] imagines himself to be the first to enter whereas he is always the last term of a preceding series even if the first term of a succeeding one, each imagining himself to be first, last, only and alone, whereas he is neither first nor last nor only nor alone in a series originating in and repeated to infinity. (*U* 731)

From a narrative point of view, the narrator's questions and answers shift the pattern of referential authority from a mimetic mode (which has been prevalent throughout Stephen's philosophizing) to a deconstructive, diegetic mode. "If he had smiled . . . [he might have smiled] To reflect that. . . ." Bloom is thus held capable of positing a theory of integration which is sig-

[68] *U* 634. It would not be farfetched to think that Stephen's attempt to "forge . . . the uncreated conscience of his race" (*P* 253) is related to the "forging" of Holy Writ. Cf. *FW* 181-182 on forgeries: "Who can say how many pseudostylic shamiana, . . . how very many piously forged palimpsests slipped in the first place by this morbid process from his pelagiarist pen?" In fact, the very process of intertextual cross-breeding is for Joyce a kind of plagiarism: "(Stoop) if you are abcedminded, to this claybook, what curios of signs (please stoop), in this allaphbed! Can you rede (since We and Thou had it out already) its world? It is the same told of all. Many. Miscegenations on miscegenation" (*FW* 18).

nificantly different from any that Stephen has articulated. Whereas Stephen's aesthetic theory and Shakespearean myth depend on the existence of an ideal, original source and guarantee of meaning, Bloom is now said to be capable of conceiving a diacritical system of reference, structured as a metonymic chain of spatial juxtapositions, underwritten by no definable origin. The indeterminacy of this chain's origin, rather than being a source of frustration and despair, as it is for Stephen, is for Bloom a situation with which one can live. Bloom sees himself as merely another cipher within that long, hidden sentence which leads neither back to the proper Word of creation, nor forward to the teleologic end of history.

A variant of this umbilical chain had already appeared in Stephen's thoughts about the human chain of history leading back by *anastomosis* to the primal Eve: "The cords of all link back, strandentwining cable of all flesh" (*U* 38), to "our mighty mother" to whom "we are linked up with by successive anastomosis of navelcords" (*U* 391). Stephen's anastomotic views of history (and narratives of history) imply that signifiers proceed from and are supported by a transcendentally self-present signified: God to Christ, Shakespeare to Hamlet, Dedalus to Icarus, in a kind of umbilical relation. From this perspective, the artist's task is simply to recover the signifiers most appropriate for the "expression" of that link between a self-present immanent core of meaning and its radiated significations. Artists conduce meanings from signifieds to signifiers, while readers deduce those meanings from the proffered signifiers. In contrast, Leopold's anastomotic network completely problematizes this unidirectional flow by making it a channel without detectable origin, and oriented toward no predictable end. Stephen's figure of "anastomosis," as reiterated by Bloom, is thus a felicitous one, designating at once a physiological interconnection between bodies of any kind, and the rhetorical process of intercommunication.[69] As a concept of displacement, of transport, anastomosis is precisely a constitutive property of metaphor.

In accordance with the semantic pattern established throughout Joyce's texts, however, it is nonetheless uncertain whether or not the word "anastomosis" communicates a determinate meaning. Since it possesses, as it does, two distinct senses, one connoting a literal transmission or propagation, the other denoting a figural dissemination of a semantic content, it is not justifiable to define *anastomosis* as the communication of any one particular meaning.

For Stephen, however, this communicating chain does form a fixed, directional, telic axis, which carries within itself the hope of transmitting some sort of life-sustaining force from an original (procreating) to a secondary (procreated) body. Bloom, in contrast, entertains no such delusion: his metaphoric chain "originates in and repeats to infinity," and in accepting the "apathy of the stars" (*U* 734), posits "nolast term" (*U* 731), no determinate end of accomplished communication. Bloom's anastomotic metaphor thus might well anticipate the notion that "History is a process without a *telos* or a subject," for he repudiates fixed master narratives and their categories of narrative closure and individual character.[70]

Ineluctably multiplying the tender relations that its linked couples implacably displace, Leopold's "infinite chain" represents the necessity of the mirage that an original source of meaning can be conceived. The act of copulation, which for Bloom forms the emblem of the anastomotic human chain, is

[69] *OED*, s. v. "anastomosis." Elliot B. Gose, Jr. notices the function of "anastomosis" in *Ulysses* and *Finnegans Wake* but does not deal with it as rigorously as, in my opinion, Joyce's text requires. See *The Transformation Process in Joyce's Ulysses* (Toronto: University of Toronto Press, 1980), pp. 88-89.

[70] Louis Althusser, *Réponse à John Lewis* (Paris: Maspéro, 1973), pp. 91-98. Cited by Fredric Jameson, *The Political Unconscious: Narrative as a Socially Symbolic Act* (Ithaca: Cornell University Press, 1981), p. 29.

the living sign of asymmetrical difference in human affairs. It is, as the narrator grandiosely puts it, the "natural act of a nature expressed or understood executed in natured nature by natural creatures in accordance with his, her, and their natured natures, of dissimilar similarity" (*U* 733). This copulative play of "dissimilar similarity" does not simply distinguish one "natural creature" from another. It separates him or her radically from "his, her" own multiple identities. As for Ishmael in another context, Bloom's "dissimilar similarity" makes the totalization of the identity of the self impossible. His difference designates, moreover, that existential meaning is a function not of an immanent core of truth within each of the copulating elements, which can be genetically transmitted through a kind of racial system of telecommunication. It is instead a function of the network of oppositions that distinguishes the dissimilar pair and relates them to one another and to every other combination of copulating pairs.[71]

As an anastomotic-minded semiotician, Bloom can thus be said to imagine with convincing equanimity that "From outrage (matrimony) to outrage (adultery) there arose nought but outrage (copulation)" (*U* 733), and that in the exchanges of terms within that chain of copulating pairs, "the natural grammatical transition by inversion involv[es] no alteration of sense."[72]

[71] In *Finnegans Wake*, "anastomosis" explicitly links the variant metaphoric systems of "flowers," "heliotrope," and "copulation." See, for instance: "Humperfeldt and Anunska, wedded now evermore in annastomoses . . ." (*FW* 585), and "letter from litter, word at ward, with sendence of sundance, since the days of Plooney and Columcellas when Giacinta, Pervenche and Margaret swayed . . . anastomosically assimilated . . ." (*FW* 615).

[72] *U* 734. The salient qualities of *contingency* and *difference* which characterize the Joycean anastomotic chain of human history also characterize the way in which language forms *value*. Ferdinand de Saussure argues that linguistic values do not emanate from pre-existing ideas which are carried over into language. Rather, values emanate from the system of juxtaposed linguistic signs. "Concepts are purely differential and defined not by their positive content but negatively by their relations with other terms of the system. Their precise characteristic is in being what the others are not. . . . Signs function, then, not through their intrinsic value but through their relative position" (*Course in*

Bloom's structural model of humanity (linked to one another by the anastomotic phallus but tied to no primal, original source) creates a provisional semantic field by contingency free of the illusion of pre-existing "ideas" and can be read as an emblem of the processes of the Joycean narrative itself in *Ulysses*. In Joyce's narratives, every metaphorical system that arises in the narrative to define an independent and authoritative truth always reveals itself to be necessarily inscribed in a relational chain or system within which it refers to other concepts, concepts which are themselves produced by the systematic by-play of the differences between them, and not by any privileged source of intrinsic value.

The effects of this anastomotic structure upon the notion of a "classical" narrative are striking indeed. Since language in *Ulysses* has not been carried down to humanity whole, significant, and free of differences by a Thoth-like heavenly messenger, it is clear that whatever meaning does exist has been produced by the interactions of Joyce's fictional characters. Stephen's words, therefore, certainly are the effects of a cause, as he imagines. But they have as their cause neither a Transcendental Subject, nor a Radiant Essence that is somewhere present (even

General Linguistics, trans. Wade Baskin [New York: McGraw-Hill, 1959]), pp. 117, 118. While Joyce will not consciously use "semiological" terms until *Finnegans Wake* (p. 465), in passages such as these in *Ulysses* he is strikingly close to the logic and methodology Saussure uses when he argues that "in language there are only differences *without positive terms*" (*Course*, p. 120). On Joyce and the semiotician Marcel Jousse, see Stephen Heath, "Joyce in Language," in MacCabe, *James Joyce: New Perspectives*, pp. 129-148. Joyce's floral and solar metaphors are examples of the production of linguistic value from the relative positionings of concepts which are themselves without positive, intrinsic value. And despite Joyce's expressed antipathy to Freud and Freudian psychoanalysis, it is worth recalling Freud's examples of "the language of flowers" in his discussion of the work of "condensation" and "displacement" ("metaphor" and "metonymy" in current Lacanian terms) in the dream work. Dream-content and dream-process are for Freud as narrative content and narrative creation are for Joyce, constructed in major part by "an ingenious interweaving of their reciprocal relations" (*The Interpretation of Dreams*, trans. James Strachey [1900; New York: Avon Books, 1965], p. 319).

if hidden) and which itself escapes the play of linguistic difference. The traces which Stephen, and sometimes Bloom, appear to find of such a Primary Cause are themselves the results of the system which gives metaphor a privileged place in the dialectical movement which is to produce that fabled "universal language" of Stephen's dream. These traces continue to break up the present moment, reconstituting it as a synthesis of past and future moments in an ineffaceable historicity of discourse.

Stephen's and Bloom's metaphoric attempt to encounter the totalizing word of that universal language forms an allegory of the indeterminacy of meaning. Though driven by a desire for transcendence, allegories always remain schematic. Allegories are emblems, not archetypes of the universal Logos within which man, woman, and God might exist in perfect unity. If at any point the narrative of *Ulysses* were to have created such a heliotropic archetype of unity, the text might have been able to cease discarding alternative narrative voices and styles. But the closing period to that multi-perspectival structure remains unattained, even beyond the final word of the "Penelope" section. Molly's "yes" answers no questions, resolves no contradictions, hypostatizes no distinct links in the copulative figural chain which is *Ulysses*. Molly's voice returns, as the narrative voices return, from its digressive movement to the central pattern of metaphor. It is a pattern, however, that cannot reduce polarities or resolve contradictions. To interpret those figures of speech as signs of consubstantial union between man and wife, father and son, word and idea, or signifier and signified, is to fall into the intoxicating delusion of Joyce's synthetic metaphors.

Stephen's "actions" in the text are the result of a nostalgia for a mythic universal language which is described in *A Portrait of the Artist* through the indirection which names the aesthetic theory as a model for the proper reading of the world. According to that theory, meaning and materiality can be reconciled in a transfigurative flash. For one fragile, heroic instant, a surge of spirit illuminates and redeems the material world from within.

In *Ulysses,* that nostalgia is named in the form of the allegory of the self-begotten son. Bloom's actions are the reciprocal movement of Stephen's word-play. The narrative of their quests for organic unity and totalization is repeatedly displaced by other narratives which parody that quest by expressing it in ever-proliferating styles and narrative modes. And perhaps we may go one step further to suggest that Stephen's and Bloom's constantly deferred goal of recreating a self-constituting, self-referential, and unmediated Word which will order the system of discourse is the analogue of the author's own attempt to encounter the proper narrative mode for the expression of their story. Had a universal language for the reconciliation of differences emerged from the text, father and son might have been reconciled and a genealogical chain linking them back to a proper origin might have been forged. But at every point in the narrative the linguistic sign marks out a systematic anarchy which does allow the creation of a provisional semantic field, but which also traces the law of arbitrariness and ambiguity which governs the creation of meaning.

Metaphor, "in the track of the sun," is not itself a presence but a simulacrum attempting to fill that semantic void. The heliotropic flowers of the Joycean narrative, always tending through metaphor toward a darkening sun, as if to form its substitute ("the condensation of spiral nebulae into suns"—*U* 700), point to no stable source. Rather, instability and effacement belong to the structure of those metaphors. And yet those metaphors are also the sources of the novel's soothing pathos, for *Ulysses* testifies on every page to the fact that there can be no essential expression, nor any understanding, of essence without metaphor. As we have noted, Nietzsche too describes this need for metaphor in human affairs: "Only by forgetting that primitive world of metaphors, only by the congelation and coagulation of an original mass of similes and percepts pouring forth as a fiery liquid out of the primal faculty of human fancy, only the invincible faith, that *this* sun, . . . is a truth in itself:

in short only by the fact that man forgets himself as subject, and what is more as an *artistically creating* subject: only by all this does he live with some repose, safety and consequence."[73]

Even in the face of such Dionysian truths, Apollonian illusions of radiance will also persist. This is the source of Joyce's, and Bloom's, comic, not to say joyous, wisdom: that outside the myth of a universal language, the paternal language belonging to the lost fatherland of plenitude and truth, only the "interstellar void" exists. It is a void that can be read, as Leopold Bloom reads it, without nostalgia, but humanely, and perhaps even with equanimity, realizing that language in "track of the sun" cannot be easily deflowered. Beneath the void, provisionally filling its space, lies only what Joyce will name later in *Finnegans Wake*, "the panaroma of all flores of speech" (*FW* 143).

[73] "On Truth and Falsehood in Their Extra-Moral Sense," *The Complete Works* 2: 184.

Afterword

Having begun by disclaiming strict thematic unity, I close by reiterating the continual relationship between semantic and narrative structures. Students of the novel widely recognize that Cervantes was the initiator of a thematic and formal line of texts which repeat and develop the quixotic attempt to fashion an imaginative world within the confines of present reality.

Cervantes contributes to the development of the novel a new insight into the manner in which language, as a temporal and phenomenal expression of the "genealogical imperative," creates authority. But Cervantes does not simply note this fact; he dramatizes it. Language is for Cervantes the anastomotic link which allows us to connect the world's indiscriminate variety of events into a rational chain that progresses from ignorance to knowledge.

Cervantes also recognizes that language is sometimes incapable of an authorized and definitive expression of the "meaning" that should mark the end of the progression from chaos to order, that language must, as a consequence, sometimes forge those rational links. Both art and life depend on the duplicity of language. This recognition leads Cervantes and other language-conscious authors to a distinctive form of pathos, which itself becomes a subject of the narration. The recognition also leads to a "tropology" of truth, which becomes a contingent means for the location of linguistic and formal authority in the novel.

My reading of *Don Quijote* reveals that the thematic aspects of the text are linked to a specific performative rhetoric. This rhetoric in turn always interrupts, detains, displaces, and, finally, renders questionable, the cognitive rhetoric that produces the intricacies of meaning and signification embodied in the story of the mad hidalgo. But my concern is as much to explore the implications of this clash of rhetorics in order to determine the nature and structure of Cervantes' intentions as a novelist as it is to locate the textual site of the clash. The close reading of Cervantes serves as a prolegomenon to an investigation of the difficult problem of the textuality of the novel in general, and is not simply an exercise in textual decipherment.

Le Rouge et le Noir, *Moby-Dick*, *Jude*, *Portrait*, and *Ulysses* all weave the thematic pattern of imaginative construction formalized by *Don Quijote*. When considered in the light of *Don Quijote*'s play with linguistic and epistemological structures, these novels also witness in different ways a persistent reenactment and deconstruction of the rhetorical quest for a universal authority upon which such imaginative self-creations are based.

Beginning with the Saussurean principle of the differential nature of signification that concepts arise not positively from the content of particular signs but rather negatively from their relations with other signs in the linguistic system, I argue that these exemplary novels display the diacritical nature of meaning. To the extent that "meaning" is a product of systematic interaction among the rhetorical forces of language, the rhetoric of the novel, extended along the diachronic axis of narration, demonstrates that meaning cannot be grounded in the consciousness of a creating author, or in the mimetic presence of a referential object. This does not deny that language can be referential, but it does deny that the referent, in either subjective or objective forms, can function as an *ultimate ground* for meaning. The loss of a transcendental signified to function as that ultimate referent imposes upon texts the need to inscribe meaning to the by-play of the literal, figural, and proper levels of the signifier. This by-play, manifested in our exemplary novels as their rhetorical form, is complex and rigorous. It is delineated by its own identifiable rules.

The novel's impulse to pose the theoretical issues of self-determination may appear under various coded forms of desire: for the security and peace of holding another in intimate love, as in *Don Quijote* and *Le Rouge et le Noir,* for self-knowledge and self-possession, as in *Moby-Dick* and *A Portrait of the Artist,* or for complete possession of self and others, as in *Jude the Obscure* and *Ulysses.*

In *Le Rouge et le Noir* Stendhal considers the transformation of the romantic themes of self-identity and willed autonomy into a "realistic" narrative about the failure of such imaginative self-realizations. While recognizing the importance of Stendhal's self-conscious and analytic narrative, I examine the disturbingly unconscious dialectic played out by Julien Sorel, the master and slave of romantic passion. Stendhal's own desire to displace his erotic disappointments by rhetorical tours de force appears as a variation of Cervantes' exemplary quest for a discourse appropriate to the magnitude and depth of the desire for fulfillment. With Stendhal, the master ironist, the novel moves into full artistic maturity.

The complex pattern of metaphors, symbols, and allegories which underlie Melville's *Moby-Dick* is the basic syntax of Ishmael's tale. Faced with the "mystical and well nigh ineffable" circumstances of the hunt for the white whale, it becomes Ishmael's task to formulate the possibility of a grammar by which his visions might be faithfully communicated to his readers. His narrative effort can thus be seen as a correlative of the force which motivates Ahab's hunt for the white whale. Captain Ahab's vow of vengeance indicates his reliance on the value of action, as his later statement that "Ahab is for ever Ahab" posits the fact of the self's identity as an ultimate generative source. But Ishmael's narrative consistently subverts our confidence in this movement toward the possibility of a definitive performance. When Ishmael's constative narrative, which assumes that knowledge of the world and certainty regarding the self can be acquired, reaches an impasse as mere constative, and becomes itself a kind of performance, it too becomes vulnerable to the critical forces it has unleashed. In this confrontation between the constative and performative modes of discourse the power of action and the certainty of identity, themes which give rise to *Moby-Dick,* are put radically in question. The figural logic of Melville's novel impels us toward allegory as the only feasible, if provisional, mediator of this narrative conflict.

Hardy's *Jude the Obscure,* as among the first modernist novels to doubt the assurance of the truth of absolute reference, also joins this line of inquiry. Hardy, as we have seen, raises the issue of proper reading and interpretation in his "Preface to the First Edition." My analysis examines Hardy's notions of "natural" and "civil" law, their relation to the "readability" of the scriptural letter of the law, and the relationship Hardy makes between rhetorically active and forensically inactive semiotic systems. It offers *Jude* as the beginning of a modernist rhetoric of reference.

Finally, I propose Joyce's *A Portrait of the Artist* and *Ulysses* as culminating elements of a formal and thematic concern first elaborated in the Spanish Renaissance. The aesthetic theory presented in *Stephen Hero* and elaborated in the subsequent novels figures the theme of the search for authority, origin, and meaning. The tropological procedures implicit in the rhetorical form of the novels examined in earlier chapters reappear in Joyce's novels in full bloom as "the flowers of speech." Joyce's novels place the burden of meaning on the metaphorical order of the signifier, as the only reliable element against the contingencies of an undetermined and ineffable universe. In a kind of ultimate dialectical reversal, Joyce piles up quantities of random significations, hoping to transform them qualitatively into essential meanings. Shorn of value or *telos* by the instrumentality of rhetoric, Joyce's novels, particularly *Ulysses* and *Finnegans Wake,* unravel, problematize, and finally dissolve the last remaining traces of faith in the bedrock of referentiality as a guide to truth, while the linguistic sign is radically released to develop its own autonomous "solar" system in all directions.

The order imposed on the world by such linguistic manipulations is mirrored by the spectral self-creation of human relationships. In Joyce, metaphor, the indirect Sign of the Father, always demonstrates an insistent verbal defense against the variability of the everyday world through an act of creation. But what is created ultimately is the illusion that the linguistic sign is capable of underwriting the stability of the ephemeral world.

This brief summary of the rhetorical patterns I have identified makes explicit what has been implicit throughout my discussion. The novel's articulation of rhetorical form exhibits no necessary homogeneity and thus cannot be represented in a general theory. There is no single point of reference for a complete understanding of all novels since it is their difference that constitutes them. It does not follow, however, that we must consider novels as the mere individual products of their idiosyncratic authors. Cervantes had already warned us about misconceiving the relationship between authors and their books as a genetic one. The relationships between authors and works do depend on definite historical and discursive conditions, but these conditions do not necessarily form homologic or essential relationships of totality open to a general theory. In rejecting a general theory and insisting on the heterogeneity of rhetorical forms and their divergent effects, I have tried to mark out a space for specific theorization and questioning of the themes and discourses of the novel. The nature of this work cannot be mandated in advance.[1] Accepting the absence of any necessary foundation for a general theory of the novel means that we must devote more care to assessing the conditions and the means of analysis, and to establishing what it is novels claim and how they go about preserving what Nietzsche called those "notions with which one can live."

In the area of narrative, the central concern of my work, those given certainties are unremittingly dissected. The novel

[1] On the limitations of general theories, see Paul Hirst, *On Law and Ideology* (London: Macmillan, 1979), pp. 1-21.

focuses the interpretive categories or codes through which we receive and read reality and texts of reality. My study turns toward the act of interpretation and presupposes, as its own organizational fiction, that we never really possess a text immediately, concretely, as a thing-in-itself. Rather, as Fredric Jameson has argued, we apprehend texts through sedimented layers of previous interpretations—the interpretations already performed by all prior readers, including the author—or, if the text is indeed radically new, through the sedimented interpretive traditions within which our readings are preserved.[2] In Frank Kermode's words: "We are in a world of which it needs to be said *not* that plural readings are possible (for this is true of all narratives) but that the *illusion of the single right reading is possible no longer.*"[3]

With its care for authenticating detail and its passion for credibility and intelligibility, the novel expresses a continuing desire for types, for monological readings, for an anachronistic mythos of common understanding and a shared universe of meaning. And yet in the same breath, the novel—the new—never ceases to express the dazzling conceptual maneuvering that we all must perform in order to conceive reality, indeed to shape reality, in ways that will make sense to the human mind. Readers thus may be said to consume texts by applying to them the perceptual schemata, those markers of untroubled temporality, unified character, or definitive closure, which go to create acceptable versions of reality.[4] The application of these schemata is the work of ideology. It is worth recalling, however, that all of these notions have been severely put into question since at least the sixteenth century. Pursuing continuities at all costs,

[2] I draw here heavily on Jameson's discussion of symbolical structures in "On Interpretation," *The Political Unconscious*, pp. 17-102.

[3] Kermode, "Novels: Recognition and Deception," *Critical Inquiry* 1 (1974): 111. Of relevance here too is Bakhtin's idea of the novel as the forum for the *dialogic* word. See "Discourse in the Novel," *The Dialogic Imagination*, pp. 259-422.

[4] Kermode, "Novels: Recognition and Deception," pp. 116-120.

readers sometimes accept the fiction of horizontal readings at the expense of the more speculative, more troubling, implications introduced by the vertical relations which metaphorical discourse and figural language always bear. Novels call us back to the force of rhetoric as it aids in the construction of simple story grammars even as it disrupts the coherence of grammar; they continuously return to the possibilities contained in the figural elements the reader may forget to consider. As part of their scrupulous protocol, novels instruct readers in the hermeneutic skills appropriate to the reading of a particular text, with the result that our interest in reading novels like *Don Quijote, Le Rouge et le Noir,* or *Moby-Dick* often lies as much on the method of interpretation, the ideological motives, through which we attempt to understand and appropriate them as on their narrated tales.

Interpretation is essentially an allegorical act that consists in receiving a text in terms of a provisional master code that accounts most rigorously for its rhetorical and formal strategies.[5] Its aim is less to elaborate some sophisticated précis of a story than to *produce* the text's epistemological and ideological concept of the real world, to instantiate the competing systems of ideas and modes of representation which structure the world at a particular place and time.[6] Cultural matrices use the signifier to create truths and set these as norms, coercive texts for meaning, that claim universality. Deconstructive readings can point out the hypostasization of these universal truths from the *con-*

[5] Paul de Man argues that an analysis of a critique of epistemological structure results in an allegorical narrative. See his *Allegories of Reading,* pp. 240-245, and also "The Epistemology of Metaphor," *Critical Inquiry* 5 (1978): 13-30.

[6] An elaboration of a Marxist theory of literary production is another story altogether. Nonetheless, one could begin by reading Louis Althusser's essays "Ideology and Ideological State Apparatuses" and "Freud and Lacan" in *Lenin and Philosophy* (New York and London: New Left Books, 1971), pp. 127-186 and pp. 195-219, respectively; Pierre Macherey's *A Theory of Literary Production* (London and Boston: Routledge & Kegan Paul, 1978), pp. 66-68; Jameson's "Towards Dialectical Criticism" in *Marxism and Form,* pp. 306-416; or Michael Ryan's *Marxism and Deconstruction,* pp. 9-42.

structed domains of a specific history and a particular culture. They allow us to see the production of ideology not as a system of formalized ideas, but as ordinary ways of thinking, as common sense. Our novels represent that what appears "natural" in the ways individuals live their roles in society is the result of a "limiting of the endless productivity of the signifying chain."[7] Cultural matrices produce specific articulations which in turn impose certain conditions on subjects in order that those subjects may participate in a culture's truth and meaning. As representations, these productive processes are necessarily figurative and cannot be abolished because they allow social formations to persist; but they can be articulated and analyzed.

I take the cases of Cervantes, Stendhal, Melville, Hardy, and Joyce as exemplars of the novel's critical interpretive task of dramatizing in "the all-informing process of *narrative*"[8] the ability of knowledge, ideology, subjectivity, desire and cultural productions in general to create the "ontologically empty but historically full"[9] forces that do constrain the course of narrative. But, not to be denied, narratives persist in uncovering this coercion by representing it as the irreducibly dialectical clash of the cultural-historical forces that surround a text and the rhetorical and formal dynamics within a text. Narratives are thus preeminently and rigorously dialectical. By insisting upon and employing all the devices of rhetoric, they situate the natural truths of precritical idealism as the local effects of "differential relations, institutions, conventions, histories, practices" and as the deferred results of the "institutionality and spatiality of language."[10] Read dialectically, our novels indicate that lan-

[7] Coward and Ellis, *Language and Materialism*, p. 67.

[8] Jameson, *The Political Unconscious*, p. 13.

[9] Lentricchia, *After the New Criticism*, p. 184.

[10] Ryan, *Marxism and Deconstruction*, p. 24. In "The Dialectics of Difference: Toward a Theory of the Chicano Novel," *MELUS* 6 (1979): 73-92, I have tried to show how the aesthetic forces of rhetoric are marshalled in the service of a contemporary, politically radical literature, and how the social implications of the conceptual breakthrough of deconstruction can be immediately called forth.

guage and discourse do affect human life in determining ways, ways that are themselves shaped by social history. Giving rise to questions concerning our proper language, our sovereign identity, and the laws that govern our behavior, they reveal the heterogeneous systems that resist the formation of a fatherland of unitary truth. It is thus in narrative, as the symbolic instance of our desires to transform the "mystical and well nigh ineffable" world into "comprehensible form," that the *aesthetic* quality of the human mind is brightly evident. With synaesthetic force, it turns toward the flowery cadenzas, those Joycean "panaromas of all flores of speech," which function as the horizons of human knowledge.

Index

Library of Congress Cataloging in Publication Data

Saldívar, Ramón.
Figural language in the novel.

Includes index.
1. Fiction—Technique. 2. Fiction—History and criticism. 3. Narration (Rhetoric) I. Title.
PN3383.N35S24 1984 809.3′922 83-16117

ISBN 0-691-06587-X (alk. paper)